Consistent Ethic of Life

Joseph Cardinal Bernardin

Richard A. McCormick, S.J.

John Finnis

James M. Gustafson

J. Bryan Hehir

Frans Jozef van Beeck, S.J.

James J. Walter

Lisa Sowle Cahill

Sidney Callahan

Thomas G. Fuechtmann, Editor

Sheed & Ward

Sheed & Ward™ is a service of National Catholic Reporter Publishing
Company, Inc.

Library of Congress Catalog Card Number: 88-61497

ISBN: 1-55612-120-2

Published by: Sheed & Ward
                 115 E. Armour Blvd. P.O. Box 419492
                 Kansas City, MO 64141

To order, call: (800) 333-7373

Contents

Part I: Addresses of Joseph Cardinal Bernardin

Part II: Symposium Papers

Part III: Response to the Symposium

Editor's Note

Joseph Cardinal Bernardin of Chicago did not originate the concept of a "consistent ethic of life," but he has certainly been its principal spokesperson in the Catholic Church in the United States. Since he delivered the Gannon Lecture at Fordham University in New York, December 6, 1983, Cardinal Bernardin has returned to the "consistent ethic" theme numerous times and in different settings.

In the addresses, Cardinal Bernardin spoke in the role of a pastor, rather than as a theologian or philosopher. Cardinal Bernardin was concerned that the consistent ethic concept—which went on to live its own life in the public policy arena—be scrutinized carefully from a scholarly point of view. This was a task of the symposium held at Loyola University of Chicago on November 7, 1987. The event was sponsored jointly by Loyola and the Archdiocese of Chicago.

Ten of the Cardinal's addresses were selected as the more important statements by the Cardinal of the "consistent ethic" theme. Richard McCormick, S.J., John Finnis, James M. Gustafson, and J. Bryan Hehir were invited to comment on the Cardinal's development of the concept out of their own expertise. Their papers were submitted to symposium participants in advance. At the symposium itself, the speakers presented a thirty-minute synopsis of their argument. The authors had the opportunity to revise their initial working papers prior to publication in this volume.

Each of the major speakers was followed at the symposium by a designated respondent. Frans Jozef van Beeck, S.J., James Walter, Lisa Cahill, and Sidney Callahan each presented a fifteen-minute response, and subsequently provided the written texts included in this volume.

Cardinal Bernardin himself attended the entire symposium, and gave the concluding address, in which he responded to the four major speakers. That address is the concluding text in this volume.

Scholars and critics will evaluate the theological and philosophical arguments about the consistent ethic on their own merits, as presented in this volume and in the series of video and audio tapes constituting the record of the event.

The symposium itself, though, is noteworthy in another respect. The event itself provided a remarkable instance of the Cardinal, as a voice of the *magisterium*, engaging in open discussion with Christian philosophers and theologians. As expected, the scholars did not all agree with the Cardinal, or with each other. But the symposium provided a model for how the pastor and the scholar can conduct a fruitful and constructive dialogue.

Finally, a note to those who may be reading the Cardinal's addresses for the first time. The first two addresses, those at Fordham University (1983) and St. Louis University (1984), develop the basic concept of the consistent ethic itself. The next six addresses apply the concept to particular situations. The last two addresses of the original ten, those at Seattle University and Portland Oregon, develop further the basic concept and apply it to religion and politics.

The editor's task would not be complete without an expression of deep gratitude to the I.A. O'Shaughnessy Foundation, of St. Paul, Minnesota, for its financial support. Loyola University and the Archdiocese of Chicago are particularly indebted to Mrs. Eileen A. O'Shaughnessy for her sponsorship.

Thomas G. Fuechtmann
Loyola University of Chicago

A Consistent Ethic of Life: An American-Catholic Dialogue

Gannon Lecture, Fordham University
Joseph Cardinal Bernardin
December 6, 1983

It is a privilege to be invited to give the Gannon Lecture at Fordham University. Fr. Gannon's life as a priest, a Jesuit and a scholar offers a standard of excellence which any Gannon lecturer should seek to imitate.

I was invited to address some aspect of the U.S. Catholic bishops' pastoral letter, "The Challenge of Peace: God's Promise and Our Response." I am happy to do so, but I want to address the topic in a very specific manner. The setting of today's lecture has shaped its substance. The setting is a university, a community and an institution committed to the examination and testing of ideas. A university setting calls for an approach to the pastoral which does more than summarize its content; six months after its publication, it is necessary to examine the document's impact and to reflect upon the possibilities for development which are latent in its various themes.

1

2 A Consistent Ethic of Life

More specifically, Fordham is an American Catholic university, an institution which has consistently fostered the work of enriching American culture through Catholic wisdom and has simultaneously sought to enhance our understanding of Catholic faith by drawing upon the American tradition.

Today I will discuss the pastoral letter in terms of the relationship of our Catholic moral vision and American culture. Specifically, I wish to use the letter as a starting point for shaping a consistent ethic of life in our culture. In keeping with the spirit of a university, I have cast the lecture in the style of an inquiry, an examination of the need for a consistent ethic of life and a probing of the problems and possibilities which exist within the Church and the wider society for developing such an ethic.

I do not underestimate the intrinsic intellectual difficulties of this exercise nor the delicacy of the question—ecclesially, ecumenically and politically. But I believe the Catholic moral tradition has something valuable to say in the face of the multiple threats to the sacredness of life today, and I am convinced that the Church is in a position to make a significant defense of life in a comprehensive and consistent manner.

Such a defense of life will draw upon the Catholic moral position and the public place the Church presently holds in the American civil debate. The pastoral letter links the questions of abortion and nuclear war. The letter does not argue the case for linkage; that is one of my purposes today. It is important to note that the way these two issues are joined in the pastoral places the American bishops in a unique position in the public policy discourse of the nation. No other major institution presently holds these two positions in the way the Catholic bishops have joined them. This is both a responsibility and an opportunity.

I am convinced that the pro-life position of the Church must be developed in terms of a comprehensive and consistent ethic of life. I have just been named the Chairman of the National Conference of Catholic Bishops' Pro-Life Committee; I am committed to shaping a position of linkage among the life issues. It is that topic I wish to develop today in three steps: (1) a reflection on the pastoral letter on war and peace; (2) an analysis of a consistent ethic of life; and (3) an examination of how such an ethic can be shaped in the American public debate.

I. The Church in Public Debate: The Pastoral in Perspective

The pastoral letter on war and peace can be examined from several perspectives. I wish to look at it today in ecclesiological terms, specifically as an example of the Church's role in helping to shape a public policy debate. Early in the letter the bishops say that they are writing in order to share the moral wisdom of the Catholic tradition with society. In stating this objective the American bishops were following the model of the Second Vatican Council which called dialogue with the world a sign of love for the world.

I believe the long-term ecclesiological significance of the pastoral rests with the lessons it offers about the Church's capacity to dialogue with the world in a way which helps to shape the public policy debate on key issues. During the drafting of the pastoral letter one commentator wrote in the editorial section of the *Washington Post:*

> The Catholic bishops. . . are forcing a public debate on perhaps
> the most perplexing nuclear question of them all, the morality of
> nuclear deterrence. . . Their logic and passion have taken them to
> the very foundation of American security policy.

This commentary accurately captures the purpose of the pastoral letter. The bishops intended to raise fundamental questions about the dynamic of the arms race and the direction of American nuclear strategy. We intended to criticize the rhetoric of the nuclear age and to expose the moral and political futility of a nuclear war. We wanted to provide a moral assessment of existing policy which would both set limits to political action and provide direction for a policy designed to lead us out of the dilemma of deterrence.

It is the lessons we can learn from the policy impact of the pastoral which are valuable today. The principal conclusion is that the Church's social policy role is at least as important in *defining* key questions in the public debate as in *deciding* such questions. The impact of the pastoral was due in part to its specific positions and conclusions, but it was also due to the way it brought the entire nuclear debate under scrutiny.

The letter was written at a time it called a "new moment" in the nuclear age. The "new moment" is a mix of public perceptions and policy proposals. The public sense of the fragility of our security system is today a palpable reality. The interest in the TV showing of "The Day After" is an example of how the public is taken by the danger of our present condition. But the "new moment" is also a product of new ideas, or at least the shaking of the foundation under old ideas.

Another commentary generated during the drafting of the pastoral letter, this one from *The New Republic*, identified the policy characteristics of the "new moment":

> The ground is not steady beneath the nuclear forces of the United States. The problem is not modes of basing but modes of thinking. The traditional strategy for our nuclear arsenal is shaken by a war of ideas about its purpose, perhaps the most decisive war of ideas in its history.

The significant fact to which this editorial points is that the "new moment" is an "open moment" in the strategic debate. Ideas are under scrutiny and established policies are open to criticism in a way we have not seen since the late 1950's. From the proposal of "no first use," through the debate about the MX, to the concept of a Nuclear Freeze, the nuclear policy question is open to reassessment and redirection. The potential contained in the "new moment" will not last forever; policies must be formulated, ideas will crystallize and some consensus will be shaped. As yet, the content of the consensus is not clear.

The fundamental contribution of *The Challenge of Peace*, I believe, is that we have been part of a few central forces which have created the "new moment." We have helped to shape the debate; now we face the question of whether we can help to frame a new consensus concerning nuclear policy.

The "new moment" is filled with potential; it is also filled with danger. The dynamic of the nuclear relationship between the superpowers is not a stable one. It is urgent that a consensus be shaped which will move us beyond our present posture. The pastoral letter has opened space in the public debate for a consideration of the moral factor. How we use the moral questions, that is, how we relate them to the strategic and political elements, is the key to our contribution to the "new moment." I could spend the entire lecture on the moral dimension of the nuclear debate, but my purpose is rather to relate the experience we have had in dealing with the nuclear question to other issues. Without leaving the topic of the war and peace discussion, I will try to show how our contribution to this issue is part of a larger potential which Catholic moral vision has in the public policy arena. This larger potential is to foster a consideration of a consistent ethic of life and its implications for us today.

II. A Consistent Ethic of Life: A Catholic Perspective

The Challenge of Peace provides a starting point for developing a consistent ethic of life but it does not provide a fully articulated framework. The central idea in the letter is the sacredness of human life and the responsibility we have, personally and socially, to protect and preserve the sanctity of life.

Precisely because life is sacred, the taking of even one human life is a momentous event. Indeed, the sense that every human life has transcendent value has led a whole stream of the Christian tradition to argue that life may never be taken. That position is held by an increasing number of Catholics and is reflected in the pastoral letter, but it has not been the dominant view in Catholic teaching and it is not the principal moral position found in the pastoral letter. What is found in the letter is the traditional Catholic teaching that there should always be a *presumption* against taking human life, but in a limited world marked by the effects of sin there are some narrowly defined *exceptions* where life can be taken. This is the moral logic which produced the "Just-War" ethic in Catholic theology.

While this style of moral reasoning retains its validity as a method of resolving extreme cases of conflict when fundamental rights are at stake, there has been a perceptible shift of emphasis in the teaching and pastoral practice of the Church in the last 30 years. To summarize the shift succinctly, the presumption against taking human life has been strengthened and the exceptions made ever more restrictive. Two examples, one at the level of principle, the other at the level of pastoral practice, illustrate the shift.

First, in a path-breaking article in 1959 in *Theological Studies*, John Courtney Murray, S.J., demonstrated that Pope Pius XII had reduced the traditional threefold justification for going to war (defense, recovery of property and punishment) to the single reason of defending the innocent and protecting those values required for decent human existence. Second, in the case of capital punishment, there has been a shift at the level of pastoral practice. While not denying the classical position, found in the writing of Thomas Aquinas and other authors, that the state has the right to employ capital punishment, the action of Catholic bishops and Popes Paul VI and John Paul II has been directed against the exercise of that right by the state. The argument has been that more humane methods of defending the society exist and should be used. Such humanitarian concern lies behind the policy position of the National Conference of Catholic Bishops against capital punishment, the opposition expressed by individual bishops in their home states against reinstating the death penalty, and the extraordinary interventions of Pope John Paul II and the Florida bishops seeking to prevent the execution in Florida last week.

Rather than extend the specific analysis of this shift of emphasis at the levels of both principle and practice in Catholic thought, I wish to probe the rationale behind the shift and indicate what it teaches us about the need for a consistent ethic of life. Fundamental to the shift is a more acute perception of the multiple ways in which life is threatened today. Obviously questions like war, aggression and capital punishment have been with us for centuries and are not new to us. What is new is the *context* in which these ancient questions arise, and the way in which a new context shapes the *content* of our ethic of life. Let me comment on the relationship of the context of our culture and the content of our ethic in terms of: 1) the *need* for a consistent ethic of life; 2) the *attitude* necessary to sustain it; and 3) the *principles* needed to shape it.

The dominant cultural fact, present in both modern warfare and modern medicine, which induces a sharper awareness of the fragility of human life is our technology. To live as we do in an age of careening development of technology is to face a qualitatively new range of moral problems. War has been a perennial threat to human life, but today the threat is qualitatively different due to nuclear weapons. We now threaten life on a scale previously unimaginable. As the pastoral letter put it, the dangers of nuclear war teach us to read the Book of Genesis with new eyes. From the inception of life to its decline, a rapidly expanding technology opens new opportunities for care but also poses new potential to threaten the sanctity of life.

The technological challenge is a pervasive concern of Pope John Paul II, expressed in his first encyclical, *Redemptor Hominis,* and continuing through his address to the Pontifical Academy of Science last month when he called scientists to direct their work toward the promotion of life, not the creation of instruments of death. The essential question in the technological challenge is this: In an age when we *can* do almost anything, how do we decide what we *ought* to do? The even more demanding question is: In a time when we can do anything technologically, how do we decide morally what *we never should do?*

Asking these questions along the spectrum of life from womb to tomb creates the need for a consistent ethic of life. For the spectrum of life cuts across the issues of genetics, abortion, capital punishment, modern warfare and the care of the terminally ill. These are all distinct problems, enormously complicated, and deserving individual treatment. No single answer and no simple responses will solve them. My purpose, however, is to highlight the way in which we face new technological challenges in each one of these areas; this combination of challenges is what cries out for a consistent ethic of life.

Such an ethic will have to be finely honed and carefully structured on the basis of values, principles, rules and applications to specific cases. It is not my task today, nor within my competence as a bishop, to spell out all the details of such an ethic. It is to that task that philosophers and poets, theologians and technicians, scientists and strategists, political leaders and plain citizens are called. I would, however, highlight a basic issue: the need for an attitude or atmosphere in society which is the pre-condition for sustaining a consistent ethic of life. The development of such an atmosphere has been the primary concern of the "Respect Life" program of the American bishops. We intend our opposition to abortion and our opposition to nuclear war to be seen as specific applications of this broader attitude. We have also opposed the death penalty because we do not think its use cultivates an attitude of respect for life in society. The purpose of proposing a consistent ethic of life is to argue that success on any one of the issues threatening life requires a concern for the broader attitude in society about respect for human life.

Attitude is the place to root an ethic of life, but ultimately ethics is about principles to guide the actions of individuals and institutions. It is therefore necessary to illustrate, at least by way of example, my proposition that an inner relationship does exist among several issues not only at the level of general attitude but at the more specific level of moral principles. Two examples will serve to indicate the point.

The first is contained in *The Challenge of Peace* in the connection drawn between Catholic teaching on war and Catholic teaching on abortion. Both, of course, must be seen in light of an attitude of respect for life. The more explicit connection is based on the principle which prohibits the directly intended taking of innocent human life. The principle is at the heart of Catholic teaching on abortion; it is because the fetus is judged to be both human and not an aggressor that Catholic teaching concludes that direct attack on fetal life is always wrong. This is also why we insist that legal protection be given to the unborn.

The same principle yields the most stringent, binding and radical conclusion of the pastoral letter: that directly intended attacks on civilian centers are always wrong. The bishops seek to highlight the power of this conclusion by specifying its implications in two ways: first, such attacks would be wrong even if our cities had been hit first; second, anyone asked to execute such attacks should refuse orders. These two extensions of the principle cut directly into the policy debate on nuclear strategy and the personal decisions of citizens. James Reston referred to them as "an astonishing challenge to the power of the state."

The use of this principle exemplifies the meaning of a consistent ethic of life. The principle which structures both cases, war and abortion, needs to be upheld in both places. It cannot be successfully sustained on one count and simultaneously eroded in a similar situation. When one carries this principle into the public debate today, however, one meets significant opposition from very different places on the political and ideological spectrum. Some see clearly the application of the principle to abortion but contend the bishops overstepped their bounds when they applied it to choices about national security. Others understand the power of the principle in the strategic debate, but find its application on abortion a violation of the realm of private choice. I contend the viability of the principle depends upon the consistency of its application.

The issue of consistency is tested in a different way when we examine the relationship between the "right to life" and "quality of life" issues. I must confess that I think the relationship of these categories is inadequately understood in the Catholic community itself. My point is that the Catholic position on abortion demands of us and of society that we seek to influence an heroic social ethic.

If one contends, as we do, that the right of every fetus to be born should be protected by civil law and supported by civil consensus, then our moral, political and economic responsibilities do not stop at the moment of birth. Those who defend the right to life of the weakest among us must be equally visible in support of the quality of life of the powerless among us: the old and the young, the hungry and the homeless, the undocumented immigrant and the unemployed worker. Such a quality of life posture translates into specific political and economic positions on tax policy, employment generation, welfare policy, nutrition and feeding programs, and health care. Consistency means we cannot have it both ways. We cannot urge a compassionate society and vigorous public policy to protect the rights of the unborn and then argue that compassion and significant public programs on behalf of the needy undermine the moral fibre of the society or are beyond the proper scope of governmental responsibility.

Right to life and quality of life complement each other in domestic social policy. They are also complementary in foreign policy. *The Challenge of Peace* joined the question of how we prevent nuclear war to the question of how we build peace in an interdependent world. Today those who are admirably concerned with reversing the nuclear arms race must also be those who stand for a positive U.S. policy of building the peace. It is this linkage which has led the U.S. bishops not only to oppose the drive of the nuclear arms race, but to stand against the dynamic of a Central American policy which relies predominantly on the threat and the use of force, which is increasingly distancing itself from a concern for human rights in El Salvador and which fails to grasp the opportunity of a diplomatic solution to the Central American conflict.

The relationship of the spectrum of life issues is far more intricate than I can even sketch here. I have made the case in the broad strokes of a lecturer; the detailed balancing, distinguishing and connecting of different aspects of a consistent ethic of life is precisely what this address calls the university community to investigate. Even as I leave this challenge before you, let me add to it some reflections on the task of communicating a consistent ethic of life in a pluralistic society.

III. Catholic Ethics and the American Ethos: The Challenge and the Opportunity

A consistent ethic of life must be held by a constituency to be effective. The building of such a constituency is precisely the task before the Church and the nation. There are two distinct challenges, but they are complementary.

We should begin with the honest recognition that the shaping of a consensus among Catholics on the spectrum of life issues is far from finished. We need the kind of dialogue on these issues which the pastoral letter generated on the nuclear question. We need the same searching intellectual exchange, the same degree of involvement of clergy, religious and laity, the same sustained attention in the Catholic press.

There is no better place to begin than by using the follow-through for the pastoral letter. Reversing the arms race, avoiding nuclear war and moving toward a world freed of the nuclear threat are profoundly "pro-life" issues. The Catholic Church is today seen as an institution and a community committed to these tasks. We should not lose this momentum; it provides a solid foundation to relate our concerns about war and peace to other "pro-life" questions. The agenda facing us involves our ideas and our institutions; it must be both educational and political; it requires attention to the way these several life issues are defined in the public debate and how they are decided in the policy process.

The shaping of a consensus in the Church must be joined to the larger task of sharing our vision with the wider society. Here two questions face us: the substance of our position and the style of our presence in the policy debate.

The substance of a Catholic position on a consistent ethic of life is rooted in a religious vision. But the citizenry of the United States is radically pluralistic in moral and religious conviction. So we face the challenge of stating our case, which is shaped in terms of our faith and our religious convictions, in non-religious terms which others of different faith convictions might find morally persuasive. Here again the war and peace debate should be a useful model. We have found support from individuals and groups who do not share our Catholic faith but who have found our moral analysis compelling.

In the public policy exchange, substance and style are closely related. The issues of war, abortion, and capital punishment are emotional and often divisive questions. As we seek to shape and share the vision of a consistent ethic of life, I suggest a style governed by the following rule: We should maintain and clearly articulate our religious convictions but also maintain our civil courtesy. We should be vigorous in stating a case and attentive in hearing another's case; we should test everyone's logic but not question his or her motives.

The proposal I have outlined today is a multi-dimensional challenge. It grows out of the experience I have had in the war and peace debate and the task I see ahead as Chairman of the Pro-Life Committee. But it also grows from a conviction that there is a new openness today in society to the role of moral argument and moral vision in our public affairs. I say this even though I find major aspects of our domestic and foreign policy in need of drastic change. Bringing about these changes is the challenge of a consistent ethic of life. The challenge is worth our energy, resources and commitment as a Church.

A Consistent Ethic of Life: Continuing the Dialogue

The William Wade Lecture Series
St. Louis University
Joseph Cardinal Bernardin
March 11, 1984

I first wish to express my appreciation to St. Louis University for the invitation to deliver the 1984 Wade Lecture. "The William Wade Lecture Series" is a fitting way to celebrate Father Wade's life as a priest, a philosopher, and a teacher. His interest in the moral issues confronting today's Church and society was an inspiration to all who knew him. I hope that my participation in this series will help to keep alive his memory and his ideals.

Three months ago I gave a lecture at Fordham University honoring another Jesuit educator, Father John Gannon, and I addressed the topic of a consistent ethic of life. That lecture has generated a substantial discussion both inside and outside the Church on the linkage of life issues, issues which, I am convinced, constitute a "seamless garment." This afternoon I would like to extend the discussion by expanding upon the idea of a consistent ethic of life.

The setting of a Catholic university is one deliberately chosen for these lectures. My purpose is to foster the kind of sustained intellectual analysis and debate which the Jesuit tradition has cultivated throughout its history. The discussion must go beyond the university but it will not occur without the involvement of Catholic universities. I seek to call attention to the resources in the Catholic tradition for shaping a viable public ethic. I hope to engage others in the Church and in the wider civil society in an examination of the challenges to human life which surround us today, and the potential of a consistent ethic of life. The Fordham lecture has catalyzed a vigorous debate; I seek to enlarge it, not to end it.

I will address three topics today: (1) the case for a consistent ethic of life; (2) the distinct levels of the problem; and (3) the contribution of a consistent ethic to the Church and society generally.

I. The Seamless Garment: The Logic of the Case

The invitation extended to me for both the Gannon Lecture at Fordham and the Wade Lecture today asked that I address some aspect of the bishops' pastoral, "The Challenge of Peace: God's Promise and Our Response." While I would gladly have spent each lecture on the question of war and peace, I decided that it was equally necessary to show how the pastoral is rooted in a wider moral vision. Understanding that vision can enhance the way we address specific questions like the arms race. When I set forth the argument about this wider moral vision—a consistent ethic of life—it evoked favorable comments, often from individuals and groups who had supported the peace pastoral but found themselves at odds with other positions the Catholic Church has taken on issues touching human life. At the same time, the Fordham address also generated letters from people who fear that the case for a consistent ethic will smother the Catholic opposition to abortion or will weaken our stance against the arms race.

Precisely in response to these concerns, I wish to state the essence of the case for a consistent ethic of life, specifying *why* it is needed and *what* is actually being advocated in a call for such an ethic. There are, in my view, two reasons why we need to espouse a consistent ethic of life: (1) the dimensions of the threats to life today; and (2) the value of our moral vision.

The threat to human life posed by nuclear war is so tangible that it has captured the attention of the nation. Public opinion polls rank it as one of the leading issues in the 1984 election campaign; popular movements like the "nuclear Freeze" and professional organizations of physicians and scientists have shaped the nuclear question in terms which engage citizens and experts alike.

The Church is part of the process which has raised the nuclear issue to a new standing in our public life. I submit that the Church should be a leader in the dialogue which shows that the nuclear question itself is part of the larger cultural—political—moral drama. Pope John Paul II regularly situates his examination of the nuclear issue in the framework of the broader problem of technology, politics, and ethics.

When this broader canvas is analyzed, the concern for a specific issue does not recede, but the meaning of multiple threats to life today—the full dimension of the problems of politics and technology—becomes vividly clear. The case being made here is not a condemnation of either politics or technology, but a recognition with the Pope that, on a range of key issues, "it is only through a conscious choice and through a deliberate policy that humanity can be saved." That quote from the Holy Father has unique relevance to nuclear war, but it can be used creatively to address other threats to life.

The range of application is all too evident: nuclear war *threatens* life on a previously unimaginable scale; abortion *takes* life daily on a horrendous scale; public executions are fast becoming weekly events in the most advanced technological society in history; and euthanasia is now openly discussed and even advocated. Each of these assaults on life has its own meaning and morality; they cannot be collapsed into one problem, but they must be confronted as pieces of a larger pattern.

The reason I have placed such stress on the idea of a consistent ethic of life from the beginning of my term as chairman of the Pro-Life Committee of the National Conference of Catholic Bishops is twofold: I am persuaded by the interrelatedness of these diverse problems, and I am convinced that the Catholic moral vision has the scope, the strength and the subtlety to address this wide range of issues in an effective fashion. It is precisely the potential of our moral vision that is often not recognized even within the community of the Church. The case for a consistent ethic of life—one which stands for the protection of the right to life and the promotion of the rights which enhance life from womb to tomb—manifests the positive potential of the Catholic moral and social tradition.

It is both a complex and a demanding tradition; it joins the humanity of the unborn infant and the humanity of the hungry; it calls for positive legal action to prevent the killing of the unborn or the aged and positive societal action to provide shelter for the homeless and education for the illiterate. The potential of the moral and social vision is appreciated in a new way when the *systemic* vision of Catholic ethics is seen as the background for the *specific* positions we take on a range of issues.

In response to those who fear otherwise, I contend that the systemic vision of a consistent ethic of life will not erode our crucial public opposition to the direction of the arms race; neither will it smother our persistent and necessary public opposition to abortion. The systemic vision is rooted in the conviction that our opposition to these distinct problems has a common foundation and that both Church and society are served by making it evident.

A consistent ethic of life does not equate the problem of taking life (e.g., through abortion and in war) with the problem of promoting human dignity (through humane programs of nutrition, health care, and housing). But a consistent ethic identifies both the protection of life and its promotion as moral questions. It argues for a continuum of life which must be sustained in the face of diverse and distinct threats.

A consistent ethic does not say everyone in the Church must do all things, but it does say that as individuals and groups pursue one issue, whether it is opposing abortion or capital punishment, the *way* we oppose one threat should be related to support for a systemic vision of life. It is not necessary or possible for every person to engage in each issue, but it is both possible and necessary for the Church as a whole to cultivate a conscious explicit connection among the several issues. And it is very necessary for preserving a systemic vision that individuals and groups who seek to witness to life at one point of the spectrum of life not be seen as insensitive to or even opposed to other moral claims on the overall spectrum of life. Consistency does rule out contradictory moral positions about the unique value of human life. No one is called to do everything, but each of us can do something. And we can strive not to stand against each other when the protection *and* the promotion of life are at stake.

II. The Seamless Garment: The Levels of the Question

A consistent ethic of life should honor the complexity of the multiple issues it must address. It is necessary to distinguish several levels of the question. Without attempting to be comprehensive, allow me to explore four distinct dimensions of a consistent ethic.

First, at the level of general moral principles, it is possible to identify a single principle with diverse applications. In the Fordham address I used the prohibition against direct attacks on innocent life. This principle is both central to the Catholic moral vision and systematically related to a range of specific moral issues. It prohibits direct attacks on unborn life in the womb, direct attacks on civilians in warfare, and the direct killing of patients in nursing homes.

Each of these topics has a constituency in society concerned with the morality of abortion, war, and care of the aged and dying. A consistent ethic of life encourages the specific concerns of each constituency, but also calls them to see the interrelatedness of their efforts. The need to defend the integrity of the moral principle in the full range of its application is a responsibility of each distinct constituency. If the principle is eroded in the public mind, all lose.

A second level of a consistent ethic stresses the distinction among cases rather than their similarities. We need different moral principles to apply to diverse cases. The classical distinction between ordinary and extraordinary means has applicability in the care of the dying but no relevance in the case of warfare. Not all moral principles have relevance across the whole range of life issues. Moreover, sometimes a systemic vision of the life issues requires a combination of moral insights to provide direction on one issue. At Fordham, I cited the classical teaching on capital punishment which gives the State the right to take life in defense of key social values. But I also pointed out how a concern for promoting a *public attitude* of respect for life has led the bishops of the United States to oppose the *exercise* of that right.

Some of the responses I have received on the Fordham address correctly say that abortion and capital punishment are not identical issues. The principle which protects *innocent* life distinguishes the unborn child from the convicted murderer.

Other letters stress that while nuclear war is a *threat* to life, abortion involves the actual *taking* of life, here and now. I accept both of these distinctions, of course, but I also find compelling the need to *relate* the cases while keeping them in distinct categories.

Abortion is taking of life in ever growing numbers in our society. Those concerned about it, I believe, will find their case enhanced by taking note of the rapidly expanding use of public execution. In a similar way, those who are particularly concerned about these executions, even if the accused has taken another life, should recognize the elementary truth that a society which can be indifferent to the innocent life of an unborn child will not be easily stirred to concern for a convicted criminal. There is, I maintain, a political and psychological linkage among the life issues—from war to welfare concerns—which we ignore at our own peril: a systemic vision of life seeks to expand the moral imagination of a society, not partition it into airtight categories.

A third level of the question before us involves how we relate a commitment to principles to our public witness of life. As I have said, no one can do everything. There are limits to both competency and energy; both point to the wisdom of setting priorities and defining distinct functions. The Church, however, must be credible across a wide range of issues; the very scope of our moral vision requires a commitment to a multiplicity of questions. In this way the teaching of the Church will sustain a variety of individual commitments.

Neither the Fordham address nor this one is intended to constrain wise and vigorous efforts to protect and promote life through specific, precise forms of action. Both addresses do seek to cultivate a dialogue within the Church and in the wider society among individuals and groups which draw on common principles (e.g., the prohibition against killing the innocent) but seem convinced that they do not share common ground. The appeal here is not for anyone to do everything, but to recognize points of interdependence which should be stressed, not denied.

A fourth level, one where dialogue is sorely needed, is the relationship between moral principles and concrete political choices. The moral questions of abortion, the arms race, the fate of social programs for the poor, and the role of human rights in foreign policy are public moral issues. The arena in which they are ultimately decided is not the academy or the Church but the political process. A consistent ethic of life seeks to present a coherent linkage among a diverse set of issues. It can and should be used to test party platforms, public policies, and political candidates. The Church legitimately fulfills a public role by articulating a framework for political choices by relating that framework to specific issues and by calling for systematic moral analysis of all areas of public policy.

This is the role our Bishops' Conference has sought to fulfill by publishing a "Statement on Political Responsibility" during each of the presidential and congressional election years in the past decade. The purpose is surely not to tell citizens how to vote, but to help shape the public debate and form personal conscience so that every citizen will vote thoughtfully and responsibly. Our "Statement on Political Responsibility" has always been, like our "Respect Life Program," a multi-issue approach to public morality. The fact that this Statement sets forth a spectrum of issues of current concern to the Church and society should not be understood as implying that all issues are qualitatively equal from a moral perspective.

As I indicated earlier, each of the life issues—while related to all the others—is distinct and calls for its own specific moral analysis. Both the Statement and the Respect Life program have direct relevance to the political order, but they are applied concretely by the choice of citizens. This is as it should be. In the political order the Church is primarily a teacher; it possesses a carefully cultivated tradition of moral analysis of personal and public issues. It makes that tradition available in a special manner for the community of the Church, but it offers it also to all who find meaning and guidance in its moral teaching.

III. The Seamless Garment: A Pastoral and Public Contribution

The moral teaching of the Church has both pastoral and public significance. Pastorally, a consistent ethic of life is a contribution to the witness of the Church's defense of the human person. Publicly, a consistent ethic fills a void in our public policy debate today.

Pastorally, I submit that a Church standing forth on the entire range of issues which the logic of our moral vision bids us to confront will be a Church in the style of both Vatican II's *Gaudium et Spes* and in the style of Pope John Paul II's consistent witness to life. The pastoral life of the Church should not be guided by a simplistic criterion of relevance. But the capacity of faith to shed light on the concrete questions of personal and public life today is one way in which the value of the Gospel is assessed.

Certainly the serious, sustained interest manifested throughout American society in the bishops' letter on war and peace provides a unique pastoral opportunity for the Church. Demonstrating how the teaching on war and peace is supported by a wider concern for all of life may bring others to see for the first time what our tradition has affirmed for a very long time: the linkage among the life issues.

The public value of a consistent ethic of life is connected directly to its pastoral role. In the public arena we should always speak and act like a Church. But the unique public possibility for a consistent ethic is provided precisely by the unstructured character of the public debate on the life questions. Each of the issues I have identified today—abortion, war, hunger and human rights, euthanasia and capital punishment—is treated as a separate, self-contained topic in our public life. Each is distinct, but an *ad hoc* approach to each one fails to illustrate how our choices in one area can affect our decisions in other areas. There must be a public attitude of respect for all of life if public actions are to respect it in concrete cases.

The pastoral on war and peace speaks of a "new moment" in the nuclear age. The pastoral has been widely studied and applauded because it caught the spirit of the "new moment" and spoke with moral substance to the issues of the "new moment." I am convinced there is an "open moment" before us on the agenda of life issues. It is a significant opportunity for the Church to demonstrate the strength of a sustained moral vision. I submit that a clear witness to a consistent ethic of life will allow us to grasp the opportunity of this "open moment" and serve both the sacredness of every human life and the God of Life who is the origin and support of our common humanity.

Linkage and the Logic of the Abortion Debate

Address for Right-to-Life Convention
Kansas City, Missouri
Joseph Cardinal Bernardin
June 7, 1984

I first wish to express my appreciation for the opportunity to address this Convention of the National Right-to-Life Committee. I take the chairmanship of the NCCB Committee for Pro-Life Activities as a very serious responsibility and a significant opportunity for service. I am convinced of the total personal commitment of each of our bishops to the philosophy and program of the pro-life movement. I am also equally convinced that the heart and soul of the movement is the personal dedication of all those who are represented at this meeting.

I thought it might be most useful for me to set forth in this address a general perspective of where we stand in the struggle against abortion, the struggle to protect the life of the unborn. It is now eleven years since the Supreme Court decisions which legalized abortion on request; there are lessons to be learned from this decade. In light of this experience, we can also examine our present choices and establish our future direction.

I. The Past: Witness for Life

An examination of the past decade generates both sadness and pride. Sadness—perhaps moral dismay is a better phrase—is a product of evaluating the abortion policy set in place by the 1973 Supreme Court decisions. Pride is the justifiable product of evaluating the efforts of thousands of volunteers who are committed to reversing the present national policy and re-establishing respect for the right to life as a national policy and practice.

First, the implications of *Roe v. Wade* bear examination. In order to grasp the dimensions of the present challenge we face, it is necessary to describe the depth of the problem created by the 1973 Supreme Court decisions. The decisions were radical in nature and systemic in their consequences. They were radical since they overturned in one stroke an existing political and legal structure which treated any form of abortion as an exception to normal practice. The end product of *Roe v. Wade* was to establish a political and legal framework with no restraint on abortion. Many of us sensed then, and all of us can be sure now, that public opinion was not at all in favor of a policy opening the floodgates to 1.5 million abortions a year. Some radical decisions are justified morally and they are necessary politically, but the Court decisions of 1973 were neither justified, necessary nor acceptable to large segments of the American public.

The Court's decisions were systemic in the sense that they changed not only a given law, but they established operating presumptions in medical practice, social service agencies and administrative policy which legitimated and facilitated access to abortion. The result of the decisions was to change the structure of this society's approach to abortion. What the decisions did not change was the substantial, broad-based and solidly grounded view of American citizens across the land that abortion on request is not a satisfactory way to address the real problems individuals and families face in this delicate area of respecting unborn life.

It was this deeply felt personal opposition to abortion which crystallized the public policy position of the pro-life movement. There has undoubtedly been a strong Catholic core to this movement, but it has cut across religious and political lines, as is evidenced by the participants in this convention. It is this pro-life constituency which is an authentic source of pride for anyone associated with it. At a time when grass roots coalitions are often talked about, the pro-life constituency has a claim second to none in demonstrating local support. At a time when citizen apathy is a serious public problem, the pro-life movement has mobilized men and women personally, professionally and politically in opposition to abortion. At a time when the moral dimension of public policy on a variety of issues is in need of a clear statement, the pro-life movement has cast the political issue in decisively moral terms. Finally, the movement has been not only political but pastoral. It has joined its public advocacy with practical efforts to provide alternatives to abortion.

For all these reasons, I maintain that the witness to life in the past decade has been a cause for hope and pride. The lessons learned in the decade of the 1970's prepare us to analyze our choices in the 1980's.

II. The Present: Shaping Public Choices for Life

The effect of the pro-life movement has not been limited to its inspirational quality; there has been a specific political impact. Eleven years after the Supreme Court decisions, and after a string of other legal actions reaffirming the Roe v. Wade philosophy, the pro-abortion philosophy has not been accepted by millions of Americans. In brief, the legal status of abortion still lacks public legitimacy. The political debate which ensued shows the nation radically divided on the state of public policy on abortion.

Normally, the force of existing law provides legitimacy for policy. Keeping the question open for reform and reversal of existing policy is a significant political victory. It is a tactical success. It should not, however, be mistaken for total success. Nonetheless, it provides space to move the nation toward a different future on abortion.

Creating space to change law and policy is a pre-condition for what must be accomplished. It is imperative in the 1980's to use the space creatively. In working to change national policy on abortion, I submit that we must cast our case in broadly defined terms, in a way which elicits support from others. We need to shape our position consciously in a way designed to generate interest in the abortion question from individuals who thus far have not been touched by our witness or our arguments.

Casting our perspectives broadly does not mean diluting its content. Quite the opposite. It involves a process of demonstrating how our position on abortion is deeply rooted in our religious tradition and, at the same time, is protective of fundamental ideas in our constitutional tradition.

Speaking from my perspective as a Roman Catholic bishop, I wish to affirm that the basis of our opposition to abortion is established by themes which should be compelling for the Catholic conscience because they are so centrally located in Catholic moral and social teaching. The basic moral principle that the direct killing of the innocent is always wrong is so fundamental in Catholic theology that the need to defend it in the multiple cases of abortion, warfare, and care of the handicapped and the terminally ill is self-evident. This is why one cannot, with consistency, claim to be truly pro-life if one applies the principle of the sanctity of life to other issues but rejects it in the case of abortion. By the same token, one cannot, with consistency, claim to be truly pro-life if one applies the principle to other issues but holds that the direct killing of innocent non-combatants in warfare is morally justified. To fail to stand for this principle is to make a fundamental error in Catholic moral thought. But the moral principle does not stand alone; it is related to other dimensions of Catholic social teaching.

The opposition to abortion is rooted in the conviction that civil law and social policy must always be subject to ongoing moral analysis. Simply because a civil law is in place does not mean that it should be blindly supported. To encourage reflective, informed assessment of civil law and policy is to keep alive the capacity for moral criticism in society. In addition, the Catholic position opposing abortion is rooted in our understanding of the role of the state in society. The state has positive moral responsibilities; it is not simply a neutral umpire; neither is its role limited to restraining evil. The responsibilities of the state include both the protection of innocent life from attack and enhancement of human life at every stage of its development. The fact of 1.5 million abortions a year in the United States erodes the moral character of the state; if the civil law can be neutral when innocent life is under attack, the implications for law and morality in our society are frightening.

These themes drawn from Catholic theology are not restricted in their application to the community of faith. These are truths of the moral and political order which are also fundamental to the Western constitutional heritage. The opposition to abortion, properly stated, is not a sectarian claim but a reflective, rational position which any person of good will may be invited to consider. Examples can be used to illustrate the convergence of our concerns about abortion with other key social questions in American society.

The appeal to a higher moral law to reform and refashion existing civil law was the central idea that Dr. Martin Luther King, Jr. brought to the civil rights movement of the 1960's. The pro-life movement of the 1980's is based on the same appeal. Pro-life today should be seen as an extension of the spirit of the civil rights movement. Similarly, the Baby Doe case has proved to be a meeting ground of principle and practice between civil rights and pro-life advocates. The common ground is as yet not sufficiently explored, but there is significant potential for development in this area.

Civil rights are the domestic application of the broader human rights tradition. The right to life is a fundamental basis of this tradition. By standing for the right to life in our society, we stand with all who argue for a strong national commitment to human rights in our domestic and foreign policy.

A final example of convergence is pertinent to your program today. Father Bruce Ritter has caught the imagination and interest of broad sectors of American society with his defense of human dignity in the face of sexual exploitation. The themes of the pro-life movement, promoting a sacred vision of sexuality and support for the family, coincide with Father Ritter's courageous and compassionate witness to life.

III. The Future: A Strategy for Witness to Life

It is precisely because I am convinced that demonstrating the linkage between abortion and other issues is both morally correct and tactically necessary for the pro-life position that I have been addressing the theme of a consistent ethic of life for Church and society. The convergence of themes concerning civil rights, human rights and family life with the abortion issue is simply an indication of deeper bonds which exist along the full range of pro-life issues.

The proposals I have made on the linkage of issues are, I submit, a systematic attempt to state the vision which has always been implicit in a Catholic conception of "pro-life." A Catholic view of the meaning of pro-life stresses the interdependence of life in a social setting, the way in which each of us relies upon the premise that others respect my life, and that society exists to guarantee that respect for each person. The interdependence of human life points towards the interrelationship of pro-life issues.

This interrelationship can be illustrated in precise, detailed moral arguments, but that is not my purpose in this address. I would simply appeal to a principle which I suspect is also an element of your own experience. It is the need to cultivate within society an attitude of respect for life on a series of issues, if the actions of individuals or groups are to reflect respect for life in specific choices. The linkage theme of a consistent ethic of life is designed to highlight the common interest and reciprocal need which exist among groups interested in specific issues—peace, abortion, civil rights, justice for the dispossessed or disabled—each of which depends upon a basic attitude of respect for life. The linkage theme provides us with an opportunity to win "friends" for the life issues. Just as we insist on the principle of the right to life, so too we must recognize the responsibility that our commitment places on us. Building bridges to people working on specific life issues demands respect and kindness toward these potential allies. An atmosphere of trust and understanding can do a great deal to promote the goals of the pro-life movement.

The consistent ethic seeks to build a bridge of common interest and common insight on a range of social and moral questions. It is designed to highlight the intrinsic ties which exist between public attitudes and personal actions on one side, and public policy on the other. Effective defense of life requires a coordinated approach to attitude, action and policy. The consistent ethic theme seeks to engage the moral imagination and political insight of diverse groups and to build a network of mutual concern for defense of life at every stage in the policies and practices of our society.

The need for such a common approach is dictated by the objective interrelationship among the life issues. The strength of the Catholic contribution to such an approach lies in the long and rich tradition of moral and social analysis which has provided us with both detailed guidance on individual moral issues and a framework of relating several issues in a coherent fashion.

If we pursue a consistent ethic systematically, it will become clear that abortion is not a "single issue," because it is not even a single kind of issue. It is an issue about the nature and future of the family, both in its own right and as a basic unit of society. It is an issue about equality under law for all human beings. And it is an issue of life or death. For this reason, developments in all these areas may not always be the direct responsibility of each person in the right-to-life movement, but they should always be of intense interest to all. Whatever makes our society more human, more loving, more respectful of the life and dignity of other, is a contribution to your struggle; for the more committed society becomes to justice and compassion, the more incongruous will be its toleration of the killing of the unborn child. And whatever promotes respect for that child cannot help but promote respect for all humanity. With that in mind, I urge you to recommit yourselves with renewed energy to this cause. Where humanity is threatened at its most defenseless, we have no choice. We must stand up on its behalf.

Address For National Consultation on Obscenity, Pornography and Indecency

Cincinnati, Ohio
Joseph Cardinal Bernardin
September 6, 1984

First let me express my gratitude for the invitation to address you this evening. It is always a pleasure to return to Cincinnati and my many friends here even if for only a few hours.

I would like also to commend the National Leadership Team for their dedicated work on behalf of the Consultation on Obscenity, Pornography and Indecency. It is indeed gratifying to hear that many church and civic leaders have shown their deep concern about the challenges that face our society on these issues.

I want to be clear at the outset that I do not come before you as a politician or a legal expert, an art critic or a psychologist. I am a believer and a pastor in the Catholic Church. Although there are behavioral, aesthetic, legal and political dimensions to the issues this Consultation seeks to address, my concern is primarily theological and religious and will reflect the Catholic heritage.

I am aware that this year's Consultation is especially geared to action. I agree that sharing ideas without acting upon them can be an exercise in frustration and futility. Nonetheless, our experience suggests that before, during, and after taking action we need to continue reflection upon the basic vision and values that have motivated our actions. This helps ensure that we are clear about our purpose and that our actions are guided by our values.

That is why my reflections will seek to address the broader perspective of our vision and values and how these should shape our strategies for facing the problems of obscenity, pornography, and indecency in our society. My reflections are basically twofold: (1) the theological basis of our opposition to these problems and (2) some guiding principles that relate to our strategies for action.

I. The Dignity of the Human Person

The theological foundation of our opposition to obscenity, pornography, and indecency is the dignity of the human person. Although we include many concerns in our social ministry, the common element that links these concerns is our conviction about the unique dignity of each human person.

The very first chapter of Genesis states unequivocally that humanity represents the summit of the creative process. The Creator places all creation in our hands, giving us the awesome responsibility of stewardship over the earth's resources, including the gift of each human life. There is more to the human story: God makes each human person in his own image and likeness—not exactly a carbon copy, but, at least, a close resemblance. The person is the clearest reflection of the presence of God among us. To lay violent hands on the person is to come as close as we can to laying violent hands on God. To diminish the human person is to come as close as we can to diminishing God. Human dignity derives both from the creative act of God and from the constant care and concern that God shows toward all people.

This is the truth about the human person, a truth that makes us free. Unfortunately, there are many individuals, institutions, and systems in contemporary life which propagate as freedom what, in reality, is slavery. True human freedom is not illusory or superficial; it is found only when we face the truth about human life—the inherent dignity of each human being in all aspects and dimensions, including sexuality.

From our recognition of the worth of all people under God flow the responsibilities of a "social" morality. Catholic social doctrine is based on two truths about the human person: human life is both sacred and social. Because we esteem human life as sacred, we have a duty to protect and foster it at all stages of development, from conception to death, and in all circumstances. Because we acknowledge that human life is also social, we must develop the kind of societal environment that protects and fosters its development.

It is clearly inadequate simply to say that human life is sacred and to explain why this is so. It is also necessary to examine and respond to the challenges to the unique dignity and sacredness of human life today. Human life has always been sacred, and there have always been threats to it. However, we live in a period of history when we have produced, sometimes with the best of intentions, a technology and a capacity to threaten and diminish human life which previous generations could not even imagine.

In the first instance, there are *life-threatening* issues such as genetics, abortion, capital punishment, modern warfare, and euthanasia. These assaults on life cannot be collapsed into one problem; they are all distinct, enormously complicated, and deserving of individual treatment. No single answer and no simple response will solve them. Still, they must be confronted as pieces of a larger pattern.

That is why I have argued frequently during the past year for the need of developing a "consistent ethic of life" that seeks to build a bridge of common interest and common insight on a range of social and moral questions. Successful resolution of *any* of these issues is dependent upon the broader attitude within society regarding overall respect for life. Attitude is the place to root a consistent ethic of life. A change of attitude, in turn, can lead to a change of policies and practices in our society.

In sum, when human life under any circumstance is not held as sacred in a society, *all* human life in that society is threatened. When it *is* held as sacred in all circumstances, all human life is protected.

In the second instance, there are *life-diminishing* issues, such as prostitution, pornography, sexism, and racism. Again, each is a distinct problem, enormously complex, worthy of individual attention and action. Nonetheless, understanding that they all contribute in some way to a diminishment of human dignity provides a theological foundation for more specific reflection and concrete action.

At the same time, we need to face the fact that life-diminishing issues can become life-threatening. News reports frequently chronicle how prostitution, pornography, sexism and racism can all too easily lead to violence and death in our society. With regard to pornography, psychological research appears to confirm this assertion. We can say then that, when human life is diminished in any circumstances in a society, it contributes to the devaluing of *all* human life in that society.

Each human person is a paradox. Each of us has the capacity for seeking and expressing what is true, good and beautiful. Each of us also has the potential for embracing what is false, evil, and ugly. We can love and we can hate. We can serve and we can dominate. We can respect and we can diminish. We can protect human life and we can threaten it.

When I say "we," I do not mean simply each of us acting on his or her own. I also include our local communities, our nation, our entire society. Every social system—east or west, north or south—should be judged by the way in which it reverences, or fails to reverence, the unique and equal dignity of every person.

Our concern is not simply individual human rights but also the common good. Individual rights are to contribute to the good of society, not infringe upon other people's legitimate rights.

Human life is diminished when women or men, and especially children, are exploited in the production of pornography, whether in print, film, or television. A sacrilegious note is added when the sacred persons and symbols of religion are exploited. Diminishment of human dignity also occurs in the lives of those who purchase or use pornography. Even more serious diminishment can occur because pornography is not so much an outlet for the baser instincts of the human person, but a stimulant. Violence, degradation, and humiliation are simply not compatible with the true sexual nature of the human person.

It is relatively easy to make a case against certain kinds of sexual propaganda as corruptive of human freedom and dignity. They destroy or diminish rational freedom either by damaging the capacity for personal reflection or by exciting the passions to the extent where they interfere with rational control of thought and behavior. They diminish human dignity by reducing human persons to sex objects.

However, we must acknowledge that pornography like prostitution seems to have a permanent attraction for some people despite the fact that it perversely and sometimes viciously profanes the sacredness of sex and the dignity of human person.

What are we to do about such propaganda? When we ask that question we reach the threshold of the problem of social freedom, an issue that is as complex as it is essential for consultations such as this.

II. The Shaping of Action Strategies

I would like to address three topics in this section: (a) the distinction between morality and law, (b) the importance of striking a balance between freedom and restraint in society, and (c) the necessity of being faithful to our vision and values in whatever response we make to obscenity, pornography, and indecency in our society.

A. Distinction between Moral Principles and Law

Morality and law are clearly related but also need to be differentiated. Although the premises of law are found in moral principles, the scope of law is more limited and its purpose is not the moralization of society. Moral principles govern personal and social human conduct and cover as well interior acts and motivation. Civil statutes govern public order and concern only external acts and values that are formally social.

Hence it is not the function of law to enjoin or prohibit everything that moral principles enjoin or prohibit. History has shown over and over again that people can be coerced only into a minimum of moral actions. It would seem, therefore, that, when we pursue a legal course of action with regard to such matters as sexual morality, our expectations may have to be somewhat more limited than in other areas of human morality.

A further corollary of this is also demonstrable from our own American history. People obey good laws because they are good. When a law is held in contempt, it can defeat its own purpose and erode respect for law itself.

I am pointing this out not as an argument against a legal response to the problems we are addressing in this Consultation, but simply to put such a response in perspective, to make sure that it is sound and supportable.

B. Striking a Balance between Freedom and Restraint

Because human freedom is such an inalienable right, any constraint in society must be for the sake of freedom; that is, the constraint must create a freedom in another respect. This means that we must search for ways to strike a balance between freedom and restraint in society.

This is especially important when the restraint in question involves the area of communication within society. When we encounter sexual propaganda that is corruptive of human freedom, we need to ask ourselves whether the corruption is such that it requires attention by organized society. A second set of questions concerns whether public or private agencies in the society should attend to the corruptive influences. And, assuming that public order is the norm whose requirements are to be enforced in this action, we have to ask what requirements of public order can be applied validly against the claims of freedom.

The reason for ensuring that restraints against the claims of freedom are valid is that the limitation of freedom has many consequences—some of them identifiable only after the restraints have been imposed. One of the main consequences possible is that we may be taking the risk of damaging freedom in a third domain with consequences more dangerous to the community. At best the effect toward which we aim can only be foreseen with probability, not certainty. We are familiar with the biblical example of "the last state of the man becoming worse than the first."

Let me expand on this a bit to avoid misunderstanding. As the recipients of the Judaeo-Christian heritage, we do not condemn every portrayal of vice. Not infrequently, the Bible itself portrays vice and violence. The biblical text not only records the history of salvation; it also wrestles with the problems associated with that history.   The biblical authors did not avoid portraying the most vicious and violent components of human behavior. They confront this dimension of human life rather than escape from it.

Similarly, as Richard Griffiths has pointed out, "a refusal to experience art that often deals with eroticism and violence may be a refusal to face the world as it really is. But experience must lead to confrontation, not compromise." Overprotection can do almost as much harm as bad example in hindering young persons who are preparing to assume their rightful role in a human society which involves the experiences of eroticism and violence. Their proper role, of course, is one of confrontation rather than compromise when human life and dignity are threatened or diminished.

I want to make it clear that I am *not* suggesting that some pornography is legitimate. What I *am* saying is that we need a well-reasoned approach to the problems we are addressing with the express purpose of striking a balance between freedom and restraint.

Only then will we find the broad base of support needed for effective action in the legal sphere. We may not find a simple formula that is applicable to all cases and similar for all segments of our society. The late Rev. John Courtney Murray, S.J., a respected authority on church-state matters, said that "in the United States we have constitutionally decided that the presumption is in favor of freedom, and that the advocate of constraint must make a convincing argument for its necessity or utility in the particular case." That is why the credibility of the argument is so essential to success in these matters.

Proceeding with great care and deliberation will help ensure an effective solution to the corruptive influences of obscenity, pornography, and indecency in our society. An uncritical approach runs the risk of grossly oversimplifying the problem and is inappropriate, given the importance of our primary concern: the worth and dignity of the human person. Public opinion can be changed regarding an issue like pornography to the extent that it encounters well-reasoned articles and oral communications as well as Christian witness on a personal level.

Having made these comments about the care with which we must proceed in addressing the problem of obscenity, pornography and indecency in our society, I wish to reaffirm the urgency of the challenge confronting us and the need to face up to it creatively and decisively. We need to take legal action against these corruptive influences in our society. I accepted your invitation to address this Consultation because I want publicly to support your efforts.

I mentioned earlier my conviction that we must approach the various life issues with a certain ethical consistency. It is precisely that consistency which brings me here this evening.

As I said in a lecture I gave at the University of St. Louis this past March,

> A consistent ethic of life does not equate the problem of taking life with the problem of promoting human dignity. But a consistent ethic identifies both the protection of life and its promotion as moral questions. It argues for a continuum of life which must be sustained in the face of diverse and distinct threats. . . Consistency rules out contradictory moral positions about the unique value (and dignity) of human life.

The comprehensive moral vision, which the consistent ethic of life promotes, demands that we work together to eliminate the evils of obscenity, pornography, and indecency even as we address the other evils which threaten and diminish life in today's society.

C. Fidelity to Vision and Values

Christian witness includes fidelity to our vision and values as we carry out our social ministry. We know that pornography is primarily directed at the weaker members of our society: the immature and the inadequate, frequently children and teenagers. Our biblical tradition calls upon us to defend the rights of the weaker members of our society—today's widows, orphans, and resident aliens—who too easily can become the objects of oppression, degradation, and de-valuing. The Scriptures also tell us that it is a serious matter indeed to lead the little ones astray. Our ministry does not imply that we are superior to these brothers and sisters; neither does it signify that we have no base instincts within ourselves.

Fidelity to our mission means that we have to be careful that we do not contribute to the diminishment or devaluation of human persons as we combat the corruptive influences of obscenity, pornography, and indecency. Fidelity to our mission means not isolating these problems from other life-threatening or life-diminishing issues in the sense of neglecting anything that threatens human life or diminishes human dignity.

One further reflection: it is important that we portray beauty and not simply unmask ugliness. It is essential that we promote virtue and not simply scorn vice. It matters that we proclaim the truth of human dignity and freedom and not simply attack falsity and illusions. In a consumer-oriented society, we need to remind each person that our worth derives from who we are rather than what we own. In a society that prizes individualism, we need to promote the common good as well. In a society that is preoccupied with sexuality, we need to stress that human value consists in more than physical attractiveness, that the value of actors and writers and film makers is more than their ability to meet particular public demands.

The concerns that we are addressing in this Consultation are important, first of all, because they concern human life and dignity. They command our attention at this point in our history because there are so many influences in our society that seek to corrupt human life and cheapen human dignity. These are complex matters that do not allow for simple solutions. Thinking and reflecting and deliberating together, I am confident that we can arrive at solutions which will improve the societal environment in which we seek to protect and foster human life and dignity in all of its circumstances and in all its stages of development.

The Face of Poverty Today: A Challenge for the Church

The Catholic University of America
Joseph Cardinal Bernardin
January 17, 1985

Let me begin by expressing my appreciation to Father Byron, President of Catholic University, for the invitation to deliver this address on the fact of poverty and the challenge it poses for the Church. Both the topic and the place of the lecture have special relevance.

The bishops of the United States are engaged in a major effort to help the Church in the U.S. in its analysis and response to the fact of poverty. The first draft of the pastoral letter, "Catholic Social Teaching and the U.S. Economy," is merely an initial step in an extended process. Its goal is to engage every level of the Church in study, discussion and decisions about how the Church can and must respond to the cry of the poor.

The opportunity for me to address an audience at Catholic University as part of this process has both symbolic and substantive significance. The Church always acts with a sense of its history and its tradition. The tradition of the U.S. Church's social teaching on poverty has been profoundly influenced by this University. To come to the intellectual home of Msgr.

John A. Ryan and Bishop Francis Haas, of Father Paul Hanley Furfey and Msgr. George Higgins is to acknowledge the U.S. Church's debt to this University. It also recognizes that the social tradition continues here, symbolized by Fr. Byron's own ministry and by the work of so many of your faculty.

My purpose this evening is to analyze the relationship of the Church to the fact of poverty in our time. I will examine where we stand as a Church, what we can bring to the struggle against poverty, and how we should proceed in this struggle precisely as the Church.

More specifically, I will address three questions: the nature of the problem we face, the role of the Church, and one aspect of the policy debate on poverty.

I. The Nature of the Problem: The Fact and The Faces of Poverty

Let me begin with two assertions: (1) much of the poverty in the world is hidden from us; (2) the poor usually live at the margin of society and too often at the margin of awareness of those who are not poor. Yet, in the world of the 1980s, although many of the poor are hidden, it is also impossible for the rest of us to hide from the poor.

The faces of poverty are all around us. Chicago and Washington are different cities, but I have lived in both of them long enough to know that the only way to hide from the poor is to stay in one's room or home. We cannot walk to work or to the bus stop, we cannot run a noontime errand without seeing the faces of poverty—on the heating grates, in the doorways, near the bus terminal and huddled in the winter around the places which serve the cheapest cup of coffee.

After walking through the poverty of the city during the day, we are confronted with the faces of poverty on a wider scale in the nightly news. Ethiopia is an extreme case, but not as extreme as we might first think. The fact of poverty is the dominant social reality for over 100 countries of the world. Numbers can be numbing in their effect, but they can also crystallize a challenge.

The fact of global poverty means:

• 800 million people live in conditions of "absolute poverty," that is, "a condition of life so limited by malnutrition, illiteracy, disease, high infant mortality, and low life expectancy as to be beneath any rational definition of human decency";

• 2.26 billion people—half of the world's population—live in countries with a per capita income of less than $400 per year;

• 450 million people are malnourished.

Statistics illustrating the global reality of poverty could be given in much greater detail, of course. But statistics do not tell us all we need to know. The Gospel points out that these poor people are our brothers and sisters. The first draft of the pastoral letter wisely devotes a substantial section to the U.S. relationship with the rest of the world because the resources of this nation and its role in the world constitute a serious responsibility in responding to the absolute poverty of our 800 million brothers and sisters.

My specific concern this evening, however, is not the faces and figures of global poverty, but poverty in the United States. The fact of world poverty is so massive that it can overwhelm us. The fact of poverty in the United States is a part of our national life, but it is not recognized as a dominant fact of our existence. It can easily blend into a larger picture which stresses—not poverty—but the power and productivity of the nation.

Poverty is surely present but, in the dominant national perspective— provided by magazines, media and movies—it is not a significant feature. Poverty is present but, when we plan for the future, the poor are not central to the planning. Poverty is present but, in the policy debates of the nation, the poor exercise little leverage.

The drafting of the pastoral letter on the economy is still in its early stages. However, it has already accomplished something which commentators have quickly noticed: The letter makes space in the policy debate for the fate of the poor in a way which has not been evident for some years now.

We need to make space for the faces of the poor in our personal consciences and in the public agenda because the facts tell us that poverty is not so marginal in this nation as we might think. At the end of 1983, by official government estimates, 35 million Americans were poor. That meant 15% of the nation was defined as poor. The hidden poor were another 20-30 million who lived just above the poverty line.

Who are the poor? They represent every race and religion in the nation. They are both men and women, and, so very often, they are children. The poor are a fluid population. People move in and out of poverty. With unemployment still affecting at least 7-8 million people, the condition of poverty touches millions for some part of their lives.

No group is immune from poverty, but not all share it equally. Some of the statistics in the pastoral letter are striking: blacks are 12% of the American population but 62% of those persistently poor; women who head households constitute 19% of the family population, but 61% of persistently poor families.

The very old and the very young know the reality of poverty in disproportionate numbers.

The causes of poverty are a subject of honest disagreement, but the fact of poverty, even in a nation of our resources, cannot be disputed. It is the Church's response to this fact which is my major concern this evening.

II. The Role of the Church

The role of the Church in this question or any other must be shaped by the perspective of the Scriptures as these are read in the Catholic tradition. The draft of the pastoral letter develops the Scriptural case in detail. Here I will simply indicate the lines of an argument which is self-evident to anyone who examines the biblical basis of our faith. The argument is quite simple: The poor have a special place in the care of God, and they place specific demands on the consciences of believers.

The biblical argument runs through both Testaments, as the draft of the pastoral letter has shown. The prophets, in particular, specify the theme. In spite of their different styles and personalities, the prophets converge on a single message: the quality of Israel's faith will be tested by the character of justice in Israel's life. For the prophets, the test cases for Israel are specific: The way widows, orphans and resident aliens are treated measures the link between faith and justice.

Jesus himself continues the prophetic tradition. He clearly identifies his ministry with the preaching of the prophets as, for example, in the fourth chapter of St. Luke's Gospel. He consciously finds those on the edge of society—the "widows, orphans and resident aliens" of his time— and lifts up their plight even as he responds to their needs. He identifies himself so concretely with the poor that the first letter of St. John can say that love of God is measured by love of neighbor.

The biblical mandate about the poor is richer and more powerful than I can convey in this address. I recommend further study of the pastoral letter because it concisely gathers these biblical themes in its first chapter. However, I can synthesize the lesson the Church is trying to learn from the biblical perspective. It is found in a phrase which runs throughout the letter: the Church must have a "preferential option for the poor." This concept, rooted in the Scriptures, developed with originality by the Church in Latin America and now becoming a guide for ministry in the universal Church under the leadership of Pope John Paul II, illustrates how the Church learns anew from the Scriptures in every age.

The power of the phrase, "preferential option for the poor," is that it summarizes several biblical themes. As the pastoral letter states, it calls the Church to speak for the poor, to see the world from their perspective, and to empty itself so it may experience the power of God in the midst of poverty and powerlessness.

This, in all honesty, is an extraordinarily demanding view of what we should be as a Church. It is clear we have a distance to go in implementing this view of the Church's mission and ministry. Nevertheless, we have begun by taking the imperative seriously.

The option for the poor, I would suggest, will be realized in different ways according to the situation of the Church in different societies and cultures. Now we need to ask what the phrase means for the ministry of the Church in the United States.

I do not have a blueprint for determining the specific meaning of the "option for the poor" or integrating the concept into our ministry in this country. However, one dimension of the task especially interests me—the role of the Church as a social institution in our society. The Church as a social institution has made two distinct responses to the fact of poverty. The first has been to organize itself to carry out works of mercy. The fulfillment of the command to feed the hungry, clothe the naked and care for the sick has found direct and immediate expression in the Church from the apostolic age until today. The methods of doing this work have varied, but all can be classified as direct, social service to the poor.

The manifestations of this dimension of ministry are well known in the United States. They include Catholic Charities and social services in every diocese, St. Vincent de Paul Societies in every parish, and institutions—such as orphanages, hospitals and shelters for the homeless—established by communities of men and women religious and others throughout the country.

This form of social ministry is well known, but it is not the only way the Church addresses the fact of poverty. The second and complementary witness to the option for the poor is the Church's role as advocate and actor in the public life of society. The roots of this dimension of social ministry are found in the prophets who teach us to ask questions about how we organize our life as a society. The prophets asked questions in Israel about patterns of land ownership and wages, about the rules and customs used to design the social life of the nation. The prophets did not stop at formulating the norm that the quality of faith is tested by the character of social justice. They pressed specific questions about the social patterns in the life of Israel.

The conditions of twentieth-century industrial society are radically different from eighth-century B.C. Israelite society. Nevertheless, the prophets' style of social questioning has been taken up in the Church's social teaching of this century. The purpose of this social teaching is to measure the social and economic life of society by the standards of social justice and social charity.

The leadership of the popes in this century has, in turn, produced a body of social teaching from the bishops. The best known example was probably drafted in some faculty residence on this campus by John A. Ryan when he authored the 1919 pastoral letter of the U.S. Bishops. The first draft of the 1984 pastoral letter on the economy stands in this tradition of social teaching.

These two dimensions of the Church's life—its ministry of direct social service and its role as an advocate for the poor in society—remain the principal channels for the Church's response to poverty. The challenge we face in making an effective option for the poor is how these two aspects of social ministry are integrated into the full life of the Church today.

In a large, complex, bureaucratic secular society like the United States, the Church's social service role is more needed than ever. We should not try to duplicate what society does well in supplying social services, but, in particular, we should bring two dimensions to the system of social care. First, the delivery of some social services is best done in a decentralized local model. For many social services today, only the taxing power of the state can raise sufficient funds to meet human needs. But the state is often not the best agency to minister services to people in need. The Church and other voluntary agencies can often deliver, in a humane and compassionate way, services that only the state can fund.

Second, the Church's agencies of direct social service should be a source not only of compassion but also creativity. Public bureaucracy is not known for creative innovation. Its size and complexity often prevent it from acting in anything but routine patterns. In every field from housing to health care to hospices, there is room for new creative methods of public-private cooperation to feed the hungry, shelter the homeless and heal the sick. We can do better what we are already doing. With 35 million poor in our midst, we can reach beyond what we are doing!

In saying this, I want to be correctly understood. I am aware that Catholic Charities, the Catholic health care system and other diocesan and national networks are already involved in significant efforts of creative and direct service. It is the very success of these efforts which will give us courage to extend our efforts.

There is another sense in which I want to be clearly understood. We cannot be consistent with Catholic tradition unless we accept the principle of subsidiarity. I fully support a pluralist social system in which the state is not the center of everything.

Nevertheless, I do not want the principle of subsidiarity used in a way which subverts Catholic teaching on the collective responsibility of society for its poor. I am not endorsing a concept of decentralization or federalism which absolves the government from fulfilling its social responsibilities.

Both the Catholic and American traditions urge a pattern of public-private cooperation. This means the state has a positive social role, and we have social responsibilities as religious organizations. The churches alone cannot meet the social needs of this nation, and we should not try to do so. We should be prepared to play a major role, but part of our role is to enter the public debate and work for a compassionate, just, social policy.

This is the second challenge which confronts the Church today: how to fulfill the role of advocate in the public debate. This is the role which the Bishops' Conference is seeking to fulfill in its pastoral letters, first on peace and now on social justice. It is the role Bishop Malone stressed in his presidential address to the bishops last November. He argued that, on issues as diverse as abortion, Central America, nuclear war and poverty, failure of the bishops to speak would be a dereliction of civic responsibility and religious duty.

It is this role which puts the bishops in the midst of public controversy. Controversy is the companion of participation in public policy debate. That is why it should not be surprising that contributions of the scope and range of our two pastoral letters cause controversies.

At the same time, it is important to understand the purpose of the bishops' interventions. In the pastoral letters—and in many other documents, such as congressional testimonies, speeches and letters of individual bishops—we speak at the level of both moral principles and the applications of these principles to particular policies. We regularly assert that we understand and want others to understand that the moral principles we present have a different authority than our particular conclusions. We invite debate and discussion of our policy conclusions. We know they must be tested in the public arena, in the academic community and in the professional community. We have been using the process of successive drafts to stimulate this discussion.

Since I was so directly involved in the pastoral letter on war and peace, I believe there is specific merit in joining principles and policy proposals in the same document. Its purpose is not to foreclose debate, but to foster it. The policy conclusions give a sense of how the moral principles take shape in the concrete situations our society faces. I think we would be mistaken as bishops if we did not distinguish principles from policy judgments. But I think we would fail to stimulate the public argument if we withdrew from the arena of policy choices.

Our role is not to design or legislate programs but to help shape the questions our society asks and to help set the right terms of debate on public policy.

We have an excellent example in the issue confronting the Administration, the Congress, and the general public as we begin 1985—the deficit debate. It is the kind of highly technical and complex question which a modern state must face. The way the question is decided will shape the life of our society. The fact is that the deficit must be cut. The choices facing the Administration and the Congress are how to cut spending to reduce the deficit.

The technical details are admittedly immense, but the general policy question is not purely technical. At the core of the deficit debate is the trade-off between military spending and social spending. How that trade-off is adjudicated requires moral discernment as well as economic competence.

In the 1980s virtually every program for the poor has been cut:

- more than 2 million poor children lost health care benefits;

- half a million disabled adults lost cash and medical assistance; and

- one million poor families lost food stamp benefits.

In general, spending for the poor is less than 1% of the federal budget, but it has sustained 33% of all budget cuts.

These cuts in social spending have been accompanied by significant, steady increases in military spending. It is the responsibility of the federal government to provide for the common defense and to promote the general welfare. Military spending will justifiably be part of the budget. But the deficit forces us as a nation to ask who will bear the burden of the deficit. Military spending should not be insulated when plans for reducing the deficit are formulated.

I have no misconceptions about bishops being competent to write a national budget. But it is not beyond our competence or role to say that the burden of reducing the deficit should not be borne by the most vulnerable among us. Programs for the poor have been cut enough! The burden must be shared by all sectors of the economy. The specifics of how to do it fall beyond my responsibility, but shaping the question of how we face the deficit is clearly part of what the Church should do as advocate in the social system.

III. The Poor and the Policy Debate—One Issue

In the deficit debate, the fate of many of the poor is at stake. This evening I would like to focus attention on a particular group by addressing a specific dimension of poverty: the feminization of poverty. This phrase has been coined by Dr. Diana Pierce, a Catholic University faculty member who has made a significant contribution to the study of poverty. She has focused her research on the plight of women who are divorced, widowed or unmarried. She has surfaced data which have special relevance for the Church in the policy debate about poverty.

Dr. Pierce's pioneering work has helped many begin to understand the severe economic consequences of motherhood and sex discrimination in this country. Of course, men, especially minorities and youths, also suffer from unemployment and poverty, and millions of intact families have inadequate income. However, poverty is growing fastest among women and children.

As we look at this issue, it will be helpful to remember that nearly all (94%) women marry and nearly all of them (95%) have children. Reducing the economic price of motherhood should be a priority for our society. This disproportionate burden of poverty on women and children is appalling. Current statistics reflect some of this grim picture:

• two out of three poor adults are women;

• three out of four poor elderly are women;

• almost half of all poor families are headed by women, and half of the women raising children alone are poor;

• one in four children under six is poor;

• one in three black children under six is poor.

Even if poverty did not weigh so disproportionately on women, the growth of both the number and percentage of the poor would be cause for alarm and action. For those of us in the Church, this situation is profoundly disturbing. The fact that poverty is so concentrated among women and children should galvanize our energies and focus our attention on the conditions that create the situation.

A closer look at poverty among women reveals that it is strongly linked to two sets of factors: (1) job and wage discrimination and (2) responsibility for the support and care of children.

Job and wage discrimination leave women concentrated in the lowest paying jobs, with more problems finding full-time year-round work. But, even when women overcome these obstacles, they still earn substantially less than men. Dr. Pierce's data indicate that women college graduates working full-time and year-round still make less than male high school dropouts! Of course, most women workers are not college graduates, and so the disparity in incomes is even greater for those in the lowest paying jobs.

While this discrimination affects most women, those whose husbands are employed are partially insulated, at least temporarily, from its worst effects. For women raising children alone, of course, the situation is much worse because they are often financially responsible for most or all of their children's support. Despite some well-reported exceptions, child care and support fall mainly on women. The increased rates of divorce and out-of-wedlock births have left more women than ever solely responsible for the support of children.

Increasingly, it appears that it now takes the earnings of two adults to support a family in the United States. A single parent—widowed, divorced or unmarried—finds it difficult to stay above the poverty line. When that parent faces additional obstacles, such as the cost of day care (which can easily take more than a fourth of an average woman's salary) and sex discrimination in employment, the cards are overwhelmingly stacked against her.

The job market often offers little hope to a single mother trying to escape poverty. Unfortunately, other potential sources of supplemental income are also very limited. Child support is paid regularly to only a very small proportion of eligible mothers. Welfare benefits are so low that, in most states, the combined value of Aid to Families with Dependent

Children (AFDC) and food stamps doesn't even approach the poverty line. For the fifty States and the District of Columbia, the median benefit is 74% of the poverty threshold.

I cite these statistics and the case of women in poverty not because it is the only issue we must face as a Church in the policy debate but because it is one we should face with special emphasis. I am also aware that there are more fundamental remedies needed to address the feminization of poverty than the programs I have just mentioned. But I wanted to raise up these specific programs because they are so often criticized.

I have argued the case for a consistent ethic of life as the specific contribution which the Church can and should make in this nation's public debate. Central to a consistent ethic is the imperative that the Church stand for the protection and promotion of life from conception to death—that it stand against the drift toward nuclear war which has been so evident in recent years—and that it stand against the trend to have the most vulnerable among us carry the costs of our national indebtedness.

To stand for life is to stand for the needs of women and children who epitomize the sacredness of life. Standing for their rights is not merely a rhetorical task! The Church has its own specifically designed social services to protect and promote life. Through them we must counsel, support and sustain women seeking to raise families alone and to provide their children with the basic necessities—necessities which the most well endowed society in history surely should be able to muster.

But the Church cannot simply address the problem of the feminization of poverty through its own resources. It must also stand in the public debate for such programs as child care, food stamps, and aid to families with children. I do not contend that existing programs are without fault or should be immune from review. My point is that something like them is a fundamental requirement of a just society.

Whenever I speak about the consistent ethic, I am always forced by time limitations to omit or neglect crucial themes. In the past, I have stressed that our concern for life cannot stop at birth, that it cannot consist of a single issue—war or abortion or anything else. I have always considered that a substantial commitment to the poor is part of a consistent ethic and a concern for women in poverty a particularly pertinent aspect of this "seamless garment." This evening I am grateful for the opportunity to spell out why and how the Church should stand on these issues.

Ultimately, the pastoral letter on peace and the letter on the economy should help us as a Church develop the specific features of a consistent ethic. In the end, every social institution is known by what it stands for. I hope that the Catholic Church in this country will be known as a community which committed itself to the protection and promotion of life— that it helped this society fulfill these two tasks more adequately.

The Consistent Ethic of Life and Health Care Systems

Foster McGaw Triennial Conference
Loyola University of Chicago
Joseph Cardinal Bernardin
May 8, 1985

We meet on an auspicious day to explore more effective ways of preserving, protecting and fostering human life—the 40th anniversary of the end of the war in Europe which claimed millions of lives, both European and American. It was also a war in which, tragically, the word Holocaust will be forever emblazoned in history. We must never forget!

This anniversary is a day not only for remembering victory over the forces of oppression which led to this savage destruction of life but also for recommitting ourselves to preserving and nurturing all human life.

Daily we encounter news headlines which reflect the growing complexity of contemporary life, the rapid development of science and technology, the global competition for limited natural resources, and the violence which is so rampant in parts of our nation and world. The problems of contemporary humanity are enormously complex, increasingly global, and ominously threatening to human life and human society. Each of them has moral and religious dimensions because they all impact human life.

At times we may feel helpless and powerless as we confront these issues. It is crucial that we develop a method of moral analysis which will be comprehensive enough to recognize the linkages among the issues, while respecting the individual nature and uniqueness of each. During the past year and a half, I have addressed this task through the development of a "consistent ethic of life"—popularly referred to as the "seamless garment" approach to the broad spectrum of life issues.

I come before you today as a pastor, not a health care professional or theoretician, not a philosopher, not a politician or a legal expert. As a pastor, I wish to share with you the teaching of the Catholic Church as it pertains to human life issues.

I am very grateful to Father Baumhart for the invitation to address you on "The Consistent Ethic of Life and Health Care Systems." I will first briefly describe the concept of a consistent ethic. Then I will explore the challenge it poses to health care systems both in terms of "classical" medical ethics questions and in regard to "contemporary" social justice issues.

I. The Consistent Ethic of Life

Although the consistent ethic of life needs to be finely tuned and carefully structured on the basis of values, principles, rules and applications to specific cases, this is not my task this afternoon. I will simply highlight some of its basic components so that I can devote adequate attention to its application to health care systems and the issues they face today.

Catholic social teaching is based on two truths about the human person: human life is both sacred and social. Because we esteem human life as sacred, we have a duty to protect and foster it at all stages of development, from conception to death, and in all circumstances. Because we acknowledge that human life is also social, we must develop the kind of societal environment that protects and fosters its development.

Precisely because life is sacred, the taking of even one human life is a momentous event. While the presumption of traditional Catholic teaching has always been against taking human life, it has allowed the taking of human life in particular situations by way of exception—for example, in self-defense and capital punishment. In recent decades, however, the presumptions against taking human life have been strengthened and the exceptions made ever more restrictive.

Fundamental to this shift in emphasis is a more acute perception of the multiple ways in which life is threatened today. Obviously such questions as war, aggression and capital punishment have been with us for centuries; they are not new. What is new is the *context* in which these ancient questions arise, and the way in which a new context shapes the *content* of our ethic of life.

One of the major cultural factors affecting human life today is technology. Because of nuclear weapons we now threaten life on a scale previously unimaginable—even after the horrible experience of World War II. Likewise, modern medical technology opens new opportunities for care, but it also poses potential new threats to the sanctity of life. Living, as we do, in an age of careening technological development means we face a qualitatively new range of moral problems.

The protection, defense and nurture of human life involve the whole spectrum of life from conception to death, cutting across such issues as genetics, abortion, capital punishment, modern warfare and the care of the terminally ill. Admittedly these are all distinct problems, enormously complex, and deserving individual treatment. No single answer and no simple response will solve them all. They cannot be collapsed into one problem, but they must be confronted as pieces of a *larger pattern*. The fact that we face new challenges in each of these areas reveals the need for a consistent ethic of life.

The pre-condition for sustaining a consistent ethic is a "respect life" attitude or atmosphere in society. Where human life is considered "cheap" and easily "wasted," eventually nothing is held as sacred and all lives are in jeopardy. The purpose of proposing a consistent ethic of life is to argue that success on any one of the issues threatening life requires a concern for the broader attitude in society about respect for life. Attitude is the place to root an ethic of life. Change of attitude, in turn, can lead to change of policies and practices in our society.

Besides rooting this ethic in societal attitude, I have demonstrated, in a number of recent addresses, that there is an inner relationship—a linkage—among the several issues at the more specific level of moral principle. It is not my intention to repeat these arguments today.

Nevertheless, I would like to examine briefly the relationship between "right to life" and "quality of life" issues. If one contends, as we do, that the right of every unborn child should be protected by civil law and supported by civil consensus, then our moral, political and economic responsibilities do not stop at the moment of birth! We must defend the *right to life* of the weakest among us; we must also be supportive of the *quality of life* of the powerless among us: the old and the young, the hungry and the homeless, the undocumented immigrant and the unemployed worker, the sick, the disabled and the dying. I contend that the viability and credibility of the "seamless garment" principle depends upon the consistency of its application.

Such a quality-of-life posture translates into specific political and economic positions—for example, on tax policy, generation of employment, welfare policy, nutrition and feeding programs and health care. Consistency means we cannot have it both ways: we cannot urge a compassionate society and vigorous public and private policy to protect the rights of the unborn and then argue that compassion and significant public and private programs on behalf of the needy undermine the moral fiber of society or that they are beyond the proper scope of governmental responsibility or that of the private sector. Neither can we do the opposite!

The inner relationship among the various life issues is far more intricate than I can sketch here this afternoon. I fully acknowledge this. My intention is merely to bring that basic linkage into focus so I can apply it to the issues facing health care systems today.

II. The Consistent Ethic and "Classical" Medical Ethics Questions

As I noted at the outset, the consistent ethic of life poses a challenge to two kinds of problems. The first are "classical" medical ethics questions which today include revolutionary techniques from genetics to the technologies of prolonging life. How do we define the problems and what does it mean to address them from a Catholic perspective?

The essential question in the technological challenge is this: In an age when we *can* do almost anything, how do we decide what we *should* do? The even more demanding question is: In a time when we can do anything *technologically*, how do we decide *morally* what we should *not* do? My basic thesis is this: Technology must not be allowed to hold the health of human beings as a hostage.

In an address in Toronto last September, Pope John Paul II outlined three temptations of pursuing technological development: (1) pursuing development for its own sake, as if it were an autonomous force with built-in imperatives for expansion, instead of seeing it as a resource to be placed at the service of the human family; (2) tying technological development to the logic of profit and constant economic expansion without due regard for the rights of workers or the needs of the poor and helpless; (3) linking technological development to the pursuit or maintenance of power instead of using it as an instrument of freedom.

The response to these temptations, as the Holy Father pointed out, is *not* to renounce the technological application of scientific discoveries. We need science and technology to help solve the problems of humanity. We also need to subject technological application to moral analysis.

One of the most recent and most critical ethical questions which impacts the quality of human life is that of genetics, genetic counseling and engineering. Perhaps no other discovery in medicine has the potential so radically to change the lives of individuals and, indeed, the human race itself.

As with most scientific achievements in medicine, there are advantages and disadvantages to the utilization of this theoretical knowledge and technological know-how. Many genetic diseases can now be diagnosed early, even *in utero*, and technology is also moving toward treatment *in utero*. Proper use of such information can serve to prepare parents for the arrival of a special infant or can allay the fears of the expectant parents if the delivery of a healthy infant can be anticipated. The accumulation of scientific data can lead to a better understanding of the marvels of creation and to the possible manipulation of genes to prevent disease or to effect a cure before the infant sustains a permanent disability.

On the other hand, people also use available diagnostic procedures to secure information for the sex selection of their children. Some may wish to use it to eliminate "undesirables" from society. Many believe that the provision of genetic information contributes to an increase in the number of abortions.

At the other end of life's spectrum is care of the elderly. Our marvelous progress in medical knowledge and technology has made it possible to preserve the lives of newborns who would have died of natural causes not too many years ago; to save the lives of children and adults who would formerly have succumbed to contagious diseases and traumatic injuries; to prolong the lives of the elderly as they experience the debilitating effects of chronic illness and old age. At the same time, some openly advocate euthanasia, implying that we have absolute dominion over life rather than stewardship. This directly attacks the sacredness of each human life.

Other new moral problems have been created by the extension of lives in Intensive Care Units and Intensive Neonatal Units as well as by surgical transplants and implants, artificial insemination and some forms of experimentation. Computers provide rapid, usually accurate, testing and treatment, but they also create problems of experimentation, confidentiality and dehumanization. Intense debate is being waged about the extension of lives solely through extraordinary—mechanical or technological—means.

The consistent ethic of life, by taking into consideration the impact of technology on the full spectrum of life issues, provides additional insight to the new challenges which "classical" medical ethics questions face today. It enables us to define the problems in terms of their impact on human life and to clarify what it means to address them from a Catholic perspective.

III. The Consistent Ethic of Life and "Contemporary" Social Justice Issues

The second challenge which the consistent ethic poses concerns "contemporary" social justice issues related to health care systems. The primary question is: How does the evangelical option for the poor shape health care today?

Some regard the problem as basically financial: How do we effectively allocate limited resources? A serious problem today is the fact that many persons are left without basic health care while large sums of money are invested in the treatment of a few by means of exceptional, expensive measures. While technology has provided the industry with many diagnostic and therapeutic tools, their inaccessibility, cost and sophistication often prevent their wide distribution and use.

Government regulations and restrictions, cut-backs in health programs, the maldistribution of personnel to provide adequate services are but a few of the factors which contribute to the reality that many persons do not and probably will not receive the kind of basic care that nurtures life—unless we change attitudes, policies and programs.

Public health endeavors such as home care, immunization programs, health education and other preventive measures to improve the environment and thus prevent disease, have all served as alternate means of providing care and improving the health of the poor and isolated populations. In the past, if patients from this sector of society needed hospitalization, institutions built with Hill-Burton funds were required to provide a designated amount of "charity care" to those in need.

In some instances, hospitals continue to follow this procedure. However, access to these alternate, less expensive types of health care is becoming more difficult. Cuts in government support for health programs for the poor, for persons receiving Medicare or Medicaid benefits, are making it increasingly more difficult for people who need health care to receive it.

Today we seem to have three tiers of care: standard care for the insured, partial care for Medicaid patients, and emergency care only for the 35 million Americans who are uninsured. Do we nurture and protect life when there appears to be an unjust distribution of the goods entrusted to our stewardship? How can Catholic hospitals continue both to survive and to implement a preferential option for the poor?

This is not merely a theological or pastoral issue. Access to standard health care is largely nonexistent for about half of the poor and very limited for the other half who are eligible for Medicaid or Medicare. The United States has the worst record on health care of any nation in the North Atlantic community and even worse than some under-developed nations.

Judith Feder and Jack Hadley, currently co-directors of the Center for Health Policy Studies at Georgetown University, have conducted research on uncompensated hospital care. Some of their findings are particularly disturbing. They concluded, for example, that *non-profit* hospitals—including Catholic facilities—do very little more for the poor than *for-profit* hospitals (which is very little, indeed). Free care provided by private, non-profit hospitals averaged only 3.85% of all charges (gross revenues) in 1982. I am aware that some dispute the accuracy of these findings in regard to Catholic hospitals, but I have not yet seen data which shows that, overall, these institutions provide substantially more free care than their counterparts.

I must also affirm, of course, that there are some inner city and other Catholic hospitals which do a great deal for the poor. Nonetheless, as the research seems to indicate, hospitals average less than 5% of patient charges for uncompensated care. Much of this is for deliveries to women who appear in heavy labor at our emergency rooms and the subsequent neonatal intensive care for their infants born with severe problems because of the lack of care given their mothers during pregnancy.

Our national resources are limited, but they are not scarce. As a nation we spend *more* per capita and a *higher* share of our Gross Domestic Product (GDP) on health than any other country in the world—nearly twice as much as Great Britain, for example. Yet our system still excludes at least half the poor. In 1982 the U.S. share of GDP devoted to health care was 10.6% against 5.9% within the United Kingdom, which has universal access to health care and a lower infant mortality rate than the U.S.

The basic problem of health care in the U.S. is managerial: the effective allocation and control of resources. The key is the underlying philosophy and sense of mission which motivates and informs managerial decisions.

As a nation, we spend enormous amounts of money to prolong the lives of newborns and the dying while millions of people don't see a doctor until they are too ill to benefit from medical care. We allow the poor to die in our hospitals, but we don't provide for their treatment in the early stages of illness—much less make preventive care available to them.

These facts are disturbing to anyone who espouses the sacredness and value of human life. The fundamental human right is to life—from the moment of conception until death. It is the source of all other rights, including the right to health care. The consistent ethic of life poses a series of questions to Catholic health care facilities. Let me enumerate just a few.

• Should a Catholic hospital transfer an indigent patient to another institution unless superior care is available there?

• Should a Catholic nursing home require large cash deposits from applicants?

• Should a Catholic nursing home transfer a patient to a state institution when his or her insurance runs out?

• Should a Catholic hospital give staff privileges to a physician who won't accept Medicaid or uninsured patients?

If Catholic hospitals and other institutions take the consistent ethic seriously, then a number of responses follow. All Catholic hospitals will have outpatient programs to serve the needs of the poor. Catholic hospitals and other Church institutions will document the need for comprehensive pre-natal programs and lead legislative efforts to get them enacted by state and national government. Catholic medical schools will teach students that medical ethics includes care for the poor—not merely an occasional charity case, but a commitment to see that adequate care is available.

If they take the consistent ethic seriously, Catholic institutions will lead efforts for adequate Medicaid coverage and reimbursement policies. They will lobby for preventive health programs for the poor. They will pay their staffs a just wage. Their staffs will receive training and formation to see God "hiding in the poor" and treat them with dignity.

I trust that each of you has an opinion about the importance or viability of responses to these challenges. My point in raising them is not to suggest simplistic answers to complex and difficult questions. I am a realist, and I know the difficulties faced by our Catholic institutions. Nonetheless, I do suggest that these questions arise out of a consistent ethic of life and present serious challenges to health care in this nation—and specifically to Catholic health care systems.

Medical ethics must include not only the "classical" questions but also contemporary social justice issues which affect health care. In a 1983 address to the World Medical Association, Pope John Paul II pointed out that developing an effective medical ethics—including the social justice dimension—fundamentally depends on the concept one forms of medicine. It is a matter of learning definitely whether medicine truly is in service of the human person, his dignity, what he has of the unique and transcendent in him, or whether medicine is considered first of all as the agent of the collectivity, at the service of the interests of the healthy and well-off, to whom care for the sick is subordinated.

He went on to remind his listeners that the Hippocratic oath defines medical morality in terms of respect and protection of the human person.

The consistent ethic of life is primarily a theological concept, derived from biblical and ecclesial tradition about the sacredness of human life, about our responsibilities to protect, defend, nurture and enhance God's gift of life. It provides a framework for moral analysis of the diverse impact of cultural factors—such as technology and contemporary distribution of resources—upon human life, both individual and collective.

The context in which we face new health care agendas generated both by technology and by poverty is that the Catholic health care system today confronts issues both of survival and of purpose. How shall we survive? For what purpose? The consistent ethic of life enables us to answer these questions by its comprehensiveness and the credibility which derives from its consistent application to the full spectrum of life issues.

The Death Penalty in Our Time

Address to Criminal Law Committee
Criminal Court of Cook County
Joseph Cardinal Bernardin
May 14, 1985

I wish to acknowledge with gratitude your considerable contribution to the quality of life among the people of Cook County as you preserve the value of justice and implement it each day. The court system is an indispensable part of our great American heritage of "justice for all under the law." I am aware that your dedicated work involves considerable frustration as you constantly encounter the seamier side of human behavior.

I am grateful for your invitation to meet with you this afternoon and to share my reflections on an issue of mutual concern: capital punishment. I come before you as a *pastor*—not a legal expert. It is my understanding that the constitutional principle of the separation of Church and State ensures religious organizations the right to engage in debate about public policy, expecting neither favoritism nor discrimination. At the same time, I firmly believe that they must earn the right to be heard by the quality of their arguments.

It has also been my longstanding conviction that civil law and social policy must always be subject to ongoing moral analysis. Simply because

a civil law is in place does not mean it should be blindly supported. En-
couraging reflective, informed assessment of civil law and policy keeps
alive the capacity for moral criticism in society.

I also come before you as a *citizen* who cares deeply about the quality
of life in our community.

I will address two dimensions of the topic this afternoon. First, I will
situate the issue of capital punishment in the context of a consistent ethic
of life and then examine the case for capital punishment in light of this
ethic.

I. The Context: A Consistent Ethic of Life

Catholic social teaching is based on two truths about the human person:
human life is both sacred and social. Because we esteem human life as
sacred, we have a duty to protect and foster it at all stages of development,
from conception to death, and in all circumstances. Because we acknowledge that human life is also social, society must protect and foster it.

Precisely because life is sacred, the taking of even one life is a momentous event. Traditional Catholic teaching has allowed the taking of human
life in particular situations by way of exception, as, for example, in self-
defense and capital punishment. In recent decades, however, the presumptions against taking human life have been strengthened and the exceptions
made ever more restrictive.

Fundamental to this shift in emphasis is a more acute perception of the
multiple ways in which life is threatened today. Obviously such questions
as war, aggression and capital punishment have been with us for centuries;
they are not new. What *is* new is the *context* in which these ancient questions arise, and the way in which a new context shapes the *content* of our
ethic of life.

Within the Catholic Church, the Second Vatican Council acknowledged
that "a sense of the dignity of the human person has been impressing itself
more and more deeply on the consciousness of contemporary man"
(Declaration on Religious Freedom, #1). This growing awareness of
human dignity has been a dominant factor within Western culture. Within
the United States, the struggle to appreciate human worth more fully is

found in the civil rights movement and in the public debate about our foreign policy toward totalitarian regimes of both the right and the left.

This deepening awareness, as I intimated above, has been precipitated in part by a growing recognition of the frailty of human life today. Faced with the threat of nuclear war and escalating technological developments, the human family encounters a qualitatively new range of moral problems. Today, life is threatened on a scale previously unimaginable.

This is why the U.S. Catholic bishops and others have been so visible and vocal in the public debate this past decade or two, asserting belief in the sacredness of human life and the responsibilities we have, personally and as a society, to protect and preserve the sanctity of life.

Nonetheless, it is not enough merely to assert such an ethical principle. If it is to be acknowledged and implemented, it must impact all areas of human life. It must respond to all the moments, places or conditions which either threaten the sanctity of life or cultivate an attitude of disrespect for it.

A consistent ethic of life is based on the need to ensure that the sacredness of human life, which is the ultimate source of human dignity, will be defended and fostered from womb to tomb, from the genetic laboratory to the cancer ward, from the ghetto to the prison.

II. Capital Punishment in Light of This Ethic

As you undoubtedly know, since the time of St. Augustine, great thinkers in the Roman Catholic tradition—St. Thomas Aquinas, for example—have struggled with such ethical questions as the right of the State to execute criminals. Through the centuries, as I noted above, the Church has acknowledged that the State *does* have the right to take the life of someone guilty of an extremely serious crime.

However, because such punishment involves the deliberate infliction of evil on another, it always needs justification. Usually this has consisted of indicating some good which would derive from the punishment, a good of such consequence that it justifies the taking of life.

As I understand the current discussion about capital punishment, the question is not whether the State still has the *right* to inflict capital punishment, but whether it should *exercise* this right. In present circumstances, are there sufficient reasons to justify the infliction of the evil of death on another human person?

This is the question which the U.S. Catholic Bishops and others have been addressing recently—the United States Catholic Conference in 1980, the Massachusetts Catholic Conference Board of Governors in 1982, the Oklahoma Catholic bishops in 1983, the Tennessee Bishops exactly one year ago today, and Florida church leaders last November. Although there are differences of presentation, basically the reasoning of these positions follows two lines of thought.

First, they review four traditional arguments justifying capital punishment: retribution, deterrence, reform and protection of the State. Based on their review, the religious leaders have argued that these reasons no longer apply in our age.

I don't have time this afternoon to present the reasoning in regard to all four areas, but I would like to use the question of retribution as an example. The 1980 USCC statement states:

> We grant that the need of retribution does indeed justify punishment. For the practice of punishment both presupposes a previous transgression against the law and involves the involuntary deprivation of certain goods. But we maintain that this good does not require nor does it justify the taking of the life of the criminal, even in cases of murder. . . . It is morally unsatisfactory and socially destructive for criminals to go unpunished, but the limits of punishment must be determined by moral objectives which go beyond the mere infliction of injury on the guilty. Thus we would argue it is as barbarous and inhumane for a criminal who had tortured or maimed a victim to be tortured or maimed in return. Such punishment might satisfy certain vindictive desires that we or the victim might feel, but the satisfaction of such desires is not and cannot be an objective of a humane and Christian approach to punishment.

Basing their judgment on this and similar lines of reasoning, many religious leaders conclude that, under our present circumstances, the death penalty as punishment for reasons of deterrence, retribution, reform or protection of society cannot be justified.

Nonetheless, our reflections on this issue do not stop at this level. As religious leaders we argue that there are gospel insights which bespeak the inappropriateness of capital punishment. First, there is the example of Jesus, offering forgiveness at the time of his own unfair death (Lk 23:24).

Another challenging gospel theme is that of "God's boundless love for every person, regardless of human merit or worthiness. This love was especially visible in Jesus' ministry to outcasts, in his acceptance of sinners" (Florida church leaders). Consistent with this theme and flowing from it is the biblical imperative of reconciliation. Wherever there is division between persons, Christ calls them to forgiveness and reconciliation.

While these themes are specifically grounded in the New Testament, I do not believe they are unique to the Christian vision. People of good will recognize that these values ennoble human experience and make it more complete. Commitment to these values changes one's perspective on the strengths and weaknesses of the human family.

This change in perspective seems to have been in mind when the ecumenical leaders of Florida stated that Jesus shifted the locus of judgment in this matter to a higher court: a court where there is absolute knowledge of the evidence, of good deeds and of evil, of faith and of works of faith, of things private and things public—a court in which there is both wrath and tenderness, both law and grace.

It is when we stand in this perspective of a "higher court"—that of God's judgment seat—and a more noble view of the human person, that we seriously question the appropriateness of capital punishment. We ask ourselves: Is the human family made more complete—is human personhood made more loving—in a society which demands life for life, eye for eye, tooth for tooth?

Let me acknowledge that your experience is probably quite different from mine. You have had to deal with heinous crimes, with persons so filled with hatred and violence as to chill the heart. You may be wondering whether my colleagues and I are naive or simplistic in our approach.

Perhaps I won't be able to dispel that perception with my response. Nevertheless, I want to affirm that the State *does* have the responsibility to protect its citizens. It deserves and merits the full support of all of us in the exercise of that responsibility. Although we don't have an adequate understanding of the causes of violent crime, society "has the right and the duty to prevent such behavior including, in some cases, the right to impose terms of lifetime imprisonment" (Florida ecumenical leaders).

I am not suggesting that society should be a prisoner of violence or violent crime. On the contrary, the consistent ethic of life requires that society struggle to eradicate poverty, racism and other systemic forces which nurture and encourage violence. Similarly, the perpetrators of violence should be punished and given the opportunity to experience a change of heart and mind.

But, having said this, I also think that capital punishment is not an appropriate response to the problem of crime in our land. To take any human life, even that of someone who is not innocent, is awesome and tragic. It seems to me and to others that, in our culture today, there are not sufficient reasons to justify the State continuing to exercise its right in this matter. There are other, better ways of protecting the interests of society.

Recently the Gallup organization conducted a poll about capital punishment—something they had done on previous occasions. In 1966 42% of those polled favored capital punishment, in 1981 66% favored it, and this year the percentage was 72%.

Why has 24% of the population turned to favoring capital punishment in the last nineteen years? This question is even more urgent because that same poll reported that fully 51% of the respondents said "they would still support capital punishment even if studies showed conclusively it does not deter crime"! This is striking because people often use deterrence as a main argument to justify capital punishment. If it is not to deter crime, why do people support capital punishment? Thirty percent of those who favored capital punishment indicated their reason was simple: revenge!

One might argue that the cycle of violence has become so intense in our society that it is understandable and appropriate for people to support capital punishment. What alternative is there, some ask, in a violent society other than to meet violence with violence?

As a citizen in a democracy whose founding dream is of human dignity and as a disciple of Jesus, I must reject this alternative. In fact, as a citizen of this city which has recently been alarmed, saddened and polarized by the senseless killing of a talented high school basketball star and a ten-year-old standing in front of his home, I assert that violence is not the answer—it is not the way to break the cycle of violence.

Pope John Paul II, speaking to Peruvians who were living in the midst of a rebel stronghold, told them: "The pitiless logic of violence leads to nothing. No good is obtained by helping to increase violence."

Capital punishment, to my mind, is an example of meeting violence with violence. What does it say about the quality of our life when people celebrate the death of another human being? What does it say about the human spirit when some suggest a return to public executions which only twenty years ago we would have considered barbaric?

We desperately need an attitude or atmosphere in society which will sustain a consistent defense and promotion of life. Where human life is considered "cheap" and easily "wasted," eventually nothing is held as sacred and all lives are in jeopardy. The purpose of proposing a consistent ethic of life is to argue that success on any one of the issues threatening life requires a concern for the broader attitude in society about respect for life. Attitude is the place to root an ethic of life.

Change of attitude, in turn, can lead to change of policies and practices in our society. We must find ways to break the cycle of violence which threatens to strangle our land. We must find effective means of protecting and enhancing human life.

The Consistent Ethic of Life: The Challenge and the Witness of Catholic Health Care

Catholic Medical Center—Jamaica, New York
Joseph Cardinal Bernardin
May 18, 1986

The very mention of "Bhopal" or "Chernobyl" sends shudders through people everywhere. While the tragic deaths and injuries caused by the Bhopal disaster were confined to a particular area, its repercussions are still being felt worldwide. The Chernobyl incident, however, affects the planet in a more direct way through the spread of radioactivity. Its destructive potential is even more worrisome.

These two disasters highlight an important fact which has enormous significance for the future of the world community: the growing interdependence of contemporary life—an interdependence which has been accelerated by the rapid development of science and technology—and the worldwide competition for limited natural resources. The problems and challenges of the human family today are enormously complex, increasingly global, and ominously threatening to human life and society. Each of them has moral and religious dimensions because they all impact human life.

It is crucial that we develop a method of moral analysis which will be comprehensive enough to recognize the linkages among the issues confronting us, while respecting the individual nature and uniqueness of each. During the past few years, I have addressed this task through the development of a comprehensive approach to the broad spectrum of life issues which I have called the "consistent ethic of life."

I am very grateful to the Catholic Medical Center and St. John's University for the invitation to address you this evening on "The Consistent Ethic of Life: The Challenge and the Witness of Catholic Health Care." As you may know, I applied the consistent ethic concept to health care systems last year in an address to the Foster McGaw Triennial Conference in Chicago. I wish to follow a similar format this evening, applying the concept, however, to different, but related, issues.

More specifically, I will first briefly describe the concept of a consistent ethic. Then I will explore the challenge it poses to health care systems both in terms of "classical" medical ethics questions and "contemporary" social justice issues.

I. The Consistent Ethic of Life

The "consistent ethic of life" has become part of our ethical vocabulary in the past three years. No doubt you are already familiar with it—at least, to some extent. However, there are many misconceptions about it. That is why I want to ensure at the outset that the basic concept is correctly understood.

Although the consistent ethic needs to be finely tuned and carefully structured on the basis of values, principles, rules and applications to specific cases, this is not my task this evening. I will simply highlight some of its fundamental components so that I can devote more attention to its application to health care systems and several of the issues they face today.

Catholic social teaching is based on two truths about the human person: human life is both *sacred* and *social*. Because God's gift of life is sacred, we have a duty to protect and foster it at all stages of development, from conception to natural death, and in all circumstances. Because we acknowledge that human life is also social, society must protect and preserve its sanctity.

Precisely because life is sacred, the taking of even one human life is a momentous event. Traditional Catholic teaching has allowed the taking of human life in particular situations by way of exception, as, for example, in self-defense and capital punishment. In recent decades, however, the presumptions against taking human life have been strengthened and the exceptions made ever more restrictive.

Fundamental to these shifts in emphasis is a more acute perception of the many ways in which life is threatened today. Obviously such questions as war, aggression and capital punishment are not new; they have been with us for centuries. Life has always been threatened, but today there is a new *context* which we must take into consideration. And this new *context* shapes the *content* of our ethic of life.

The principal factor responsible for this new context is modern technology. Technology induces a sharper awareness of the fragility of human life. Speaking in Ravenna last Sunday, Pope John Paul II acknowledged that technical progress makes it possible to transform the desert, to overcome drought and hunger, to lighten the burden of work, to resolve problems of underdevelopment, and to render a more just distribution of resources among people of the world. But he also warned that the same technology has brought us to see "the land uninhabitable, the sea unserviceable, the air dangerous and the sky something to fear."

The discovery of nuclear energy, for example, is one of the most important scientific developments of this century. Despite its benefits to the human family, however, we have become painfully aware of its potential to destroy life on a scale previously unimaginable. Likewise, while modern medical technology opens new opportunities for care, it also poses new threats to life, both immediate and potential. The extraordinary technological development of this century has brought with it a qualitatively new range of moral problems.

My basic thesis is this: Technology must not be allowed to hold human beings as hostages. The essential questions we face are these: In an age when we *can* do almost anything, how do we decide what we *should* do? In a time when we can do almost anything *technologically,* how do we decide *morally* what we should not do?

Asking these questions along the whole spectrum of life from conception to natural death creates the need for a consistent ethic, for the spectrum cuts across such issues as genetics, abortion, capital punishment, modern warfare, and the care of the terminally ill. Admittedly these are all *distinct,* enormously complex problems, and they deserve individual treatment. No single answer and no simple response will solve them all. *But they are linked.* Moreover, we face new challenges in each of these areas. This combination of challenges is what cries out for a consistent ethic of life.

We desperately need an *attitude* or climate in society which will sustain a comprehensive, consistent defense and promotion of life. When human life is considered "cheap" or easily expendable in one area, eventually nothing is held as sacred and all lives are in jeopardy. The purpose of proposing the need for a consistent ethic of life is to argue that success on any one of the life-threatening issues is directly related to the attitude society has generally toward life. Attitude is the place to root an ethic of life, because, ultimately, it is society's attitude—whether of respect or non-respect—that determines its policies and practices.

At the same time, I hasten to add that ethics concerns itself with principles which are supposed to guide the *actions* of individuals and institutions. That is why I have demonstrated, in a number of recent addresses, that there is also an inner relationship—a linkage—among the several issues at the more specific level of moral principle. It is not my intention to repeat these arguments this evening.

Nevertheless, I would like to examine briefly the relationship between "right to life" and "quality of life" issues. If one contends, as we do, that the right of every unborn child should be protected by civil law and supported by civil consensus, then our moral, political and economic responsibilities do not stop at the moment of birth! We must defend the *right to life* of the weakest among us: we must also be supportive of the *quality of life* of the powerless among us: the old and the young, the hungry and the homeless, working mothers and single parents, the sick, the disabled and the dying. The viability and credibility of the "consistent ethic" principle depend primarily upon the consistency of its application.

Such a quality-of-life posture translates into specific political and economic positions—for example, on tax policy, generation of employment, welfare policy, nutrition and feeding programs, and health care. Consistency means we cannot have it both ways: we cannot urge a compassionate society and vigorous public and private policy to protect the rights of the unborn and then argue that compassion and significant public and private programs on behalf of the needy undermine the moral fiber of society or that they are beyond the proper scope of governmental responsibility or that of the private sector. Neither can we do the opposite!

As I acknowledged earlier, the inner relationship among the various life issues is far more intricate than I can sketch here this evening. I fully acknowledge this. My intention is merely to bring that basic linkage into focus so I can apply it to some of the issues facing health care systems today.

II. Ordinary vs. Extraordinary Medical Procedures

As I noted earlier, the consistent ethic of life poses a challenge to two kinds of problems. The first are "classical" medical ethics questions which today include revolutionary techniques ranging from genetics to the prolonging of life. How do we define the problems, and what does it mean to address them from a Catholic perspective?

One of the most critical moral questions today is the appropriate use of ordinary and extraordinary medical procedures, especially in the care of the terminally ill. I would like to explore this issue with you in some detail.

Two fundamental principles guide the discussion. The first is the principle which underlies the consistent ethic: Life itself is of such importance that it is never to be attacked directly. That is why the Second Vatican Council taught:

All offenses against life itself, such as murder, genocide, abortion, euthanasia, or wilful suicide. . . all these and the like are criminal; they poison civilization. (*Pastoral Constitution on the Church in the Modern World*, 31)

Consequently, even in those situations where a person has definitively entered the final stages of the process of dying or is in an irreversible coma, it is not permitted to act directly to end life. In other words, euthanasia—that is, the intentional causing of death whether by act or omission—is always morally unjustifiable.

The *second* guiding principle is this: Life on this earth is not an end in itself; its purpose is to prepare us for a life of eternal union with God. Consistent with this principle, Pope Pius XII, in 1957, gave magisterial approval to the traditional moral teaching of the distinction between *ordinary* and *extraordinary* forms of medical treatment. In effect, this means that a Catholic is not bound to initiate, and is free to suspend, any medical treatment that is extraordinary in nature.

But how does one distinguish between ordinary and extraordinary medical treatments? Before answering that question, I would like to point out that the Catholic heritage does not use these terms in the same way in which they might be used in the medical profession. That which is judged *ethically* as extraordinary for a given patient can, and often will, be viewed as ordinary from a *medical* perspective because it is ordinarily beneficial when administered to most patients. That being said, it is, nevertheless, possible to define, as Pope Pius XII did, what would *ethically* be considered as extraordinary medical action: namely, all "medicines, treatments, and operations which cannot be obtained or used without excessive expense, pain, or other inconvenience or which, if used, would not offer a reasonable hope of benefit."

This distinction was applied by the Congregation for the Doctrine of the Faith to the care of the terminally ill in its 1980 Declaration on Euthanasia, which states:

When inevitable death is imminent in spite of the means used, it is permitted in conscience to take the decision to refuse forms of treatment that would only secure a precarious and burdensome prolongation of life, so long as the normal care due the sick person in similar cases is not interrupted.

In other words, while the Catholic tradition forcefully rejects euthanasia, it would also argue that there is no obligation, in regard to care of the terminally ill, to initiate or continue extraordinary medical treatments which would be ineffective in prolonging life or which, despite their effectiveness in this regard, would impose excessive burdens on the patient.

Recently the American Medical Association's Council on Ethical and Judicial Affairs adopted a policy statement on withholding or withdrawing life-prolonging medical treatment. Earlier this year the National Conference of Commissioners on Uniform State Laws adopted a "Uniform Rights of the Terminally Ill Act" for proposed enactment by state legislatures. While containing some helpful insights, this latter document raises serious moral questions which could result in ethically unsound legislative efforts that would further undermine the right to life and the respect for life in American society.

In addition, there has been a good deal of media attention given to certain cases involving seriously ill patients. In light of all this, there is need for serious reflection on the question of our ethical responsibilities with regard to the care of the dying.

Again, the consistent ethic of life will prove useful in such reflection. Here I will limit myself to two observations. First, an attitude of disregard for the sanctity and dignity of human life is present in our society both in relation to the end of life and its beginning. There are some who are more concerned about whether patients are dying fast enough than whether they are being treated with the respect and care demanded by our Judaeo-Christian tradition.

To counteract this mentality and those who advocate so-called "mercy killing," we must develop societal attitudes, policies, and practices that guarantee the right of the elderly and the chronically and terminally ill to the spiritual and human care they need. The process of dying is profoundly human and should not be allowed to be dominated by what, at times, can be purely utilitarian considerations or cost-benefit analyses.

Second, with regard to the manner in which we care for a terminally ill person, we must make our own the Christian belief that in death "life is changed, not ended." The integration of such a perspective into the practice of a medical profession whose avowed purpose is the preservation of life will not be easy. It also is difficult for a dying person's family and loved ones to accept the fact that someone they love is caught up in a process that is fundamentally good—the movement into eternal life.

In order that these and other concerns may be addressed in a reasoned, Christian manner, the dialogue must continue in forums like this. The consistent ethic, by insisting on the applicability of the principle of the dignity and sanctity of life to the full spectrum of life issues and by taking into consideration the impact of technology, provides additional insight to the new challenge which "classical" medical ethics questions face today. It enables us to define the problems in a broader, more credible context.

III. Adequate Health Care for the Poor?

The second challenge which the consistent ethic poses concerns "contemporary" social justice issues related to health care systems. The primary question is: How does the gospel's preferential option or love for the poor shape health care today?

Some regard the problem as basically financial: How do we effectively allocate limited resources? A serious difficulty today is the fact that many persons are left without basic health care while large sums of money are invested in the treatment of a few by means of exceptional, expensive measures. While technology has provided the industry with many diagnostic and therapeutic tools, their inaccessibility, cost and sophistication often prevent their wide distribution and use.

Government regulations and restrictions, cut-backs in health programs, and the maldistribution of personnel to provide adequate services are but a few of the factors which contribute to the reality that—unless we change attitudes, policies, and programs—many persons probably will not receive the kind of basic care that nurtures life.

A significant factor impacting health in the U.S. today is the lack of medical insurance. The American Hospital Association estimates that nearly 33 million persons have no medical insurance. They include the 60% of low-income persons who are ineligible for Medicaid; nearly half of the "working poor"; the unemployed, seasonally employed, or self-employed; and middle-income individuals denied coverage because of chronic illnesses. They include disproportionate numbers of young adults, minorities, women, and children.

According to the most recent federal data, only one-third of the officially poor are eligible for the "safety net" of Medicaid. The Children's Defense Fund estimates that two-thirds of poor or near-poor children are never insured or insured for only part of the year. It is shocking, but not surprising in light of what I have just said, that the U.S. infant mortality rate is the same as that of Guatemala! Forty thousand infants die each year in the U.S. and others are kept alive by surgery and technology—only to die in their second year of life. The principal causes are well known: poverty and lack of adequate medical care. Moreover, many argue that the situation worsens as hospitals become more competitive and prospective pricing holds down the reimbursement rate.

I assume that we all share a deep concern in regard to adequate health care for the poor, but we also recognize that providing this is much easier said than done. Between 1980 and 1982 the number of poor and near-poor people without health insurance increased by 21%. During the same period, free hospital care increased by less than 4%.

A related concern is sometimes referred to as "dumping." An article in a recent issue of the *New England Journal of Medicine* reported the results of a study of 467 patients transferred to Cook County Hospital in Chicago in a 42-day period in late 1983. The conclusions were disturbing for a number of reasons. First, the primary reason for a majority of the transfers was economic rather than medical. Second, at least one-fourth of these patients were judged to be in an unstable condition at the time of transfer.

In addition, only 6% of the patients had given written informed consent for transfer. Thirteen percent of the patients transferred were not informed beforehand about the transfer. When the reason for the transfer was given, there was, at times, a serious discrepancy between the reason given to the patient and that given to the resident physician at Cook County Hospital during the transfer-request phone call.

The problems facing Chicago hospitals are by no means unique. They can be found across the nation. Another article in the same issue of the journal described the Texas attempt to eliminate "dumping" of patients without valid medical reason. However, the same article summarized the ongoing dilemma which continues to face all segments of our society: "Who will pay for the medical care of the poor?"

Although each hospital must examine its own policies and practices in regard to uncompensated care of the poor, some recent studies suggest that such care of itself may not be an effective substitute for public insurance. Arizona, as you may know, is the only state without Medicaid. Recent studies reveal that the proportion of poor Arizona residents refused care for financial reasons was about *double* that in states with Medicaid programs. On the other hand, poor elderly Arizona residents—covered by Medicare—were found to have access to health care *comparable* to that of other states.

These facts are disturbing to anyone who espouses the sacredness and value of human life. The fundamental human right is to life—from the moment of conception until natural death. It is the source of all other rights, including the right to health care. The consistent ethic of life poses a series of questions and challenges to Catholic health care facilities. Let me enumerate just a few.

- Should a Catholic hospital transfer an indigent patient to another institution unless superior care is available there?

- Should a Catholic nursing home transfer a patient to a state institution when his or her insurance runs out?

- Should a Catholic hospital give staff privileges to a physician who won't accept Medicaid or uninsured patients?

If Catholic hospitals and other institutions take the consistent ethic seriously, then a number of responses follow. All Catholic hospitals will have outpatient programs to serve the needs of the poor. Catholic hospitals and other Church institutions will document the need for comprehensive pre-natal programs and lead legislative efforts to get them enacted by state and national government. Catholic medical schools will teach students that medical ethics includes care for the poor—not merely an occasional charity case, but a commitment to see that adequate care is available. If they take the consistent ethic seriously, Catholic institutions will lead efforts for adequate Medicaid coverage and reimbursement policies. They will lobby for preventive health programs for the poor.

My point in raising these issues is not to suggest simplistic answers to complex and difficult questions. I am a realist, and I know the difficulties faced by our Catholic institutions. Nonetheless, the consistent ethic does raise these questions which present serious challenges to health care in this nation—and specifically to Catholic health care systems.

To face these challenges successfully, Catholic health care institutions, together with the dioceses in which they are located, will have to cooperate with each other in new and creative ways—ways which might have been considered impossible or undesirable before. No longer can we all be "lone rangers." I know what you have done (and are doing) here in the Brooklyn diocese to maximize the effectiveness and outreach of your hospitals and other health care institutions. I commend you for this. In the very near future the Archdiocese of Chicago and its Catholic hospitals hope to announce the establishment of a new network which will provide a structure for joint action aimed at the hospitals' *market competitive position*, promoting *governance continuity*, and ensuring *maximum mission effectiveness*.

In short, today's *agenda* for Catholic health care facilities is new. The *context* in which we face this agenda is also new because, unlike the past, the Catholic health care system today confronts issues of survival and of purpose. How shall we survive? For what purpose? The consistent ethic helps us answer these questions. It is primarily a theological concept, derived from biblical and ecclesial tradition about the sacredness of human life, about our responsibilities to protect, defend, nurture and enhance this gift of God. It provides us with a framework within which we can make a moral analysis of the various cultural and technological factors impacting human life. Its comprehensiveness and consistency in application will give us both guidance and credibility and win support for our efforts. The challenge to witness to the dignity and sacredness of human life is before us. With God's help and our own determination, I am confident that we will be equal to it.

Address at Seattle University

Joseph Cardinal Bernardin
March 2, 1986

I wish to express my sincere appreciation to Seattle University, to its President Fr. William Sullivan, S.J., and to the Board of Trustees for the honor bestowed on me today. The relationship between centers of scholarship and learning and the episcopacy is one of the pre-eminent issues in the Church in the United States today. I accept your honorary degree with he pledge that I will do all I can to strengthen that relationship—to keep it based on standards of intellectual honesty, professional respect, and a shared concern for the welfare of the church and its witness in society.

It is the Church's witness to life that I wish to address this afternoon. It is now over two years since I first proposed consideration of a "consistent ethic of life" in the Gannon Lecture at Fordham University. Since that time there has been a sustained process of reflection and analysis in the Church about the multiple issues which come under the umbrella of the consistent ethic.

Last November, the National Conference of Catholic Bishops adopted the consistent ethic theme in its revised Plan for Pro-Life Activities. Obviously, I find that step particularly significant, for it gives the consistent ethic the status of policy within the Episcopal Conference. Nevertheless, I believe the concept and consequences of the consistent ethic must be examined more deeply, its implications make clearer within the Church and in the wider civil society. So I am returning to the theme this afternoon at another Catholic university, seeking to press forward the dialogue of several disciplines in the quest for a comprehensive and consistent ethic of life.

During the past two years, as I have followed the commentary on the consistent ethic in journals and the media, and as I have carried on a wide-ranging personal correspondence with many bishops, theologians, philosophers, and social scientists, three topics emerged about the theme which I wish to address: its theological foundation, its ethical logic, and its political consequences.

I. The Theological Foundation: Systematic Defense of the Person

Some commentators, while very positive about the substance and structure of the call for a consistent ethic, have urged me to focus on its underlying theological foundations. I see the need for this and will comment here on two aspects of its theological substance, leaving for the next section some more detailed moral commentary.

The consistent ethic grows out of the very character of Catholic moral thought. By that I do not mean to imply that one has to be a Catholic to affirm the moral content of the consistent ethic. But I do think that this theme highlights both the systematic and analogical character of Catholic moral theology. The systematic nature of Catholic theology means it is grounded in a set of basic principles and then articulated in a fashion which draws out the meaning of each principle and the relationships among them. Precisely because of its systematic quality, Catholic theology refuses to treat moral issues in an *ad hoc* fashion. There is a continual process of testing the use of a principle in one case by its use in very different circumstances. The consistent ethic seeks only to illustrate how this testing goes on when dealing with issues involving the taking of life or the enhancement of life through social policy.

The analogical character of Catholic thought offers the potential to address a spectrum of issues which are not identical but have some common characteristics. Analogical reasoning identifies the unifying elements which link two or more issues, while at the same time it recognizes why similar issues cannot be reduced to a single problem.

The taking of life presents itself as a moral problem all along the spectrum of life, but there are distinguishing characteristics between abortion and war, as well as elements which radically differentiate war from decisions made about care of a terminally ill patient. The *differences* among these cases are universally acknowledged; a consistent ethic seeks to highlight the fact the differences do not destroy the elements of a *common moral challenge.*

A Catholic ethic which is both systematic in its argument and analogical in its perspective stands behind the proposal that, in the face of the multiple threats to life in our time, spanning every phase of existence, it is necessary to develop a moral vision which can address these several challenges in a coherent and comprehensive fashion.

If the theological style of the consistent ethic is captured by the two words, systematic and analogical, the theological rationale for the ethic is grounded in the respect we owe the human person. To defend human life is to protect the human person. The consistent ethic cuts across the diverse fields of social ethics, medical ethics, and sexual ethics. The unifying theme behind these three areas of moral analysis is the human person, the core reality in Catholic moral thought.

It is precisely the abiding conviction of Catholic ethics about the social nature of the person that ties together the emphasis—in the pastoral letter on the economy—on society's responsibility for the poor, the insistence of the bishops that abortion is a public not a purely private moral question, and the constant refrain of Catholic ethics that sexual issues are social in character.

The theological assertion that the person is the *imago dei,* the philosophical affirmation of the dignity of the person, and the political principle that society and state exist to serve the person all these themes stand behind the consistent ethic. They also sustain the positions that the U.S. Catholic Bishops have taken on issues as diverse as nuclear policy, social policy, and abortion. These themes provide the basis for the moral perspective of the consistent ethic. It is the specifics of that moral perspective which now must be examined.

II. The Ethical Argument: The Logic of Linkage

The central assertion of the consistent ethic is that we will enhance our moral understanding of a number of "life-issues" by carefully linking them in a framework which allows consideration of each issue on its own merits, but also highlights the connections among distinct issues. This is the moral logic of an analogical vision.

In essence the consistent ethic is a moral argument, and, therefore, its principles and perspective must be constantly measured and tested. The consistent ethic rejects collapsing all issues into one, and it rejects isolating our moral vision and insulating our social concern on one issue. What has been the response to the moral argument of the consistent ethic?

First, it has generated precisely the kind of substantive debate in the Catholic community and in the wider society which I believe is needed. The response began immediately after the Gannon Lecture in the press and weekly journals; it has now moved also to scholarly journals. Second, the range of the commentary has run from the ethical theory of the consistent ethic, to debate about its specific conclusions, to assessment of its contribution to the public witness of the Church in U.S. society.

A particularly extensive analysis of the theme appeared in the "Notes on Moral Theology" in *Theological Studies* last March. This annual review of scholarly writing on moral theology has been highly respected for many years. Among the many commentaries on the consistent ethic, I cite this one because it engages bishops and theologians in the kind of disciplined debate which is needed if our theology is to be authentically Catholic, intellectually responsive to contemporary moral challenges, and pastorally useful to the Catholic community and civil society.

In a time when continuing respectful dialogue is urgently needed between bishops and theologians, I believe the kind of theological interest generated by the two pastoral letters of the U.S. bishops and the consistent ethic proposal is a healthy sign. The Theological Studies articles on the consistent ethic were a wide-ranging survey of several specific questions. On the whole, I found the commentary quite positive and very helpful. I lift it up for consideration by others even though I do not agree with every conclusion drawn by others.

One of the areas where I differ is the critique of the moral theory made by Fr. Richard McCormick, S.J. He supports the perspective of the consistent ethic, calling it "utterly essential," but he believes that I give the prohibition of direct killing of the innocent too high a status. Rather than calling it a basic principle of Catholic morality, Fr. McCormick would designate it a moral rule, "developed as a result of our wrestling with concrete cases of conflict." Furthermore, he argues that the rule has been formulated in teleological fashion, by a balancing of values which yield some exceptions to the presumption against killing.

While I do not consider it my role to engage in a full review of the moral theory of the consistent ethic, I think the reduction of the prohibition against the intentional killing of the innocent to a status less than an absolute rule is not correct. As I argued in the Gannon lecture, the justification of the use of force and the taking of human life is based on a presumption against taking life which then allows for a series of exceptions where the presumption is overridden. But within this general structure of reasoning, for example in the Just War doctrine, the direct killing of the innocent has not been regarded as a legitimate exception.

This means, as Fr. John Connery, S.J. and others have observed, that Catholic teaching has not ruled out the taking of life in all circumstances. There is a *presumption* against taking life, not an *absolute prohibition*. But the cutting edge of the Just War argument has been its capacity to place a double restraint on the use of force. One limit is based on the calculation of consequences (the principle of proportionality) and the other based on an absolute prohibition of certain actions (the principle of non-combatant immunity).

As I read Fr. McCormick's proposal, both principles would become proportional judgements. My experience in addressing the nuclear question leads me to conclude that such an interpretation will weaken the moral strength of the ethic of war. In assessing the strategy of deterrence, having two distinct criteria of moral analysis provided the bishops with a perspective on the policy debate which was different from what a totally proportionalist view would have offered.

Because of my experience with this specific moral dilemma of deterrence and because I find the prohibition against the intentional killing of the innocent a crucial element across the spectrum of the consistent ethic, I find myself not persuaded by Fr. McCormick's recommendation, even though I appreciate the care with which he reviewed my lectures. I know adherence to the absolute prohibition creates very complex and difficult choices, not least in deterrence theory, but testing the absolute prohibition across the spectrum of life leads me to reaffirm it rather than reduce its status.

A very different objection to the consistent ethic arose—primarily from persons active in the right-to-life movement—immediately after the Gannon Lecture. The critique continues to this day. The objection is raised against the way I called for relating our defense of innocent life to support for social policies and programs designed to respond to the needs of the poor. The passage of the Gannon Lecture which attracted the most criticism read this way:

If one contends, as we do, that the right of every fetus to be born should be protected by civil law and supported by civil consensus, then our moral, political and economic responsibilities do not stop at the moment of birth. Those who defend the right to life of the weakest among us must be equally visible in support of the quality of life of the powerless among us: the old and the young, the hungry and the homeless, the undocumented immigrant and the unemployed worker. Such a quality of life posture translates into specific political and economic positions on tax policy, employment generation, welfare policy, nutrition and feeding programs, and health care. Consistency means we cannot have it both ways: We cannot urge a compassionate society and vigorous public policy to protect the rights of the unborn and then argues that compassion and significant public programs on behalf of the needy undermine the moral fiber of the society or are beyond the proper scope of governmental responsibility.

Reviewing those words in light of the criticisms of the last two years, I still find what I said to be morally correct and, if anything, politically more necessary to say than it was two years ago. In the first half of the 1980s we have seen many of the programs designed to meet basic needs of poor people systematically cut. Perhaps the prototypical example is what is happening to children—precisely those who first evoke our right-to-life defense. In the second draft of the pastoral letter on the economy the bishops graphically describe the situation of children in our country:

Today one in every four American children under the age of 6 and one in every two black children under 6 are poor. The number of children in poverty rose by 4 million over the decade between 1973-1983, with the result that there are now more poor children in the United States than at any time since 1965.

In a recent book of far-reaching significance, Senator Patrick Moynihan has made the point that children are the most vulnerable group in our society.

In the face of this evidence it is precisely the function of a consistent ethic to gather a constituency which stands against those social forces legitimating the taking of life birth, *and* stands against other social forces legitimating policies which erode the dignity of life after birth by leaving children vulnerable to hunger, inadequately housing, and insufficient health care.

The criticism of my Gannon Lecture was twofold: that it confused two different moral issues and that it expected everyone to do everything. I have responded to this critique previously, but I wish to expand upon my response. Surely we can all agree that the taking of human life in abortion is not the same as failing to protect human dignity against hunger. But having made that distinction, let us not fail to make the point that both are moral issues requiring a response of the Catholic community and of our society as a whole.

The logic of a consistent ethic is to press the moral meaning of both issues. The consequences of a consistent ethic is to bring under review the position of every group in the Church which sees the moral meaning in one place but not the other. The ethic cuts *two* ways, not one: It challenges pro-life groups, and it challenges justice and peace groups. The meaning of a consistent ethic is to say in the Catholic community that our moral tradition calls us beyond the split so evident in the wider society between moral witness to life before and after birth.

Does this mean that everyone must do everything? No! There are limits of time, energy and competency. There is a shape to every individual vocation. People must specialize, groups must focus their energies. The consistent ethic does not deny this.

But it does say something to the Church: It calls us to a wider witness to life than we sometimes manifest in our separate activities. The consistent ethic challenges bishops to shape a comprehensive social agenda. It challenges priests and religious to teach the Catholic tradition with the breadth it deserves. And it challenges Catholics as citizens to go beyond the divided witness to life which is too much the pattern of politics and culture in our society. Responding to this multiple challenge requires consideration of the public consequences of the consistent ethic.

III. The Political Consequences: Shaping Public Choices

Some commentators on the consistent ethic saw it primarily as a political policy. They missed its primary meaning: It is a moral vision and an ethical argument sustaining the vision. But the moral vision does have political consequences. The consistent ethic is meant to shape the public witness of the Catholic Church in our society.

The first consequence is simply to highlight the unique place which Catholic teaching on a range of issues has given the Church in the public arena. As I have said before, no other major institution in the country brings together the positions the Catholic bishops presently hold on abortion, nuclear policy, and economic policy. Our positions cut across party lines, and they contradict conventional notions of liberal and conservative. I find that a healthy contribution to the public debate, and I believe we ought to stress the point.

The second public consequence of a consistent ethic is to establish a framework where we can test the moral vision of each part of the Church in a disciplined, systematic fashion. We will not shape an ecclesial consensus about the consistent ethic without the kind of vigorous public debate which has gone on in the Church in the last two years. But our debate will sharpen our ecclesial moral sense, and it can also be a public lesson to the wider society if it is marked by coherence, civility, and charity.

The third public consequence of a consistent ethic is that it provides a standard to test public policy, party platforms, and the posture of candidates for office. Here is where the challenge to moral reasoning, pastoral leadership, and political sensitivity reaches its most delicate level. But we should not shrink from the need to make specific the logic of the consistent ethic.

We are a multi-issue Church precisely because of the scope and structure of our moral teaching. But it is not enough to be interested in several issues. We need to point the way toward a public vision where issues can be understood as morality and politically interdependent. I propose the consistent ethic not as a finished product but a framework in need of development. I invite more debate about it, precisely at this concrete level where specific choices on issues are made, where candidates take positions, and where citizens must evaluate them.

I believe our moral vision is broader and richer than we have made it appear at this concrete, practical level of politics. Precisely because we are not yet in a national election year, we need to think about how a consistent ethic can be set forth in a convincing way. It will cut across conventional party lines, and it will not lead to crystal clear judgments on candidates, but it may give the Church, as an institution and a community, a better way to engage the attention of the nation regarding the intersection of moral vision, public policy, and political choices.

To think through the meaning of such a position, we need bishops who foster the debate, political leaders who enter the discussion, professors and policy analysts who can clarify categories, and members of the Church who exercise the supremely important role of citizens. It is my hope that we can have this kind of ecclesial and public debate in the months ahead.

Address: Consistent Ethic of Life Conference

Portland, Oregon
Joseph Cardinal Bernardin
October 4, 1986

I am deeply grateful for the invitation to address you on a topic to which I have devoted much time and energy during the past three years: the "consistent ethic of life."

This morning I will (1) give an overview of the concept, (2) explore the movement from moral analysis to public policy choices, and (3) identify issues needing further development: the implications of the consistent ethic for citizens, office seekers, and office holders.

I. The Consistent Ethic of Life: An Overview

The idea of the consistent ethic is both old and new. It is "old" in the sense that its substance has been the basis of many programs for years. For example, when the U.S. bishops inaugurated their Respect Life Program in

1972, they invited the Catholic community to focus on the "sanctity of human life and the many threats to human life in the modern world, including war, violence, hunger, and poverty."

Fourteen years later, the focus remains the same. As the 1986 Respect Life brochure states, "The Pastoral Plan is set in the context of a consistent ethic that links concern for the unborn with concern for all human life. The inviolability of innocent human life is a fundamental norm."

Moreover, the bishops' pastoral letter, "The Challenge of Peace: God's Promise and Our Response," emphasized the sacredness of human life and the responsibility we have, personally and as a society, to protect and preserve its sanctity. In paragraph 285, it specifically linked the nuclear question with abortion and other life issues:

> When we accept violence in any form as commonplace, our sensitivities become dulled. When we accept violence, war itself can be taken for granted. Violence has many faces: oppression of the poor, deprivation of basic human rights, economic exploitation, sexual exploitation and pornography, neglect or abuse of the aged and the helpless, and innumerable other acts of inhumanity. Abortion in particular blunts a sense of the sacredness of human life. In a society where the innocent unborn are killed wantonly, how can we expect people to feel righteous revulsion at the act or threat of killing non-combatants in war?

However, the pastoral letter—while giving us a starting point for developing a consistent ethic of life—does not provide a fully articulated framework.

It was precisely to provide a more comprehensive theological and ethical basis for the Respect Life Program and for the linkage of war and abortion, as noted by the pastoral letter, that I developed the theme of the consistent ethic. Another important circumstance which prompted me to move in this direction was that I had just been asked to serve as Chairman of the Bishops' Pro-Life Committee. It was October of 1983, and I knew that both abortion and defense-related issues would undoubtedly play an important role in the upcoming presidential campaign.

It was urgent, I felt, that a well-developed theological and ethical framework be provided which would link the various life issues while, at the same time, pointing out that the issues are not all the same. It was my fear that, *without* such a framework or vision, the U.S. bishops would be severely pressured by those who wanted to push a particular issue with little or no concern for the rest. *With* such a theological basis, we would be able to argue convincingly on behalf of all the issues on which we had taken a position in recent years.

I first presented the theme in a talk at Fordham University in December, 1983. At that time, I called for a public discussion of the concept, both in Catholic circles and the broader community. In all candor I must admit that the public response greatly exceeded my hopes and expectations.

Since that time there has been a lively exchange by both those who agree and disagree with the theme and its implications. By far, the majority of the reactions have been supportive. Nonetheless, it has been used and misused by those who have tried to push their own, narrower agendas. I myself have made further contributions to the discussion through subsequent talks and articles.

The concept itself is a *challenging* one. It requires us to broaden, substantively and creatively, our ways of thinking, our attitudes, our pastoral response. Many are not accustomed to thinking about all the life-threatening and life-diminishing issues with such consistency. The result is that they remain somewhat selective in their response. Although some of those who oppose the concept seem not to have understood it, I sometimes suspect that many who oppose it recognize its challenge. Quite frankly, I sometimes wonder whether those who embrace it quickly and whole-heartedly truly understand its implicit challenge.

Last November, when the U.S. bishops updated and reaffirmed the Pastoral Plan for Pro-Life Activities, they explicitly adopted the "consistent ethic" for the first time as the theological context for the Plan.

In sum, to the delight of those who agree with its theological reasoning and to the dismay of the small minority who do not, the "consistent ethic" has entered into our theological vocabulary.

Let me now explain in greater depth the theological basis and strategic value of the "consistent ethic." Catholic teaching is based on two truths about the human person: human life is both sacred and social. Because we esteem human life as sacred, we have a duty to protect and foster it at all stages of development, from conception to natural death, and in all circumstances. Because we acknowledge that human life is also social, society must protect and foster it.

Precisely because life is sacred, the taking of even one life is a momentous event. Traditional Catholic teaching has allowed the taking of human life in particular situations by way of exception—for example, in self-defense and capital punishment. In recent decades, however, the presumptions against taking human life have been strengthened and the exceptions made ever more restrictive.

Fundamental to these shifts in emphasis is a more acute perception of the many ways in which life is threatened today. Obviously, such questions as war, aggression, and capital punishment are not new; they have been with us for centuries. Life has always been threatened, but today there is a new *context* that shapes the *content* of our ethic of life.

The principal factor responsible for this new context is modern *technology* which induces a sharper awareness of the fragility of human life. War, for example, has always been a threat to life, but today the threat is qualitatively different because of nuclear and other sophisticated kinds of weapons. The weapons produced by modern technology now threaten life on a scale previously unimaginable. Living, as we do, therefore, in an age of extraordinary technological development means we face a qualitatively new range of moral problems. The essential questions we face are these: In an age when we *can* do almost anything, how do we decide what we *should* do? In a time when we can do anything *technologically,* how do we decide *morally* what we should not do?

We face new technological challenges along the whole spectrum of life from conception to natural death. This creates the need for a consistent ethic, for the spectrum cuts across such issues as genetics, abortion, capital punishment, modern warfare, and the care of the terminally ill. Admittedly, these are all *distinct* problems, enormously complex, and deserve individual treatment. Each requires its own moral analysis. No single answer or solution applies to all. *But they are linked!*

Given this broad range of challenging issues, we desperately need a societal *attitude* or climate that will sustain a consistent defense and promotion of life. When human life is considered "cheap" or easily expendable in one area, eventually nothing is held as sacred and all lives are in jeopardy. Ultimately, it is society's attitude about life—whether of respect or non-respect—that determines its policies and practices.

The theological foundation of the consistent ethic, then, is defense of the person. The ethic grows out of the very character of Catholic moral thought. I do not mean to imply, of course, that one has to be a Catholic to affirm the moral content of the consistent ethic. But I do think that this theme highlights both the systematic and analogical character of Catholic moral theology.

The *systematic* nature of Catholic theology means it is grounded in a set of basic principles and then articulated in a fashion which draws out the meaning of each principle and the relationships among them. Precisely because of its systematic quality, Catholic theology refuses to treat moral issues in an *ad hoc* fashion. There is a continual process of testing the use of a principle in one case by its use in very different circumstances. The consistent ethic seeks only to illustrate how this testing goes on when dealing with issues involving the taking of life or the enhancement of life through social policy.

The *analogical* character of Catholic thought offers the potential to address a spectrum of issues which are not identical but have some common characteristics. Analogical reasoning identifies the unifying elements which link two or more issues, while at the same time recognizing why similar issues cannot be reduced to a single problem.

The taking of life presents itself as a moral problem all along the spectrum of life, but there are differences between abortion and war, just as there are elements that radically differentiate war from decisions made about the care of a terminally ill patient. The *differences* among these cases are universally acknowledged. A consistent ethic seeks to highlight the fact that differences do not destroy the elements of a *common moral challenge*.

A Catholic ethic which is both systematic in its argument and analogical in its perspective stands behind the proposal that, in the face of the multiple threats to life in our time, spanning every phase of existence, it is necessary to develop a moral vision which can address these several challenges in a coherent and comprehensive fashion.

The theological assertion that the human person is made in the image and likeness of God, the philosophical affirmation of the dignity of the person, and the political principle that society and state exist to serve the person—all these themes stand behind the consistent ethic. They also sustain the positions that the U.S. Catholic bishops have taken on issues as diverse as nuclear policy, social policy, and abortion. These themes provide the basis for the moral perspective of the consistent ethic.

II. From Moral Analysis to Public Policy Choices

Some commentators on the consistent ethic saw it primarily as a political policy. They missed its primary meaning: It is a moral vision and an ethical argument sustaining the vision. But the moral vision *does* have political consequences. The consistent ethic is meant to shape the public witness of the Catholic Church in our society.

Before exploring some of the political consequences, I would like to comment briefly on some related issues which provide a broader context for such a discussion. The movement from moral analysis to public policy choices is a complex process in a pluralistic society like ours.

First, civil discourse in the United States is influenced, widely shaped, by *religious pluralism.* The condition of pluralism, wrote John Courtney Murray, is the coexistence in one society of groups holding divergent and incompatible views with regard to religious questions. The genius of American pluralism, in his view, was that it provided for the religious freedom of each citizen and every faith. However, it did not purchase tolerance at the price of expelling religious and moral values from the public life of the nation. The goal of the American system is to provide space for a religious substance in society but not a religious State.

Second, there is a *legitimate secularity* of the political process, just as there is a legitimate role for religious and moral discourse in our nation's life. The dialogue which keeps both alive must be a careful exchange which seeks neither to transform secularity into secularism nor to change the religious role into religiously dominated public discourse.

John Courtney Murray spent a substantial amount of time and effort defending the Church's right to speak in the public arena. But he also stressed the *limits* of the religious role in that arena. Today religious institutions, I believe, must reaffirm their rights and recognize their limits. My intent is not, of course, to produce a passive Church or a purely private vision of faith. The limits relate not to *whether* we enter the public debate but *how* we advocate a public case. This implies, for example, that religiously rooted positions somehow must be translated into language, arguments, and categories which a religiously pluralistic society can agree on as the moral foundation of key policy positions.

Third, all participants in the public discourse must face the test of *complexity.* From issues of defense policy through questions of medical ethics to issues of social policy, the moral dimensions of our public life are interwoven with empirical judgments where honest disagreement exists. I do not believe, however, that empirical complexity should silence or paralyze religious or moral analysis and advocacy of issues. But we owe the public a careful accounting of how we have come to our moral conclusions.

Fourth, we must keep in mind the relationship between *civil law and morality*. Although the premises of civil law are rooted in moral principles, the scope of law is more limited and its purpose is not the moralization of society. Moral principles govern personal and social human conduct and cover as well interior acts and motivation. Civil statutes govern public order; they address primarily external acts and values that are formally social.

Hence it is not the function of civil law to enjoin or prohibit *everything* that moral principles enjoin or prohibit. History has shown over and over again that people cherish freedom; they can be coerced only minimally. When we pursue a course of legal action, therefore, we must ask whether the requirements of public order are serious enough to take precedence over the claims of freedom.

Fifth, in the objective order of law and public policy, how do we determine which issues are *public* moral questions and which are best defined as *private* moral questions?

For Murray, an issue was one of public morality if it affected the *public order* of society. Public order, in turn, encompassed three goods: public peace, essential protection of human rights, and commonly accepted standards of moral behavior in a community. Whether a given question should be interpreted as one of public morality is not always self-evident. A rationally persuasive case has to be made that an action violates the rights of another or that the consequences of actions on a given issue are so important to society that the authority of the State and the civil law ought to be invoked to govern personal and group behavior.

Obviously, in a religiously pluralistic society, achieving consensus on what constitutes a public moral question is never easy. But we have been able to do it—by a process of debate, decision-making, then review of our decisions.

Two cases exemplify how we struggled with public morality in the past. First, Prohibition was an attempt to legislate behavior in an area ultimately decided to be beyond the reach of civil law because it was not sufficiently public in nature to affect the public order. Second, civil rights, particularly in areas of housing, education, employment, voting, and access to public facilities, were determined—after momentous struggles of war, politics, and law—to be so central to public order that the State could not be neutral on the question.

Today, we have a public consensus in law and policy which clearly defines civil rights as issues of public morality, and the decision to drink alcoholic beverages as clearly one of private morality. But neither decision was reached without struggle. The consensus was not automatic on either question. Philosophers, activists, politicians, preachers, judges, and ordinary citizens had to state a case, shape a consensus, and then find a way to give the consensus public standing in the life of the nation.

The fact that a spontaneous public consensus is lacking at a given moment does not prohibit its being created. When he was told that the law could not legislate morality, Dr. Martin Luther King, Jr., used to say that the law could not make people love their neighbors but it could stop their lynching them. Law and public policy can also be instruments of shaping a public consensus; they are not simply the product of consensus.

In sum, in charting the movement from moral analysis to public policy choices, we must take into account the facts that (1) civil discourse in this nation is influenced and shaped by religious pluralism; (2) there is a legitimate secularity of the political process; (3) all participants in it must face the test of complexity; (4) there is a distinction between civil law and morality; and (5) some issues are questions of public morality, others of private morality.

This brings us to the third part of my address.

III. Implications of the Consistent Ethic for Citizens, Office Seekers and Office Holders

In light of the nearly three-year debate about the consistent ethic, questions have surfaced at the level of theological principle and ethical argument. As noted earlier, I have addressed these as they have arisen. The area that now needs attention is precisely how the framework of the consistent ethic takes shape (a) in the determination of public policy positions taken by the Church and (b) in the decisions that legislators and citizens take in light of the Church's positions.

Let me hasten to acknowledge that I do not have all the answers to the next set of questions. At this point in the dialogue I have chosen simply to identify questions which need further reflection and discussion. I also acknowledge that others have raised some of the questions; they are not all mine. Although I am not prepared to give answers to these questions, I do intend to address them at a later date.

What role does consensus play in the development of public policy and civil law? Earlier I suggested that its role is essential in the long run. But what about the short term? Moreover, what are the appropriate roles of civic and religious leaders in providing moral leadership in the public policy debate within a pluralistic community? What is the difference between a bishop's role and a politician's in the public debate about moral issues which the consistent ethic embraces? Should a politician wait until a consensus is developed before taking a stand or initiating legislation?

Must a Catholic office seeker or office holder work for all clearly identified Catholic concerns simultaneously and with the same vigor? Is that possible? If such a person need not work for all these concerns aggressively and at the same time, on what basis does one decide what to concentrate on and what not? Does theology provide the answer or politics or both? What guidelines does one use to determine which issues are so central to Catholic belief that they must be pursued legislatively regardless of the practical possibilities of passage? What are the consequences if a Catholic office seeker or office holder does not follow the Church's teaching in the campaign for or exercise of public office?

What is a Catholic office holder's responsibility in light of the Second Vatican Council's Declaration on Religious Liberty to protect the religious beliefs of non-Catholics? What is his or her responsibility under the Constitution? How are these responsibilities related?

How is the distinction between accepting a moral principle and asking prudential judgments about applying it in particular circumstances—for example, in regard to specific legislation—worked out in the political order? What is the responsibility of a Catholic office holder or office seeker when the bishops have made a prudential judgment regarding specific legislation? How are Catholic voters to evaluate a Catholic office holder or office seeker who accepts a moral principle and not only disagrees with the bishops regarding specific legislation but supports its defeat?

Until questions like these are explored and ultimately answered, using the consistent ethic of life to test public policy, party platforms, and the posture of candidates for office will remain problematic and controversial. I firmly believe, however, that the consistent ethic, when pursued correctly and in depth, can make a genuine contribution. Solid, credible answers to the questions raised above will require an honest exchange of the best there is to offer in theological, political and social thought.

I assure you that the Catholic bishops will remain in the public debate, and we need help. Public officials will remain in the line of fire, and they need help. Citizens will ultimately make the difference, and they, too, need help if the dialogue about how we are to respond to the broad range of contemporary issues is to proceed in a constructive fashion.

As the debate proceeds, we have a wonderful opportunity to bring together the best of our religious, political and social traditions in the service of each other and the wider society to which we are bound in hope and love.

The Consistent Ethic of Life: Is There an Historical Soft Underbelly?

Richard A. McCormick, S.J.
John A. O'Brien Professor of
Christian Ethics
Department of Theology
University of Notre Dame

I am very grateful to Cardinal Bernardin for having picked the "consistent ethic of life" as the theme around which he has developed so many of his rich presentations since the Gannon and Wade lectures. Cardinal Bernardin has made points that are, in my judgement, utterly essential if the moral vision that is the "consistent ethic of life" is to shape not only an ecclesial consensus, but public policy. For instance, he repeatedly grounds this ethic in the dignity of the human person. He sees it applicable to life-*enhancing* issues as well as life-*preserving* ones. He sees it as cutting across social, medical and sexual ethics. He sees the need to develop in a way that is systematic but also analogical (as being different but having common characteristics). In this way he challenges all of us to rise above our one-eyed enthusiasms, to become multi-issue persons while always remembering that the issues are unavoidably interdependent.

I have been asked to treat the consistent ethic of life in its historical perspective. I will freely interpret "history" to comprise both remote and recent dimensions. My reflections are entitled "Is There a Soft Underbelly?" By this title I mean in no way to undermine the validity of the moral vision captured in the phrase "the consistent ethic of life." I mean only to suggest that, if this vision is to become a true ecclesial and political leaven, it must face squarely factors that are likely to undermine or weaken it. It is precisely because I endorse the general thrust of the "consistent ethic" that I think it worthwhile lifting out in all honesty possible vulnerable points. Cardinal Bernardin certainly agrees; for he has repeatedly emphasized the desirability of vigorous but civil and charitable debate in this area.

I will develop these reflections under two headings: 1) Global prescientific convictions; 2) The rule "no direct killing of the innocent."

I. Global Prescientific Convictions

This phrase is borrowed from Karl Rahner.[1] He uses it to refer to the unexamined assumptions, mostly cultural in character, that shape our moral perceptions and analyses. He was discussing bad moral arguments and explaining how they often trace to such assumptions. Philip Rieff had something very similar in mind when he referred to "reasons" that form the "unwitting" part of a culture and give shape to its habits, customs, policies and procedures.[2]

I will mention six such "unwitting assumptions"—three with more remote historical roots, three more contemporary in origin—that can easily act as obstacles to the effectiveness of a consistent ethic of life.

1. Biological Givenness as Normative

It is clear that in Cardinal Bernardin's various presentations on the consistent ethic of life, the human person is absolutely central. This is as it should be. Vatican II similarly placed the human person front and center at the very outset of *Gaudium et spes*. Further on, it stated that "the moral aspect of any procedure...must be determined by objective standards which are based on the nature of the person and the person's acts."[3] The official commentary on this wording noted two things: (1) In the expression there is formulated a general principle that applies to all human actions, not just to marriage and sexuality; (2) The choice of this expression means that "human activity must be judged insofar as it refers to the human person integrally and adequately considered."[4] So far so good.

But such integral personalism was a conciliar achievement. It did not reflect the way decisive thinkers in the Catholic tradition proceeded. Furthermore, official teaching, not-withstanding the deliverances of Vatican II, still reproduce the basic anthropological assumptions of these decisive thinkers, as I shall try to indicate. That means that in some areas of practical moral instruction, the person is not really decisive. And if that is true, a "consistent ethic of life" rooted in the centrality of the person is somewhat undermined.

Let St. Thomas be the example here.[5] In his treatment of the content of natural law, Thomas pointed out that the order of our tendencies and the goods which are their objects determine the order of the precepts of the natural law. He identified three levels of natural tendencies and three corresponding goods. (1) The tendency to the good corresponding to the nature the person has in common with all beings (self-conservation). (2) The tendency to goods relating to the nature we share with animals. Here that pertains to the natural law which nature teaches to all animals (coitus and care of offspring). (3) The tendency to the good corresponding to the rational nature proper to human beings (knowledge of truth and social life).

All of these tendencies and goods relate to the natural law in the measure that they can be regulated by reason. Formally, natural law is the law of reason. But the content of natural law at the *generic* (n.2) level is that which is natural, i.e. given in biological nature. The content of the natural law at the *specific* (n.3) level is that which is proper to human beings as spiritual. At this specific level that is natural which reason dictates to us. But at the generic level, the task of reason is to discern the demands of the natural order, that order inscribed by God in biological reality. At one level, we *recognize*. At another we *invent* or discover.

When Thomas applies this to marriage, he sees marriage at two distinct levels: as founded on the *generic* natural law, as founded on the *specific* natural law. With regard to the former, the division of sexes is for procreation; the genital organs have as their proper finality procreation; woman is a helper to man via procreation. At the generic level marriage is a good for the species (*matrimonium officium naturae*).

Thus we can understand Thomas' notion of an *actus naturae*. Its demands are inscribed in biological function. Of the goods at this generic level, some pertain to the individual (eating), others to the species (coitus). Just as eating is sinless and good when done in the order and measure required for bodily health, so coitus is sinless and good on condition that it is performed in the manner required by procreation.

In summary, then, for Thomas sexual intercourse is an act of nature relating to the order common to man and animal. Its finality is inscribed by the Creator in its very biological function, and it is procreation. It follows, of course, that couples must pursue procreation and limit themselves to acts necessary to it. Any practice that impedes conception is a sin against nature because it vitiates an *act of nature*. It is clear, therefore, that the order of nature has a very foundational value in Thomas because a notion of natural law at whose heart the biological function of an act receives the value of a first principle, and one that is absolute because inscribed by God. *Deus nihil facit inane.*

As the subsequent centuries unfolded, there were serious modifications made in this notion of *actus naturae*. One thinks of the long (4 centuries) controversy on the motive of pleasure, the acceptance of mutual love as a subjective motive (in the textbooks by ca.1850), the acceptance of "periodic continence." One can summarize the moments in this development as follows: (1) The couple must positively pursue procreation. (2) Intercourse is licit if they do not positively exclude procreation. (3) Intercourse is licit even though there is the intent to avoid procreation.[6]

Now enter *Casti connubii*. It reproduces the Thomistic distinction between the *generic* and *specific* levels of natural law in different words, *strict* and *broad*.

> This mutual interior formation of the partners, this earnest desire of perfecting one another, can be said in a certain very true sense, as the Roman Catechism teachers, to be the primary cause and reason of marriage—if only marriage is taken not strictly as an institution for the proper procreation and rearing of children, but in a broader sense as a sharing, a community, a union of their whole life.[7]

The encyclical condemned contraception, but justified intercourse even when conception is not possible "providing always that the intrinsic nature of that act is preserved and therefore its proper ordination to the primary end."[8] In summary, *Casti connubii* reproduced the argumentation of earlier centuries elaborated on the notion of *actus naturae* without showing that the intervening modifications had seriously undermined that notion.

Then, of course, came the Council, with its emphasis on the centrality of the person and its adoption of the themes that had been developed since *Casti connubii* (responsible parenthood and the personal notion of sexual intercourse—sc., an action whose intrinsic sense is to be an expression of love). This development we may characterize in stages: *actus naturae, natura actus, actus personae.*[9]

Against this developmental background *Humanae vitae* appeared in 1968. It rejected all contraception appealing to the "inseparable connection, willed by God and unable to be broken by man on his own initiative, between the two meanings of the conjugal act: the unitive meaning and the procreative meaning."[10] The obvious and unavoidable implication of this analysis is that every act of sexual intimacy is somehow procreative.

Many have seen this notion of inseparability and its implication as a linear descendent, indeed a prolongation of the analysis of intercourse as an *actus naturae* with a single procreative purpose. They are confirmed in this by the repeated references in the encyclical (as well as in the subsequent document of John Paul II, *Familiaris consortio*) to "natural laws of fecundity" (n.11), "biological laws" (n.10), "natural processes" (n.16), "the human body and its natural endowments" (n.17) as if these were normative.

In summary, then, while the basic values of marriage remain constant, the way in which they are explained and protected has gone through an evolutionary process. I agree with Joseph Selling when he notes that "the realization of the procreative end had become totally detached from the individual act of intercourse. Sexual relations were licit on the basis of their connection with expressing conjugal love alone. Consequently, a new set of norms was necessary to evaluate those relations."[11] Yet *Humanae vitae* represents a continuation of the notion of an *actus naturae*, with a decisive finality and significance located in biological facticity. How else explain the inseparability of the unitive and procreative *in every act* when the act is known to be infertile (because of age) or intended to be as in natural family planning? In another context, moral theologians John C. Ford, S.J. and Gerald Kelly, S.J. remarked:

> The marriage act has other natural and intrinsic ends in addition to procreation *which are separable* from actual procreation or any intention of actual procreation.[12]

Then comes the recent (March 1987) instruction of the Congregation for the Doctrine of the Faith on reproductive technologies.[13] There are many excellent points in this instruction and they should not be overlooked. But when dealing with procedures between husband and wife (e.g., in vitro fertilization using their own gametes), the instruction reproduces verbatim the words of *Humanae vitae* on the inseparability of the unitive and procreative and rejects on this basis any procedure that is a replacement for sexual intercourse.

In detailing these points, I am in no way interested in provoking and continuing arguments about birth regulation. Most theologians have, in one way or another, rejected the perspectives of Franciscus Hurth, S.J., who was profoundly influential in the time of Pius XII. Hurth viewed procreativity as the exclusive primary finality of human sexual expression. This was, in his view, "the intention of nature inscribed in the organs and their functions."[14] This is St. Thomas *redivivus* or better, *continuatis*. Thus he argued: "This end for man thus is both the biological law and the moral law, such that the latter obliges him to live according to the biological law."

The rejection of these perspectives is expressed in a variety of ways. For instance, John Wright, S.J., states: "Immediate finality is always subordinate to the total finality of a reasonable human life."[15] The German theologian, Franz Scholz, states: "These natural ends are not the last word. They stand under the judgement of reason, as Thomas clearly emphasized."[16] Finally, English moralist Brendan Soane writes:

> Theologians seem to be generally agreed that the French hierarchy was right when it taught that the integrity of the marriage act is one value which can be balanced by others when couples decide what they should do.[17]

My purpose is not to rehearse such arguments. It is rather metaethical, and indeed with regard to two points: criterion and method. These two points are central in Cardinal Bernardin's presentation of a consistent ethic of life.

As for criterion, let the CDF's instruction on reproductive technologies be the example. It explicitly adopts, and repeatedly, the person as the key criterion in judging reproductive technologies—yet at a key point, when dealing with husband-wife artificial insemination and in vitro fertilization, it adopts as its key criterion the inseparability of the unitive-procreative as found in *Humanae vitae*. In other words, it fails to *use and apply*, in its practical moral reasoning, the criterion it had explicitly endorsed.

Then there is method. In his stimulating book, *An Inconsistent Ethic: Teachings of the American Catholic Bishops*, Kenneth R. Overberg, S.J., has amply documented the difference in approach of the bishops to social and so-called personal morality.[18] In the first instance their teachings amply reflect the characteristics of sound moral reasoning: biblical, communal, dynamic, personal. Thus the teachings are empirically oriented, tentative, open to change, collaborative, etc.

By contrast, matters of personal morality are deductive, nontentative, authoritarian, non-collaborative, heavily reliant on past statements, etc.

Let me illustrate this by reference to a study by the editors of *Civiltá cattolica* on the encyclical *Rerum novarum*. They note that in a sense *Rerum novarum* is a document that has to be "written on an ongoing basis." It is a kind of dynamic presence in all the social encyclicals that followed it. This dynamic presence and the real novelty of *Rerum novarum* is found not in its conclusions, many of which are dated, but in the fact that for the first time the Church's social concerns were given a systematic philosophical and theological justification. Thus its continuing relevance consists in the method in which it approached social problems.[19]

However, that encyclical must be continually reworked, because the social teaching of the Church developed in stages. *Rerum novarum* represents the first stage. It was dominated by "Christian philosophy" and a "rigidly deductive" method. This had two shortcomings. First, it left no room for the relevance of the sciences (political science, sociology, economics). Second, and a consequence, doctrinal elaboration was seen as an exclusively hierarchical task, lay persons being merely "faithful executors."

The second stage covers the pontificates of Pius XI and Pius XII and might be called the stage of "social doctrine." Indeed, *Quadragesimo anno* used this term for the first time. It referred to an organic corpus of universal principles still rigidly deduced from social ethics and constituted a kind of third way between liberalism and socialism. However, there is greater emphasis on the historical moment and applications of principles to practice, hence the beginnings of a re-evaluation of the place of lay persons in the process. Pius XI distinguished "unchangeable doctrine" from social action, this latter being the competence of lay persons.

The third stage began with John XXIII. John moved from the deductive to the inductive method, his point of departure being the "historical moment," to be viewed in light of the gospel. This led to a complete re-evaluation of the place of lay persons vis-a-vis social teaching, a re-evaluation completed by Vatican II. Lay persons do not simply apply the Church's social teaching; they must share in its very construction.

The novelty of this third stage is clear in the fact that the social teaching of the Church no longer refers to an immutable corpus of doctrine. Even the term "social doctrine" has fallen into disuse and is reserved for the period from Leo XIII to John XXIII. It is also clear in the new emphasis on the responsibility of the Christian community in the elaboration and application of the Church's social teaching, an emphasis most completely stated at Puebla (no.473).

This extremely interesting and very realistic analytic chronicle suggests a question: Has such a development occurred in the area of the Church's approach to familial and sexual morality? The answer is rather clearly no. Perhaps the question were better worded as follows: Should not such a development occur in the approach to these other questions? If a clearly deductive method, one that left little room to the sciences and lay experience, prevailed in the elaboration of social teaching, it is reasonable to think that the same thing occurred in familial and sexual morality. And if this method has evolved and changed during the pontificates of John XXIII, Paul VI, and John Paul II, as the editors of *Civiltá cattolica* correctly note, it is reasonable to think that the same thing ought to happen in all areas of Church teaching. Yet two things seem clear about the Church's teaching on sexual and familial morality. First, earlier popes are invariably cited for their conclusions, not simply their systematic method. Second, the sciences and lay experience remain marginal factors in the continuing reflection of the Church on familial and sexual matters, as noted above.

In summary, if, as Cardinal Bernardin rightly asserts, a consistent ethic of life cuts across social, medical and sexual ethics, that consistency is threatened, even undermined when we have different criteria and different methods used in approaching these matters, a kind of double standard. As long as a double standard is perceived by large segments of the community to operate, consistency is gone. This is the first dimension of the soft underbelly that I fear.

2. Sexism

Cardinal Bernardin has rightly insisted that a consistent ethic of life is incompatible with racism or sexism. Yet here again we must deal with the remnants, at the very least, of a "global prescientific conviction"—that women are subordinate. Theology itself, as Jaroslav Pelikan points out, has had its role to play, providing justification for the inferiority of women in the twofold assertion that Eve was created after Adam and was the one responsible for bringing sin into the world.[20] Thus Joseph A. Grassi, after reviewing the New Testament evidence, concludes that "many statements about women are time- bound to the inferior economic, social and religious position of woman in the ancient world, as well as time-bound to an old theology that held this to be the result of woman's sin."[21]

Time-bound or not, sexism persisted in the Church for centuries. The record of this can be read in any number of sources. It is found in some of the great fathers and doctors of the Church. For instance, Thomas attributed the conception of woman to the indisposition of the reproductive materials or to adverse weather conditions. When writing of women and the sacrament of orders, Thomas states:

> Since, therefore, it is not possible in the female sex that any eminence of degree be signified, for a woman is in the state of subjection, she cannot receive the sacrament of order.[22]

For centuries women were socially defined as limited by male definitions. Women who aspired to something unrelated to men and children were regarded as "masculine." And, of course, once a woman is defined in terms of sex-based stereotypes, the doors of political, economic, educational and ecclesiastical opportunity are closed one by one. Historically, then, we find no consistent ethic of life if such consistency has to include equality of women.

But the *Kinder-Kirche-Küche* syndrome has continued into the present and is still with us, perhaps in the Church more so than in western social life in general. For two years the U.S. bishops' Committee on Women in Society and in the Church dialogued with representatives of the Women's Ordination Conference.[23] The NCCB representatives acknowledged sexist attitudes as pervasive among members of the Church and its leadership.

They noted the discrepancy about the Church's teaching on women as applied in civil society and within the Church itself. The notion of "complementarity" often practically translates into subordination of women. Finally, they admitted that patriarchy had "deeply and adversely influenced the Church in its attitude toward women as reflected in its laws, theology and ministry." It has now become common to speak of the "sin of sexism," so much so that the usage is found in a recent pastoral letter by Bishops Victor Balke and Raymond Lucker.[24]

To mention such a fact is to deplore it. My only point here is that Catholic history does not provide much support for a consistent ethic of life if that ethic is to include the full dignity of women. And to the extent that this history continues into the present, it constitutes a credibility- barrier to that consistency. Pointedly, many women still feel that fetuses fare better, in official Church teaching and practice, than do women.

3. Theological Anthropomorphism

This may seem a strange "global instinctive conviction" to introduce here. This is especially so since all notions of God are bound to be anthropomorphic to a greater or lesser extent. I have the "greater extent" in mind. In this context by anthropomorphism I refer to the tendency to conceive God as another categorical actor in the world alongside other human actors. We are familiar with this phenomenon in a variety of ways in modern medicine. There are frequent examples of good people who refuse certain medical treatments for themselves or others on the grounds that "when God decides He will take me." There are also those who continue futile medical interventions to "give God a chance to perform a miracle." I mean in no way to belittle the genuine depth of religious faith and piety in such expressions and actions. I mean only to call attention to the fact that such notions contain two important implications: (1) That God is a direct actor on the human scene, like any other human agent; (2) That our own often anguishing decisional responsiblities can be postponed or transferred by such an approach.

Let Carlo Caffara be an example of this tendency.[25] Caffara attempts to provide theological backing to the *Hauptthese* of *Humanae vitae*. The human person, he argues, cannot be a direct product of the biological procreative act, but must originate in God's creative intervention. Thus, in the procreative act God and the parents are co-operative. This co-operation supposes that the partners are open to procreation. From this perspective contraceptive intervention contravenes the rights of God. Those who intervene in this way into God's active presence in the procreative act understand procreation as a merely human undertaking and prevent God "from being God."

Behind this analysis Joseph Fuchs sees a concept of God as directly and immediately involved in human causality, a kind of creationism. According to this understanding of God, conflicts can indeed arise between the two causes at work (God, parents). But Fuchs argues that this notion of God's creative activity is inadequate. Instead, he suggests the analysis originally proposed by Rahner and now widely accepted. God, the transcendental ground of all created reality, is causally active only through created secondary causes. He is not causally active in the way Caffara's analysis supposes.

I introduce this subject here because there are numerous appeals in historical Catholic thought to God's permissions and authorizations where human life is concerned. Thus martyrs who rushed into the flames were often said to be acting by divine inspiration, or permission. More to the point, the direct taking of innocent human life was said to be morally wrong because of a "lack of divine authorization." The implications of this analysis are interesting and far-reaching, as I shall attempt to indicate below.

4. The Dominance of Independence in Western (Especially American) Thought.

Here I shall rely on and briefly summarize some remarks of Theodore Minnema.[26] Of June Spencer Churchill's death by suicide, the coroner stated: "She had cancer in all her bones and there was no cure...It would seem to me she died before she became totally dependent upon others...something she couldn't bear."

"Something she couldn't bear" is a good description of the attitude of many people toward dependence on others. Independence is felt and viewed as essential to human dignity. Dignity highlights the active virtues. There is a pronounced negativity that attaches to the passive virtues (meekness, humility, patience) in our cultural and personal consciousness. Active virtues arise directly from the moral agent whereas passive virtues are reactions to what is outside the agent.

This personal repugnance to dependence has historical roots in our national self-image. We define ourselves nationally through the "Declaration of Independence" and live it out boisterously every July 4th.

Our abhorrence of dependence is only deepened even as we increasingly practice it, all the while proclaiming independence, for example in matters of energy. Similar things are overtaking our individual social experience. We proclaim our independence, yet act more dependently all the time (sedation, drugs, acclaim from others).

This "unwitting" absolution of independence has formidable effects on our moral consciousness and judgments, effects that can seriously affect a consistent ethic of life. In this sense, such a consistent ethic cries out for the incorporation of dependence as essential to our notion of human dignity. As a passive virtue, dependence refers to the ability to receive other persons and their achievements into our lives. That which is other than myself is freely accepted. Christians should know this down their pulses. Christ's dignity was manifested supremely in His dependence: "Not my will, but thine be done." The vulnerability of dependence can lead, as every lover knows, to the power of new life. The communal nature of life (cf. the body metaphor of 1 Cor. 12) means that others become the completion of my incompletion.

In one specific area, the canonization of independence in our cultural consciousness means that "Death with Dignity" translates as follows: To die *my way*, at *my time*, by *my hand*. Yet the Anglican Study Group was surely correct when it wrote:

> There is a movement of giving and receiving. At the beginning and at the end of life receiving predominates over and even excludes giving. But the value of human life does not depend only on its capacity to give. Love, *agape*, is the equal and unalterable regard for the value of other human beings independent of their particular characteristics. It extends especially to the helpless and hopeless, to those who have no value in their own eyes and seemingly none for society. Such neighbor-love is costly and sacrificial. It is easily destroyed. In the giver it demands unlimited caring, in the recipient absolute trust. The question must be asked whether the practice of voluntary euthanasia is consistent with the fostering of such care and trust.[27]

5. The Interventionist Mentality.

By this I refer to the bias of a highly technologized culture to believe that interventionist manipulations are genuine (i.e. human) solutions to problems. Thus the solution to the problems of environmental pollution is more technology—the very source of the problem. We face the problem of the elderly by segregating them in leisure worlds where too often they have everything but what they really want, human companionship. We "solve" the problems of agriculture infestation with pesticides—only to learn later that they are carcinogens. We abort to make the problem go away. And on it goes.

I have always felt that a kind of ultimate symbol of this mentality is the judgment of Joseph Fletcher:

> Laboratory reproduction is radically human compared to conception by ordinary heterosexual intercourse. It is willed, chosen, purposed and controlled, and surely these are among the traits that distinguish *Homo sapiens* from others in the animal genus, from the primates down. Coital reproduction is, therefore, less human than laboratory reproduction...[28]

This is the ultimate in theology-by-incantation. The surest sign of its inhumanity is that the fun has gone out of things. But if it is a symbol—as I believe it is—then it stands as a sign of deeper cultural attitudes with historical roots in the Enlightenment. Daniel Callahan has adverted to something very similar when he contrasts the power-plasticity model of attitudes toward the world with the sacro-symbiotic model. That these attitudes will affect a consistent ethic of life is beyond question.[29]

6. Individualism

I can be brief here. This is an unexamined attitude that sees the pre-condition of the human and the moral as being left alone to do one's own thing. People are islands of self-conviction and self-direction. The good life—and eventually the morally right and wrong—is irreducibly pluralistic, because it is tied to individual preferences, which are precisely individual. Morality is eroded into the etiquette of "living and let live." Symbols of this dreary isolationism abound in our actions and language. "I didn't want to get involved" is the response of many onlookers as Kitty Genovese is stabbed to death in Central Park. "I am personally opposed but will not impose my view." "Who am I to judge?" Yes, even "you must follow your own conscience" as if its *formation* occurred in isolation. "He was just doing what he thought was best." And on and on, until abortion itself is seen as a "private" matter. What is done in private or done from personal conviction is therefore a "private matter." *Individual* dignity can easily become an *individualism* that threatens the very dignity in which the claims originate.

These then are but six unexamined assumptions of which we must be aware and with which we must contend if a consistent ethic of life is to be more than a fancy phrase.

II. The Rule: "No Direct Killing of the Innocent"

First, let me recall the importance this rule plays in the Bernardin papers, especially the earlier ones. Cardinal Bernardin insists on the inner connection among life issues at the level of principle. Where war and abortion are concerned, Bernardin states that the connection "is based on the principle which prohibits the directly intended taking of innocent human life." This principle, he states, is "at the heart of Catholic teaching on abortion." It also "yields the most stringent, binding and radical conclusion of the pastoral letter (*The Challenge of Peace*): That directly intended attack on civilian centers is always wrong."[30] Bernardin insists that this principle cannot be successfully sustained on one count and simultaneously eroded elsewhere. "I contend the viability of the principle depends on the consistency of its application." Practically I suppose that means that if one ever allows a direct abortion, one must entertain the possibility of allowing direct attacks on civilian populations in warfare.

If there is an inner connection between life issues—thus a consistent ethic of life—and if this connection is precisely the consistent application of the principle "no direct taking of innocent human life," then there are problems significant enough to merit the description "soft underbelly." The history of traditional Catholic reflection will point up these problems. I will gather this reflection under three titles: (1) "No direct killing of the innocent" as a principle; (2) The meaning and relevance of "direct;" (3) The meaning of "innocent."

1. *"No direct killing of the innocent" as a principle.* I suggest here that the dictum is a concrete rule teleologically narrowed to its present form, rather than a principle. Where did such a qualified and circumscribed description come from? Why is only *direct* killing of an *innocent* person regarded as morally wrong? Why is this not true of *any* killing? The only answer seems to be that in some instances of conflict (e.g., self-defense, warfare) killing can represent the better protection of life itself. Obviously such a conclusion roots in the weighing of the effects of two alternatives. It traces to a judgment about what would happen if some killing were not al-

lowed. Now if such a calculus is necessarily implied in the sharpening of forbidden killing down to "*direct* killing of the *innocent*," then it seems that this sharpened category itself must be similarly tested—and by the very measure or criterion that shaped the narrowing in the first place (the better protection and service of life itself). In other words "no direct killing of the innocent" is a derivative application of a more formal principle. Such applications do not have the same stability, sweep and exceptionless character as more general principles.[31]

Let me use Franz Scholz's study of St. Thomas to illustrate this point.[32] Scholz begins by noting several problem areas where earlier formulations are undergoing modification. For instance, the formulations of many manualists (e.g., Prummer, Noldin-Schmidt, Zalba, Ermecke) and of the magisterium (e.g., Pius XII) forbade direct abortion even to save the life of the mother. Now, however, we see statements similar to that of J. Stimpfle, Bishop of Augsburg: "He who performs an abortion, except to save the life of the mother, sins gravely and burdens his conscience with the killing of human life."[33]

Here we see a process of adjustment, according to Scholz, a shifting of marginal instances which, logically speaking, converts an exceptionless behavioral norm into a rule of thumb. Is such development justified? Scholz thinks so and cites St. Thomas as his authority.

For Thomas, the order of reason is the criterion of the morally right and wrong. It is reason that constitutes the natural moral law. Thomas distinguished two senses of the natural moral law, the strict (and proper) and the broader. In the strict and proper sense it refers to those principles of practical reason that are intuitively clear (we must act according to reason, good is to be done and evil avoided, etc.) and to those conclusions that follow from them without discursive reflection. These are exceptionless principles because they correspond to the initial intention of the lawgiver or law. In the broader sense there are derivative applications of these formal principles (e.g., "Thou shalt not directly kill an innocent human being"). Such concrete norms can suffer exceptions.

Thomas treats the matter when asking about the possibility of dispensations from the Decalogue. An exception is possible only when there is a difference between the original sense of the norm and its verbal formulation. Thomas seems to deny this possibility of "dispensation" in the corpus of the article, but his final word appears to be in the answer to the third objection, where the distinction between original sense and formulation appear.

Scholz takes the fifth Commandment as an example. The formulation of this prohibition forbids the taking of human life. Yet there are the instances of war and capital punishment. How do these make sense if the Decalogue is "beyond dispensation" (exceptionless)? For Thomas, the divine intention is aimed only at the unjust destruction of life ("occisio hominis...secundum quod habet rationem indebiti"). Thus the verbal formulation is not precise enough. As imprecise, it must be viewed as conditional, that is, applicable to those cases in which the taking of human life contradicts the original divine intent. For this reason the formulated norm must be regarded as a rule of thumb where exceptions cannot be excluded.

On this basis, Thomas distinguishes the factual notion (*occisio*, killing) from the value notion (*homicidium*, murder). The only thing that is exceptionless is the sense of the norm that underlies the notion of murder. It is our responsibility to determine what actions fit this category, what do not—a determination that cannot be made a priori.

2. *The meaning and relevance of "direct"*. Here I will but repeat what I have proposed elsewhere about the meaning and relevance of the notion of "direct."

First, the meaning. Traditional interpretations of the notion applied it to all cases of pregnancy-interruption except those where the interruption occurred as a result of a therapeutic procedure with a different description and purpose (e.g., cancerous uterus, ectopic pregnancy). The result of such an understanding was the prohibition of abortion even where the only alternative was the death of both fetus and mother, an understanding we find in the *Declaration on Procured Abortion* of the Congregation for the Doctrine of the Faith.

Germain Grisez has argued that this is too narrow an understanding. He proposes the following. If the very same act (abortion) is indivisible in its behavioral process (the saving effect does not require a subsequent act), then he regards the abortion (even a craniotomy in earlier days) as indirect and justified.[34] The upshot of this is that the principle that Bernardin sees "at the heart of Catholic teaching on abortion" is not clear in one of its most relevant and urgent terms; for Grisez's understanding is certainly not that of popes and theologians who appealed to the rule.

Second, there is the relevance of the notion of "direct." When the Belgian bishops were discussing this matter, they adverted to the direct-indirect distinction but finally concluded: "The moral principle which ought to govern the intervention can be formulated as follows: since two lives are at stake, one will, while doing everything possible to save both, attempt to save one rather than allow two to perish." If that is the relevant principle—and I believe it is—then it is clear that the direct-indirect distinction is not functioning here—indeed, is redundant. What is functioning, in both Grisez's move and that of the Belgian hierarchy, is the common-sense assessment that we need not stand by and lose two lives (the fetus is doomed anyway) when by intervention one (the mother) can be saved. That constitutes the intervention as the only proportionate response in these tragic circumstances, whether it is direct or not.

The dictum "no *direct* killing of the innocent" implies, of course, the decisive moral character of the principle of double effect in this area. The very relevance of this principle has been challenged in a variety of ways for the past twenty years or so, most especially in the writings of theologians like Peter Knauer, Bruno Schüller, Louis Janssens, *et al*. If the rule of double effect turns out to be redundant, then clearly the consistent ethic of life is leaning on a precarious reed to the extent that it supposes this rule.

Let me give but a single example here, that again of Franz Scholz.[35] He approaches the moral relevance of the direct- indirect distinction through the study of two sets of notions: object-circumstances, essential effect and side effect. In the narrow sense of the word, found in the manual tradition, "circumstance" referred to an aspect of human action which was "extra substantiam existens" (Thomas). Thus there grew a gradual association of the notion of circumstances with that of accident. But, as Scholz points out, some circumstances affect the very essence or substance of human action. This variability of circumstance is too easily overlooked when the idea is associated with "accident."

Scholz next turns to the notions of accidental and essential effects. Essential effects are those that proceed from the substance of the action. Accidental effects are not produced by the substance but indicate that more than one cause is at work. Now when circumstances pertain to the very essence or object of the act, they cannot be said to produce side effects that are merely accidental. Thus the key question is: Which circumstances in a given case be counted in the object itself, which remain accidental? This cannot be determined a priori; rather, reality itself is the test. Once we have determined this, we will know which actions are necessarily direct and which indirect.

To illustrate these rather fine speculative points (which he gives in considerable detail), Scholz cites three examples from the manual tradition. (1) An unarmed person meets a deadly enemy intent on killing him. The only escape is by horse and on a road occupied by a group of blind and crippled persons. He rides down the road, killing and maiming people as he escapes. Traditional manuals argued that the presence of the cripples was accidental; thus there is question of a circumstance that remains external to the object; hence the deaths were side effects. (2) Innocent persons are present in a fortress attacked by the enemy. The attacker says he does not will their deaths, but only the cause (the explosion) and not the effect. (3) A person performs an act *minus rectum* (scandal) and foresees that another will thereby be given an occasion of sin.

Scholz asks: Are we concerned with side effects in these examples, which are patient of indirectness? To the first two he says no; to the third, yes. In the first case, e.g., some authors describe the act as "fleeing down the road on a horse." By what principle do they set the boundaries between object and circumstances? Excluding the blind and the crippled from the object contradicts reality. Scholz sees this as "preprogrammed object." One degrades what is essential to the action to a side effect, but at the cost of a mistaken reading of reality. The presence of the blind and crippled on the road is of such significance that it pertains to the very *object*. And if it does, it is a part of essential effects, not side effects. The escaper cannot say he only "permitted" the deaths. The deaths and injuries are means. "But the means, just as the ends, can only be directly intended." We would have a true side effect if, in the case described, the victims threw themselves at the last moment unavoidably into the path of the horse. In that case the rider could say: "I must permit what I cannot prevent."

As for the second case, the attacking general might say that he wishes only to kill combatants. But actually the one natural effect of the bombing is destruction—of soldiers, civilians, beasts. His regret at the death of innocents means only that their deaths are not *propter se sed propter aliud*. Their deaths are a *conditio sine qua non*. But "he who is ready—under the call of the end—to realize the condition *sine qua non*, acts exactly as the one who chooses the appropriate means, scil., directly." Therefore, in these first two cases Scholz does not believe the deaths are indirect. Rather, they are a modified form of direct willing (scil., *secundum quid*, with regrets).

In the third case (scandal) we have a true side effect. He who seeks his goal by an *actio minus recta* does not cause the neighbor's sin. The operation of another cause is necessary for a true side effect. Therefore, the psychology of the will does not demand that the evil effect be willed either as a means or as a *conditio sine qua non*.

Since so many of the conflicts that were previously solved by the direct-indirect distinction really represent qualified forms of direct willing, Scholz moves to another model and espouses it: "direct, yes, but only for a proportionate reason." He sees this as not only more honest to reality but as advantageous. First, the direct confrontation of the will with the evil caused by it "ought to be to the benefit of a weighing of values" (Guterabwägung). Secondly, looking evil in the eye is healthy. It avoids development of an "exoneration mentality" associated with phrases such as "not directly willed," "only permitted." Finally, "the broken human condition with its tragic character appears more starkly. Unavoidably we become conscious of the fact that man not only cannot have, hold, and protect all goods simultaneously, but that he can be called, in the service of higher goods, to injure lesser premoral values, and that without any *animus nocendi*.

Here, then, is yet another theologian who argues that every human choice is the resolution of a conflict, that the direct-indirect distinction is only descriptive, and that when actions were legitimated as indirect permitting of evil, actually they were morally direct in most cases, even if in qualified form (*secundum quid*, with regrets: "I would not be prepared to do this unless I had to"). Hence Scholz is arguing that there is no morally significant difference between direct and indirect actions where nonmoral evils are concerned.

3. *The meaning of "innocent"*. Over the centuries the term "innocent" has been used to limit the prohibition against killing to cases where no *material* injustice was involved. Thus the term left open the possibility of killing in cases of aggression (personal or national [war]) and capital punishment.

However, the term "innocent" may seem tighter than it actually is. There is historical reason to believe that it comprised those who had done nothing against the common good and therefore were *unwilling that their lives by taken*.[36]

That it comprised those who *consented to* or *even requested* lethal action against themselves is far from clear. This unclarity, if it is sustainable, means that in two of the most anguishing and controversial contemporary instances, the dictum may be being applied beyond the historical warrants that generated it. I refer to the cases of *voluntary* euthanasia of terminal patients and termination of pregnancy where the medical condition is incompatible with postnatal life—at least for more than an extremely brief period (e.g., anencephaly, Potter's Syndrome). In such situations one thinks immediately of the axiom *consentienti non fit injuria* and of the fact that termination of pregnancy is hardly an injury if post-natal life is impossible.

In other words, by conceptualizing permitted killings within the innocent and non-innocent categories (and meaning by this latter the presence of at least material injustice), the tradition by implication limits permitted killing to the *ratio* of injustice. Where such injustice is absent, the individual is "innocent" and taking such a life is injustice. But this overlooks the fact that there can be instances where there is "innocence" (no injustice), yet killing would involve no *injuria*. I am not arguing that killing in the two cases mentioned above is morally right. (That is another matter.) I am arguing only that the classical dictum tied to the notion of justice as it is, may not be as all-encompassing and far-reaching as making it "bed-rock" would suggest.

In summary, then, there are some serious lingering speculative problems with the apparently neat and airtight dictum "No direct killing of the innocent." I want to return to these in a moment.

Here a word about Cardinal Bernardin's earlier (the Seattle lecture) response to reflections similar to the above. His response is two-pronged. First, he refers to them as a "reduction of the prohibition against the intentional killing of the innocent to a status less than an absolute rule" and sees this as wrong.[37] A possible response, especially in light of the foregoing considerations, is: it is one thing to *reduce* a prohibition; it is quite another to *recognize* its possible theoretical limitations, all the while admitting its enormous pedagogical and political utility. If the reflections I have offered have any validity—and I believe they do—they have but a single effect: a reminder that concrete formulations are really derivative applications that do not exempt us from wrestling with marginal and truly exceptional cases.

The second prong of Cardinal Bernardin's response is that the just war theory's cutting edge is its capacity "to place a double restraint on the use of force" (principle of proportionality, principle of non-combatant immunity). But viewing "no direct killing of the innocent" as a teleologically developed derivative application means that "both principles would become proportional judgments." But that will "weaken the moral strength of the ethic of war."

For continued reflection, I propose the following. First, whether an understanding "weakens" the moral strength of the ethic of war is secondary. To view an analysis dominantly in terms of its power to prevent or curtail war is to subordinate its analytic validity to a high utilitarian purpose. The rule "no direct killing of the innocent" either admits exceptions or it does not. That is determined not by its greater or lesser power in achieving this or that desirable purpose, but by the warrants available to support it as all-inclusive and exceptionless.

Second, the fact that "no direct killing of the innocent" would be subject to proportional judgment does not mean, as Cardinal Bernardin states, that both principles (proportionality, non-combatant immunity) are the same. We may still maintain two distinct criteria, a "double restraint on the use of force," remembering only that one ("no direct killing of the innocent") is as exceptionless as we can show it to be.

That brings me to some further problematic points that still need attention. They all gather around the notion of "intending death." I will simply mention them here without going into any prolonged discussion. They constitute agenda for the future.

The philosophical unclarity of "intending death"

I simply record here a puzzling disagreement among philosophers and theologians. There are those (e.g., Grisez, Ramsey) who argue that *any* morally permissible killing must be indirect. I take that to mean that it must be, in some sense, unintended. On the other hand, there are many theologians in the past who argued that *direct* killing in self-defense, capital punishment and war was permissible. That is, intending death in the actions was seen as morally permissible. This means that the very moral relevance of "intending death" is unclear.

The direct intention of lesser (than death) harms, disvalues

There are many instances where theologians, both past and present, would permit direct (intentional) doing of harm. For instance, many (e.g., Gerald Kelly, S.J.) would understand the mutilation of life-saving surgery as directly done, but justifiably so. Many understand deception (falsehood) in a similar manner, as well as the taking of another's property. This suggest that the intention of death can be shown to be morally wrong only on the assumption that causing death is causing an *absolute* disvalue.

The wrongfulness of directly killing the innocent

Catholic tradition argued that intentional killing of the innocent was wrong because of a lack of divine authorization. To the point, Bruno Schüller, S.J.:

> Intentional killing of a human being, if considered only as such, allows of no definite moral appraisal. The executioner cannot dispatch a murderer without intending death as a result of his action. This intention does not impair the rightness of his action. Hence, if intentionally killing an innocent person is said to be invariably wrong, *the wrongness of the action cannot be derived from the intention of causing death, a nonmoral evil.* The proposition: 'It is wrong intentionally to kill an innocent person' is a synthetic one. Tradition accounts for the wrongness of this action by the attempt to show that it is not authorized by God.[38]

Thus, if this is the case, then when tradition accepts killing in self-defense and capital punishment, it must see them as "authorized by God." But under examination (of the arguments), that means that certain human goods are otherwise unprotected, and left worse off. By inference, "unauthorized by God" means "unnecessary to such protection."

It is here that the anthropocentrism mentioned above becomes operative. If God's providence and causality in the world are conceived in a highly anthropocentric way, "divine authorization" is likely to be viewed in a positive, interventionist way. A less anthropocentric way would view such "authorization" (or its lack) in terms of the struggle of human *reason* as it attempts to serve basic human values in a conflicted world.

The weakness of the moral arguments

Attempts to show the absoluteness of "no direct killing of the innocent" reveal fundamental flaws. Let a recent attempt by Joseph M. Boyle, Jr. be an example here.[39] Boyle attempts to show that the difference between intending and permitting certain disvalues or evils constitutes the difference between good and bad persons. Here is the way he puts it:

In freely choosing to do something a person determines himself or herself to be a certain kind of person. For example, those who choose, however reluctantly, to end the life of an unborn baby by abortion make themselves killers, set themselves against life. But when the evil one brings about is a side effect only, one's self is not defined by the bringing about of the evil. For in this case one does not act for the sake of the evil but despite it; one does not set one's heart on it as one does when one resolves to do it in order to realize some ulterior state of affairs. Thus, in the case of indirect abortion, the child's death is not anything one seeks to realize but is reluctantly accepted and would be avoided if possible.

What is to be said of this? It could be reduced to the following syllogism: One who sets one's heart on evil (abortion) sets himself against life. But where one directly intends an abortion, one sets one's heart on evil. Therefore one who directly intends abortion, sets oneself against life. Aside from the loose terminology ("set oneself against life," "set one's heart on evil"), it must be said that this involves a straightforward *petitio principii*. It asserts what is to be proven: that there is a fundamentally different moral attitude involved when abortion is directly intended and where it is only permitted though fully foreseen.

Furthermore, how does one establish that those who choose to end the life of an unborn baby by abortion always "set themselves against life"? If abortion is the only life-saving, life-serving option available (as in the classical case: allow both to die vs. save the one [mother] that can be saved), one would think that the intervention is just the opposite of "setting oneself against life." Certainly this is what the Belgian bishops implied when they said "the moral principle which ought to govern the intervention can be formulated as follows: since two lives are at stake, one will, while doing everything possible to save both, attempt to save one rather than allow two to parish."

From a more positive perspective, Bruno Schüller, S.J., along with Franz Scholz, cited above, have argued that the identical moral attitudes of disapproval are revealed in life-saving abortions whether the effect is permitted or intended as a means: "I would not carry it out if it were possible to achieve the good effect without causing the bad one."[40] This is just about identical with Boyle's "reluctantly accepted and would be avoided if possible." As Schüller words it, "Intending a nonmoral evil as a mere means and permitting a nonmoral evil, considered as attitudes of will, differ in degree, not in kind." Put differently, Boyle seems to me to have overlooked the possibility that something can be chosen *in se sed non propter se*. When it is and there is a truly proportionate reason, how does one possibly establish the conclusion that one "sets oneself against life"? One sets oneself against life when one chooses an abortion *propter se*, or, if not *propter se*, then without a truly justifying reason. In either case we may justifiably infer something resembling an attitude of approval, or Boyle's "setting oneself against life."

I believe it was a similar point that John Langan, S.J., had in mind when he critiqued John Finnis' notion of turning against a basic good as presented in *Natural Law and Natural Rights*. Langan wrote:

> One thing that is not clear in Finnis' approach is the connection between a basic value in its general form and its particular ex- emplifications. It is hard to see a reason why one should accord overriding importance to any particular instance of sociability or aesthetic experience or play or knowledge or why one should con- clude that acting against a particular instance of any of these basic values entails disrespect for the value in general. Certainly the tradition did not draw such a conclusion even with regard to the taking of a particular life.[41]

The difficulty of establishing as absolute the prohibition of direct killing of the innocent is seen in the analysis of suicide. Many moralists, follow- ing the third argument of St. Thomas against suicide, argue that as creator, God alone is Lord over life and death. Man himself has only the right to the use of his life (*dominium utile*), not a dominion over his life (*dominium in substantiam*). Let me cite Schüller once more on this argument.

> As it stands this argument is no argument at all; it is only an analytic explanation of that which it is meant to establish. If one supposes that a man may not kill himself except in the case of a positive divine permission, it follows that man cannot have dominion over the substance of his life. For such dominion means precisely the power to decide whether an end should be placed to this life or not. Indeed, 'not to be able to kill oneself' and 'not to have dominion over the substance of one's life' are synonymous phrases. If we may say God alone is Lord over the life and death of a man, this is in the context merely an expression of that which is to be proved.[42]

In conclusion, then, I repeat my agreement with Cardinal Bernardin that, if we are to face successfully the many problems touching human life in our time, we must do so with a moral vision whose key ingredient is consistency. This means that the dignity of the human person must be supported in a variety of settings that cut across social, medical and sexual ethics.

The challenges we face come from two historical sources. The first source is a grouping of "global prescientific convictions" that dim our view of the centrality and dignity of the person and infect our deliberative processes. The second is the problematic character of translating the presumption against taking human life into viable derivative applications for practice. To the extent that these challenges are not acknowledged and squarely faced, the consistent ethic of life will be vulnerable to analytic attack. Briefly, it will retain a soft underbelly.

Notes

1. Karl Rahner, "Über schlechte Argumentation in der Moral-theologie," in *In Libertatem Vocati Estis,* ed. by H. Boelaars and R. Tremblay (Roma: M. Pisani, 1977) 245-257.

2. Philip Rieff, *The Triumph of the Therapeutic: Uses of Faith After Freud* (New York: Harper & Row, 1966).

3. "The Church in the Modern World," *Documents of Vatican II,* ed. by Walter Abbott, S.J. (New York: America Press, 1966) n. 51, p. 256.

4. *Schema constitutionis pastoralis de ecclesia in mundo huius temporis: Expensio modorum partis secundae* (Vatican Press: 1965) 37-38.

5. For a more detailed analysis, cf. Louis Janssens, *Mariage et fecondite* (Paris: J. Duculot, 1967). *Summa theologica,* Ia IIae, q. 94, art. 2.

6. Janssens, *loc.cit.,* 66-68.

7. AAS 22 (1930) 539-592 at 548.

8. *Ibid.,* 561.

9. Joseph A. Selling, "Moral Teaching, Traditional Teaching and 'Humanae vitae,'" *Louvain Studies* 7 (1978) 24-44.

10. AAS 60 (1968) 488-489.

11. Cf. note 9.

12. John C. Ford, S.J., and Gerald Kelly, S.J., *Contemporary Moral Theology II: Marriage Questions* (Westminster: Newman, 1963) 405.

13. "Instruction on Respect for Human Life in Its Origin and on the Dignity of Procreation," (Vatican City: Vatican Polyglot Press, 1987).

14. F. Hurth, S.J., "La fecondation artificielle: Sa valeur morale et juridique," *Nouvelle revue Theologique* 68 (1946) 402-426 at 413.

15. John H. Wright, S.J., "An End to the Birth Control Controversy?" *America* 144 (1981) 175-178.

16. Franz Scholz, "Innere, aber nicht absolute Abwegigkeit," *Theologie der Gergenwart* 24 (1981) 163-172 at 170.

17. Cf. *Theological Studies* 43 (1982) 73, footnote 13.

18. Kenneth R. Overberg, S.J., *An Inconsistent Ethic? Teachings of the American Catholic Bishops* (Lanham, Md.: University Press of America, 1980).

19. "Dalla 'Rerum novarum' ad oggi," *Civiltá cattolica* 132 (1981) 345-357.

20. Jaroslav Pelikan, Jr., "Eve or Mary: A Test Case in the Development of Doctrine," *Christian Ministry* 2 (1971) 21-22.

21. Joseph A. Grassi, "Women's Liberation: The New Testament Perspectives," *Living Light* 8 (1971) 22-34.

22. Note 18, In IV Sent., dist. 25, q. 2, art. 1; also of S.T., Suppl., q. 39, art. 1.

23. For a report, Cf. "The Future of Women in the Church," *Origins* 12 (1982) 1-9.

24. Victor Balke and Raymond Lucker, "Male and Female God Created Them" *Origins* 11 (1982) 333-338.

25. Cf. Josef Fuchs, S.J., "Das Gottesbild and die Moral innerweltlichen Handelns," *Stimmen der Zeit* 202 (1984) 363-382

26. Theodore Minnema, "Human Dignity and Human Dependence," *Calvin Theological Journal* 16 (n. 1, 1981) 5- 14.

27. *On Dying Well* (Church Information Office, Church House, Dean's Yard, SWIP 3NZ, 1975) 1-67 at 22.

28. Joseph Fletcher, "Ethical Aspects of Genetic Controls," *New England Journal of Medicine* 285 (1971) 776-783 at 781.

29. Daniel Callahan, "Living with the New Biology," *Center Magazine* 5 (1972) 4-12.

30. Cf. the Gannon and Wade lectures in this volume, pp. 1-19.

31. Cf. Richard A. McCormick, S.J., "Moral Norms: An Update," *Theological Studies* 46 (1985) 50-54. Also Daniel Callahan, "The Sanctity of Life," in *Updating Life and Death*, ed. by Donald R. Cutler (Boston: Beacon, 1968) 181-223.

32. Franz Scholz, "Durch ethische Grenzsituationen aufgeworfene Normenprobleme," *Theologisch-praktische Quartalschrift* 123 (1975) 341-355.

33. From the Kirchenzeitung für die Diozese *Augsburg*, cited in Scholz, p. 342.

34. Germain Grisez, *Abortion: the Myths, the Realitites, and the Arguments* (New York: Corpus, 1966).

35. Franz Scholz, "Objekt und Umstände, Wesenswirkungen und Nebeneffekte," in *Christlich Glauben und Handeln*, ed. by Klaus Demmer and Bruno Schüller, S.J. (Düsseldorf: Patmos, 1977) 243-260.

36. Cf. Lisa Cahill, "Natural Law Reconsideration of Euthanasia," *Linacre Quaterly* 44 (1977) 47-63. "In Thomas the adjective 'innocent' refers primarily to the man who is

122 A Consistent Ethic of Life

'righteous' in the sense that he has *not forfeited* his right to life so that he may be deprived of it by lawful authority. To have lost one's innocence means to have injured the common good." (55) y. II-II, Q. 64, a. 2, 6.

37. Cf. in this volume p. 81.

38. Bruno Schüller, S.J., "The Double Effect in Catholic Thought: A Reevalution," in (eds.) Richard A. McCormick, S.J., and Paul Ramsey, *Doing Evil to Achieve Good* (Lanham, Md.: University Press of America, 1985) 165-192 at 189.

39. Joseph M. Boyle, Jr., "The Principle of Double Effect: Good Actions Entangled in Evil," *Moral Theology Today* (St. Louis: Pope John XXIII Center, 1984) 243-260.

40. Cf. note 38.

41. John Langan, S.J., in a review of Finnis in *International Philosophical Quaterly* 21 (1981) 217 ff.

42. Bruno Schüller, S.J., "Zur Problematik allgemein verbindlicher ethischer Grundsätze," *Theologie und Philosophie* 45 (1970) 1-23.

Weaknesses in the Consistent Ethic of Life? Some Systematic-Theological Observations

Frans Jozef van Beeck, S. J.
Loyola University of Chicago
November 1, 1987

1. Introduction

(1) Cardinal Bernardin has repeatedly invited a broad, discerning debate on a range of crucial themes, which he has brought together under the rubric of "the consistent ethic of life."[1] This paper is meant as a small contribution to that debate. Let me begin with a personal comment. No one has

appointed me to approve of, or otherwise judge, the activities of the bearers of the Church's teaching office, but I cannot refrain from professing my deep satisfaction with the entire process. I want to note that what has been set afoot is, in my opinion, fine instance of the practical implementation of two important documents of Vatican II, the Dogmatic Constitution on the Church *Lumen Gentium* (LG) and the Pastoral Constitution on the Church in the Modern World *Gaudium et Spes*. The discussion on the consistent life-ethic involves the Catholic Church in the United States, under the magisterial and critical leadership of the Apostolic Office, in a process of discerning the will of God as well as the true well-being of humanity, in the setting of a fast-moving and not always very considerate or conscientious world—a world which the Church must very much help create and guide. It is attempting to do so in frank, respectful dialogue with other Christians, Jews, and conscientious seekers after truth—all of them enumerated by the Council as the Catholic Church's spiritual relatives (LG 15-16). The debate has also led to a welcome exemplification of the exercise of collegiality in a concrete, institutional shape: the conference of bishops.[2] Finally, the debate has one feature that I have come to consider a characteristic strength of public authority and credibility not so much from the position you occupy as from *the urgency of the issue that you have the moral courage to address*; once that kind of authority is established, your position will be respected and *what* you have to say will find a hearing, too.[3]

It would appear, too, that the process initiated by Cardinal Bernardin's addresses is already yielding measurable results. While ugly strong-arm tactics by militant one-issue alliances have by no means disappeared,[4] a recent article has alleged evidence that—contrary to stereotypes still current in the public press—people with compassionate attitudes toward AIDS-patients and unfavorably disposed towards capital punishment are likely to be found at pro-life rallies rather than at pro-choice rallies.[5]

(2) This paper is also happily set in the context of the much-needed search for a constructive relationship between what Thomas Aquinas calls the two "chairs" in the Church: *the cathedra pastoralis* (that is—to use a relatively recent expression—the "magisterium," which authentically exercises the apostolic teaching office) and the *cathedra magistralis* (the theologians, whose teaching authority depends on "sufficiency of learning," which entitles them to seek licence to instruct others, as an office of charity).[6] I also welcome the opportunity to make a contribution to the further development of a constructive relationship between Christian dogmatics and systematics and Christian ethics—separate and even estranged

relatives for far too long. In fact, the organizers of this conference have encouraged me to take my cues, unashamedly, from doctrinal and systematic theology.

(3) This paper takes as its point of departure Cardinal Bernardin's ten addresses on the consistent ethic of life given between December 6, 1983 and October 4, 1986, published in this volume. More specifically, it serves as a partial response to Richard A. McCormick's paper *The Consistent Ethic of Life: Is There an Historical Soft Underbelly?* By phrasing the issue in this fashion, Fr. McCormick has indicated that his remarks are mainly *cautionary*; his essay does not attack the Cardinal's basic conception. In fact, McCormick's whole approach presupposes the intellectual legitimacy and coherence of the consistent ethic as proposed by the Cardinal. To remove any lingering doubts about this, we have Fr. McCormick's own affirmation of "the validity of the moral vision captured in the phrase 'the consistent ethic of life'";[7] the Cardinal in turn is on record as having taken note of Fr. McCormick's support of the perspective of the consistent life-ethic as "utterly essential."[8]

(4) Fr. McCormick's cautions involve two sets. He starts by reminding us that if you want to be consistent you have to be consistent. McCormick then proceeds to point out that *current Catholic teaching can not unreasonably be charged with inconsistency*, due to its partial dependence on "global (= unspecified, unthematic) prescientific convictions" that are opposed widely enough (inside the Catholic Church and outside it) to prevent widespread assent to the main proposition.[9] Fr. McCormick's second caution illustrates *the difficulties involved in formulating and interpreting absolute principles*.[10] The present paper addresses both issues, starting with the second.

2. Magisterium and Theologians: Consistency and Formulability

(1) The difference between Cardinal Bernardin and Father McCormick on the status of the proposition "no direct killing of innocent human life" is, in my view, largely a matter, not of substance, but of *function*, or, to use the term introduced by Wittgenstein, of *use*.[11] This makes it, again in my view, a classic instance of the difference between the ministries, and hence the concerns, and hence the language-uses, of the *cathedra pastoralis* on

the one hand, and the *cathedra magistralis* on the other. Unless this is grasped, what is a quite normal misunderstanding resulting from a difference of *function* can easily degenerate into an unnecessary debate on what, or which, or who, is *right*.

(2) First of all, I wish to submit that one feature of the difference of opinion between Cardinal Bernardin and Fr. McCormick must be evaluated *positively*: it shows, thank God, that there is contact between the authentic teaching office in the Church and the theological academy. Now for contact to become dialogue, there must be mutual appreciation of each other's *tasks*.

(3) Fr. McCormick asks that the "theoretical limitations" of the principle "no direct killing of innocent human life" be recognized. In the mean- time, however, he does admit its "enormous pedagogical and political utility"[12] (even though he emphasizes that this utility contributes nothing to the principle's validity as a proposition). I suggest that this is understating the issue; there is much more than utility involved here. At the hands of the bishops, the affirmation of the principle primarily serves the purposes of *witness*, since authentic (that is, authoritative) witness is one of the teaching office's primary responsibilities. Now witness involves both the profession of, and the call to, a *self-commitment* to a high, ultimately divine reality, on the part of communities of persons—Catholics and non-Catholics. Theologians, I think, can be expected to acknowledge, respect, honor, and even share in some way the magisterium's ministry of authentically professing commitments and calling others to them, also in the form of insisting, for instance, that legal protection be given to the unborn.

(4) Now the fact is that such commitments, whether they concern teaching, conduct, or worship,[13] can never be adequately formulated. There is always more to be expressed; there is always much that is left unexpressed; as a matter of fact, positive attempts at non-expressing are part and parcel of the articulation of a faith-commitment, to do justice to its mystery. "In the *language* of faith, much remains unsaid; in parallel fashion, *the Christian commitment to the good life* involves behavioral commitments too deep to be entirely brought to the surface, and while the Church's *worship*, which is her response to God's Presence, does indeed prompt her every word and gesture of prayer, the basic act of worship eludes the grasp of those who pray."[14] This is not to encourage a pious, but basically lazy form of homiletic ignorance. On the contrary, in matters of faith-commitment we are rightly articulate, yet we also acknowledge that in the final analysis the object of our statement remains in a kind of "darkness of ig-

norance, by which ...we are best united with God," as Aquinas observes in a different context.[15] For the purposes of public witness, therefore, the relative inconclusiveness of the language of faith-commitment is not really a weakness, but a strength. And in any case (and this is a second, more general point), no proposition is ever formulated to foster interest in itself. Aquinas acknowledges this when he explains that

> the object of a believer's act (of faith) is not a proposition, but a reality. For we do not formulate propositions except in order that through them we may have knowledge of reality; this applies to faith just as it does to knowledge.[16]

On the analogy of this insight, we can say that the object of a moral agent's commitment is not a principle, but a course of action. For we do not formulate moral principles except in order that through them we may involve ourselves and others in actions.

(5) All authentic witness and all commitment, however, does inexorably give rise to *thought*; faith-commitment seeks understanding, and understanding intrinsically seeks articulate expression. Hence, the Church's teaching office wisely practices and encourages *informed* discussion. Teaching faith-commitments, however, also inexorably provokes debate, disagreement, and even contention. Now I wish to submit that the magisterium would do well and wisely not unnecessarily to occasion this latter type of response. It should stick to its last: authentic teaching by witness, with the aim of fostering commitment. This leads to a conclusion about magisterial language. It would seem wise to refrain from claims that are liable to unnecessarily provoke analytic debate, casuistry, quibbling, and contentiousness. Let me give an example. Calling *any* proposition "absolute" is, I submit, asking for just that kind of reaction, for to the extent that a proposition is really "absolute" it cannot be adequately formulated. Hence, some people will be quick to point out that the very language of the proposition belies the claim to absolute validity. This should not surprise or disconcert us, for if there is anything that is absolute, it is not the proposition, but the *commitment* intended by the proposition. So *in order not to jeopardize assent to the commitment, it is often wise not to claim too much in behalf of the proposition*: saying less is sometimes saying more. For analogous reasons, therefore, might I suggest that the qualifier "direct" be avoided, since it is a straight invitation of casuistry, as Fr. McCormick's treatment shows? Could it be replaced by a word like "self-serving"? And might I suggest that the new, simpler formula "no self-serving killing of innocent human life" be referred to as the "ground rule," or the "first rule,"

or the "fundamental rule," or (even better) the "basic commitment" of the consistent ethic of life?

(6) A complementary comment on the theologian's responsibility. It is the theologian's task to serve the *intellectus fidei*, and testing a magisterial pronouncement's *meaning* and its *application* is a responsible way to do this. The second half of Fr. McCormick's paper is a good example of this procedure, in the interest, ultimately, of "wrestling with marginal and truly exceptional cases."[17] But here we have to be realistic—on two scores, I would like to suggest. Let me explain.

(7) Part of the risk inherent in scholarship is the "internal reference" of its language. The language-philosopher J. Verhaar has explained this well. He points out that conceptualized thinking, and the technical terminology associated with it, are characterized by a tendency toward *internal reference of thought*. Scholars rightly get interested in the *immanent consistency* of their reflections and thoughts, and in due course they develop a tendency *to treat their concepts as if they were the reality* that is the object of their study. In Verhaar's words:

> The law operating here is that the more we are concerned with what is meant by what we say, the more we seem to be separated from what we are speaking, and thinking, *about*. From transparent, our words become opaque. The clearer the meanings, the more arbitrary. In this shifting spectrum of increasing reflexivization we finally arrive at the level where words have become terms, and meanings concepts; natural language has been left behind.[18]

To put it differently, discussion among professionals about the meaning and the terms of a proposition does not necessarily lead to a better *public* proposition, whether in the Church or in the public arena. In the process of scholarly refinement, the truer the proposition gets, the more it tends to lose its ability to serve the non-scholar as a means to articulate and convey a commitment; a fine, generous moral principle "may thus be killed by inches, the death by a thousand qualifications."[19] This may generate an atmosphere of intellectual discouragement: there appears to be no point in trying to establish articulate moral maxims. On the rebound, some bishops may feel they have no alternative but to fill the vacuum by asserting their teaching authority. Scholars are not always aware of this dynamic inherent in scholarship. Hence, a second point concerning realism must be made.

(8) Ethicists reflecting on principles rightly worry about "marginal and truly exceptional cases." *Opponents* of the *commitment* implicit in the consistent life-ethic also tend to seize upon those cases. In doing so, they *seem* to do what scholars do: argue that the *principle* has "theoretical limitations."[20] However, what really matters is their *agenda*: what they frequently do—unfortunately, mostly by caricature—is argue that *the commitment is unsound in itself*, and thus deserves to be rejected as a reliable, shared value. Typically they argue from the anticipated dire consequences that would ensue, were the commitment accepted as normative.[21] We have all heard the whole wearisome array: without the death-penalty known killers will be stalking the streets with impunity; without legal abortion on demand poor women, pregnant from rape or incest, will be forced back into the hands of back-alley operators; programs to assist the poor will aid and abet laziness and irresponsibility, sap the nation's moral fibre, and introduce socialism; questioning the unconditional use of every available artificial life-support system to keep the irreversibly comatose alive will bring to the United States Hitler's plans for compulsory euthanasia for the handicapped and the elderly; and cutting back on nuclear armaments will have the Soviet army marching down Pennsylvania Avenue. Unfortunately, moralists and ethicists on both sides of the conservative-liberal divide sometimes allow themselves to be unreasonably impressed by such dubious rhetoric. This often does little more than serve the vested interests or prejudices of pressure groups that tend to equate morality with their own security; even more often, it would seem, it simply serves the needs of the media, so interested in featuring the struggle about values primarily for its entertainment value.

(9) In the face of this situation, ethicists and moral theologians, I submit, have *two tasks*. The first one is *constructive*, and consists in arguing reasonably to command true, permanent, and *coherent* moral commitments, lest human values die the death of the human propensity to act in a merely convenient fashion. Only if they positively articulate and commend reasoned moral generosity can ethicists also safely practice their second task, which is *critical*: to point out the *limitations* of moral principles, lest unreasonable burdens be placed on people's shoulders, especially by moral authorities unwilling to touch them themselves (cf. Mt 23, 4).

(10) Let me conclude this section with a proposal for cooperation between the *cathedra pastoralis* and the *cathedra magistralis*—a cooperation that would leave their several tasks intact. Allow me to take my inspiration from Cardinal Newman. He writes:

> Religious Truth is neither light nor darkness, but both together; it
> is like the dim view of a country seen in the twilight, with forms
> half extricated from the darkness, with broken lines and isolated
> masses.[22]

Cardinal Bernardin has repeatedly, and in my view rightly, stated that
the consistent ethic of life is a matter of *systematic coherence* and *analogy*.[23] Cardinal Newman, writing about Christian doctrine, adds something
to that: the coherence of the faith is *not entirely manifest*; conveying
religious truth is not a matter of balance between revelation and mystery,
of using a pattern of prominence and recessiveness. Bearing authentic witness to the coherence—the "linkage"—among the life-issues, I wish to
suggest, is not wholly dissimilar; there is analogy between expression of
faith and expression of moral commitment. Magisterial teaching on a consistent ethic of human life need not rely on the massive fixity of explicit
principle; it may be achieved by conveying *convergence*. This is best done,
not by insisting on one absolute principle, but the use of *several convergent formulas*. Such formulas can, precisely by their convergence, point to
the total commitment that lies at the basis of the consistent ethic of life,
without expressing it in one standard formula.[24] One such life-ethic formula could be analytic and cumulative, like the following: "No intentional,
self-serving, undeserved termination, by disproportionate force, of any
human life." Another could be broader and more confessional, like: "Do
not *ever* do to the life of others what Jesus did not do, or what you do not
now want done to your own life." While the incompleteness of each individual maxim could be readily acknowledged, their common point of
convergence would place the basic commitment beyond cavil. Such an approach would appeal to common sense, fairness in understanding, and
moral generosity. Modernist quibbling, equivocating, and rationalizing,
and (on the other extreme) dogmatic integralism and ideological zealotry
would betray themselves as acts of prejudice and determination to
misunderstand.

3. Consistency, Profession of Faith, and the Appeal to Reason

(1) The words "Christian confession" have come up incidentally a few
times already in the previous section; they are at the heart of a second concern I wish to raise with regard to the consistent life-ethic. It takes the form

of a question: Where lies the *root* of the consistency? This second concern is much wider in scope; in the present context, all I can do is make a basic observation, explain it, and, perhaps, suggest avenues for further development.

(2) In his speeches on the subject of the consistent ethic of life, Cardinal Bernardin has consistently and intentionally addressed the wider culture. In doing so, he has positioned himself squarely in the mainstream of the Catholic tradition, which has always been appreciative of everything that is naturally valuable. The ethics of the New Testament incorporate a great many naturally virtuous practices readily available in the culture. Ever since Justin Martyr's *Apologies*, the Christian Church has professed to be, by divine grace, the fulfillment of all that is positive in the world; this enables it to recognize Christ in the features of the great souls of all times, and it will appeal to all men and women of good will, with the intention of sharing the moral wisdom of the Catholic tradition with society.[25] Catholicity is inherently anti-sectarian.

(3) At the same time, the Christian faith, while continuous with the world, involves a specific vision of the world: the fulfillment also incorporates a difference. The second-century *Letter to Diognetus* orchestrates the many New Testament warnings against conformity with the world with great realism and clarity:

> Christians are distinguished from the rest of people neither by country, nor by language, nor by customs. For nowhere do they live in cities of their own, nor do they use some different form of speech, nor do they practice a peculiar way of life. ...They do not champion, like others, a human philosophy of life. Yet ...they make no secret of the remarkable and admittedly extraordinary constitution of their citizenship. ...They marry like everybody and beget children; but they do not expose their newly-born. The table they provide is common, but not the bed. *They obey the established laws, and in their own lives they surpass the laws.*[26]

Thomas Aquinas was but reformulating the great Tradition when he taught that grace, far from "cancelling" nature, both "pre-supposes" and "perfects" it; hence, reason must recognize the superiority of faith.[27] Not surprisingly, therefore, he also taught, again with the great Tradition, that "the gift of grace exceeds every power of created nature."[28] It is consonant with this to say that the Church's witness to the world is credible only if it *integrates* grace and nature—that is to say, if it *combines* its profession of faith with the demonstration, by means of an appropriate apologetic, that the beliefs and practices involved in its profession are also naturally attractive and reasonable. From his lecture on the consistent life-ethic onward, Cardinal Bernardin has been no stranger to this truth, as is evident from the following passage:

> The substance of a Catholic position on a consistent ethic of life is rooted in a religious vision. But the citizenry of the United States is radically pluralistic in moral and religious conviction. So we face the challenge of stating our case, which is shaped in terms of our faith and our religious convictions, in non-religious terms which others of different faith convictions might find morally persuasive.[29]

(4) Now I wish to suggest that all of this implies that for Christians, *the profession of the Christian faith is the principal source of the consistency of their approach to life*. But if this is on the mark, then I have a confession to make: as a Catholic theologian, I think Cardinal Bernardin's addresses have been somewhat irresolute in putting this principle into practice. I say this with regret as well as respect for the difficulty of the task. Let me add at once that I have this problem with much of the recent teaching of the Catholic bishops in the United States: the bishops' eagerness to address important public ethical issues (nuclear strategy, socio-economic policy, etc.) which are outside their primary magisterial competence is not matched by an equally eager ministry as teachers of the Christian faith. What I mean to imply is that they have taught too much as if the Catholic Church community and American society at large constitute only *one single audience*. In saying this, I do not mean to advocate that the bishops simply limit their teaching to Catholics, nor that they draw moral precepts exclusively from revealed sources; I am calling into question the theological balance of their approach, and I wish to suggest that this has led to problems.[30] Let me repeat, this area of concern is a very large one, and it is essentially predicated on the way in which one interprets the concrete relationship between Church and society—a relationship with a long and extremely varied history. Yet the issue itself is a perennial one; let me at least try very briefly to sketch some of its features, to stimulate (in my view) much-needed discussion.

(5) The New Testament, of course, contains no immediately applicable warrants for the development of a Christian public ethic. It does, however, set standards for living; and while these standards primarily concern life in the community, they also address Christian behavior vis-à-vis the outside

world. The New Testament sets these standards by *addressing and stirring the Christian conscience* (occasionally even under threat of penalties). Having been set free, by Christ's death and resurrection, from the enslavement to the powers of the present age,[31] Christians are now to use their freedom, not by way of licence, to do what they want, but by way of service.[32] That service is empowered by the gift of the Spirit, and guided by the example of Christ, who came to save and not to judge, and who bequeathed to his followers his own commitment to abandonment of self-will and to universal, responsible stewardship in behalf of the world and humanity.[33] This stewardship is far from romantic: sin and death are still real, but Christ's resurrection enables his disciples to look them straight in the face—they have lost their sting,[34] and yielded to hope. From all of this results a most striking, yet integral feature of the Christian responsibility in the world: the Christian faith simply refuses to recognize violence as a divinely warranted means to set things straight;[35] it renounces the use of violence, even to the point of willingness to suffer unjustly and to give one's life for others, including enemies.[36] *Dedication to compassionate service in imitation of Christ, not appeal to natural law or natural rights is the primary source of Christian life-ethics.*[37]

(6) In light of this, a minimal conclusion must be drawn: even if there should *arguably* be situations, whether exceptional or habitual, in which intentional abortion, the rejection of public policies to assist the poor and the elderly, the administration of capital punishment, the use of every possible technological means to affect physiological life at all costs,[38] and the manufacturing and stockpiling of idiotically expensive and indiscriminately murderous nuclear arms should responsibly be judged ethically permissible, *still no positive Gospel warrant can be alleged for them.* In other words, the Church could (*perhaps*) *concede* or *tolerate* them;[39] it can never *commend* them. Thus *the consistent ethic of life positively draws its consistency from the Christian faith*; the principle "no self-serving killing of innocent human life" is not so much a ground-rule as the negative expression of the limits of the Christian, Catholic community's moral tolerance on human-life issues. It draws its primary inspiration, not from any alleged *rights* of unborn human life, the poor and the elderly, perpetrators of heinous crime, the marginally alive, and the defenseless citizens threatened by military power, but from *the commitment of Christians as moral agents viewing themselves as well as humanity and the world in the light of Christ.* Only on that basis does the Catholic tradition reliably seek coherent, compelling arguments for its moral commitments as well as its moral tolerance by recourse to natural reason.

(7) Cardinal Bernardin has not tired of pointing out that consistency on life-issues is essential, and I for one agree. And while ideally, "in the public arena we should always speak and act like a Church,"[40] in practice the Catholic community has borne "divided witness"[41] to the consistent ethic of life—something that has weakened the bishops' public witness. How to interpret this or account for this? Let me offer a hypothesis, and let me try to concretize it with the help of one well-known, burning example. There has been outright dissent in the Catholic community on the legitimacy of the availability of choice for women who want an abortion. Could it be that this is in (large?) part due to the fact that Catholics *de facto* view the ethics of abortion exclusively in terms of a public policy issue, to be argued solely on natural grounds, with only an incidental reference to the Gospel and to the tradition of the undivided Church? Public policy issues are freely and publicly debated in this country; could it be that the Catholic dissenters were concerned, not with the moral issue, let alone with the Catholic faith-response to the widespread practice of abortion on demand, but with the civil liberties of all Americans, and especially of American women?[42] Remember, the American Catholic experience, from bishop John Carroll to Fr. John Courtney Murray and beyond, has learned to appreciate these civil liberties, even if it means living with some public policies that are imperfect, and even sinful from a Catholic point of view. If the United States bishops in their wisdom have decided that the distinction between what is tolerable in public life and what is moral among Catholics does not apply to the abortion issue, what are the grounds for that decision? Or did the bishops mean to prohibit the free participation of Catholics in the *public, civic* debate about abortion? I think that it is possible to give excellent reasons why Christians and Catholics should publicly oppose abortion as it is so demoralizingly available today; I also think that they have a right to be taught, not just by recourse to natural-reason arguments (which *ex supposito* are also compelling to non-Catholics), but by recourse to the faith that identifies them specifically as Catholics. The effectiveness of such teaching, I suggest would be very dependent on the suasiveness of the Catholic bishops' conviction that the Catholic Church *cannot* be prepared to live with anything short of a total legislative ban on all abortions. Such a teaching effort, I submit, would also have to deal with the alarming profession of "private opposition" to public availability of abortion on the part of Catholics in public life. It looks as if many of them, in interpreting the abortion debate in purely civic terms, have also adopted some of the American tendency to consider religion a private affair; but in all fairness, have the bishops done enough to spell out the specifically *Christian, Catholic* commitments to compassion and against violence that must lie at the root of the Church's *communal* position in the public

debate? And have Catholics heard enough about the possibility of *practical* commitments to back up the Catholic rejection of abortion with compassionate action?[43] Some of the darker sides of American civil religion are its almost entirely theoretical concept of God and its glorification of the individual conscience[44]—rationalistic Deism is still with us. The Christian commitment to active compassion *as a community obligation*, in the name of "the interdependence of human life"[45] and "the collective responsibility of society for its poor,"[46] could well enlighten American society on the limitations of its otherwise admirable tradition of voluntarism.

(8) Let me conclude with a final, more philosophical observation. I admit to a certain unease with regard to the prominence of the *rights*-argument in Cardinal Bernardin's addresses: *rights* of the unborn, the poor, and so forth. My hesitation is partly historical, partly philosophical. There are good reasons to place the origin of the rights-argument in the mid-sixteenth century—the decades of the rage for *definition* by means of objectification and hardening of boundaries.[47] I distrust that approach, since it tends to construe the world as a collection of objects, truth as a collection of truths, and human nature as a closed system, as Henri de Lubac has pointed out in his critique of Cajetan's interpretation of Aquinas' definition of human nature.[48] My preference is to support the consistent ethic of life by means of the traditional *natural-law* approach. The concept of natural law is better able to accommodate what is required of the *agent* (human persons must act in accordance with what they *are*) as well as the demands of the *object* of the agent's action (reality demands that justice be done to it according to what it *is*). This, of course, does not completely solve every problem. It is not for nothing that Fr. McCormick has indicated that there are real problems with the *application*, by the Church's magisterium, of the nature concept in individual, and especially in sexual, morality;[49] but where the problem is one of application only, there is hope for development. An ethic rooted, as a matter of principle, in natural rights would seem to be inherently and rigidly tied to the (authoritarian?) affirmation of a patternless miltiplicity of totally objective values that simply demand that justice be done to them. That would seem to preclude the possibility of any kind of *internally consistent* ethic of life—which, I find, contradicts the Christian and Catholic experience from the New Testament on.

References

1 Cf., for instance, the address at Seattle University, March 2, 1986, p. 77.

2. It is worthy of repeated emphasis that Vatican II, at least in one instance, intentionally gave true power to decide to "the various kinds of competent regional episcopal conferences legitimately constituted" (*Sacrosanctum Concilium*, 22, §2; cf. 36, §3). Piet Fransen rightly concludes from this that "the Council thus created a new ecclesial institution." Cf. his "Episcopal Conferences: Crucial Problem of the Council," in: *Ecumenism and Vatican II*, Charles O'Neill, ed., Milwaukee, Bruce, 1964, pp. 98-126, quotation p. 108.

3. Cf. Cardinal Bernardin's words: "...the Church's social policy role is at least as important in *defining* key questions in the public debate as in *deciding* such questions" ("A Consistent Ethic of Life: An American Catholic Dialogue," Gannon Lecture, Fordham University, December 6, 1983, p. 3)—The bishops in most of continental Europe (and Ireland), whose positions are still residually shaped by the tradition of establishments and concordats, tend to be more directly (if discreetly) influential in matters of public policy; hence, they tend to be reluctant to engage in open processes that involve the Church and society at large, as some of the European reactions to the process leading to the United States bishops' Peace pastoral have proved.

4. Cf., for example, "League Wins Protest in Episcopal Use of Holy Name," *Action News—Publication of the Pro-life Action League*, Vol. 7, N° 5, July, 1987, p. 1.

5. James R. Kelly, "AIDS and the Death Penalty as Consistency Tests for the Prolife Movement," *America* 157 (1987)151-155.

6. *Quodlib.* III, 4, 1; the *cathedra pastoralis* is also called *cathedra pontificalis* and *cathedra episcopalis* in the same article. Theologians who are also priests share, in a derivative way, in virtue of their ordination, the bishop's pastoral teaching responsibility; this makes it often hard for them to decide that they can occupy their chairs of theology with authority while not appearing to occupy the bishop's. I suppose it may be even harder for a bishop-theologian to recall that his theological judgments were not consecrated along with his person.

7. Richard A. McCormick, S.J., *The Consistent Ethic of Life: Is There an Historical Soft Underbelly?*, p. 97.

8. Joseph Cardinal Bernardin, Address at Seattle University, March 2, 1986, p. 80.

9. Richard A. McCormick, S.J., *The Consistent Ethic of Life: Is There an Historical Soft Underbelly?*, pp. 97-98.

10. Richard A. McCormick, S.J., *The Consistent Ethic of Life: Is There an Historical Soft Underbelly?*, pp. 109-120.

11. As in the proposition: "The meaning of a word is determined by its use." Note that the proposition does not say that meaning is *exclusively* determined by use.

12. Richard A. McCormick, S.J., *The Consistent Ethic of Life: Is There an Historical Soft Underbelly?*, p. 115-116.

13. For these three, cf. Vatican II, Dogmatic Constitution on Divine Revelation *Verbum Dei*, 8:"...and thus the Church, in its *teaching, life, and worship,* perpetuates and hands on to all generations all it is itself, all it believes."

14. F. J. van Beeck, *Catholic Identity Since Vatican II—Three Types of Faith in the One Church*, Chicago, Loyola University Press, 1985, pp. 5-6.

15. *In I Lib. Sent.*, 8, 1, 1, *ad* 4:"...et tunc remanent in quadam tenebra ignorantiæ, secundum quam ...optime Deo conjungimur... ."

16. *S. Th.* II-II, 1, 2, *ad* 3: "Actus autem credentis non terminatur ad enuntiabile, sed ad rem. Non enim formamus enuntiabilia, nisi ut per ea de rebus cognitionem habeamus, sicut in scientia, ita et in fide."

17. Richard A. McCormick, S.J., *The Consistent Ethic of Life: Is There an Historical Soft Underbelly?*, p. 115-116.

18. J. Verhaar, S.J., "Language and Theological Method," *Continuum* 7(1969)3-29; quotation p. 22. By "arbitrary" Verhaar means to indicate that terminological language is largely dependent on *definition*, having lost much of its connection with natural language.

19. This expression is borrowed from Anthony Flew's famous parable and his commentary on it, reprinted in: *New Essays in Philosophical Theology*, Anthony Flew and Alasdair MacIntyre, New York, Macmillan, 1970, pp. 96-99; quotation p. 97.

20. Richard A. McCormick, S.J., *The Consistent Ethic of Life: Is There an Historical Soft Underbelly?*, p. 115-116.

21. This form of "consequentialism" deserves, of course, rejection. However, it would seem to be unfair and unreasonable to tar all reasoned teleological and consequential arguments with the brush of consequentialism.

22. The context: "Revelation, as a Manifestation, is a doctrine variously received by various minds, but nothing more to each than what each mind comprehends it to be. Considered as a Mystery, it is a doctrine enunciated by inspiration, in human language, to be received in that language; a doctrine *lying hid* in language, to be received in that language from the first by every mind, whatever be its separate power of understanding it; entered into more or less by this or that mind, as it may be; and admitting of being apprehended more and more perfectly according to the diligence of this mind and more perfectly according to the diligence of this and that. ...A Revelation is religious doctrine viewed on the side unilluminated. Thus Religious Truth is neither light nor darkness, but both together; it is like the dim view of a country seen in the twilight, with forms half extricated from the darkness, with broken lines and isolated masses. Revelation, in this way of considering it, is not a revealed *system*, but consists of a number of detached and incomplete truths belonging to a vast system unrevealed, of doctrines and injunctions mysteriously connected together; that is, connected by unknown media, and bearing upon unknown portions of the system" (*Essays Critical and Historical*, Vol. I, London, Basil Montagu Pickering, ˆ1877, pp. 40-42).

23. Joseph Cardinal Bernardin, "A Consistent Ethic of Life: Continuing the Dialogue" (St. Louis, March 11, 1984), pp. 14-15; Address at Seattle University, March 2, 1986, pp. 77; Address at the Consistent Ethic of Life Conference, Portland, Oregon, October 4, 1986, pp. 89-90.

24. Karl Rahner has given an example of how theologians may be of service to the magisterium's witness here, by his proposal of several converging creeds. Cf. *Foundations of Christian Faith*, William V. Dych, Trans., (*A Crossroad Book*), New York, Seabury, pp. 448-460.

25. Joseph Cardinal Bernardin, "A Consistent Ethic of Life: An American-Catholic Dialogue," Gannon Lecture, Fordham University, December 6, 1983, p. 3.

26. The Epistle to Diognetus, V, 1-4, 6-7, 10 (*Sources chrétiennes* 33, pp. 62-65).

27. *S. Th.* I, 1, 8, *ad* 2: "Since grace does not cancel nature, but perfects it, natural reason must pay homage to faith" ("cum enim gratia non tollat naturam, sed perficiat, oportet quod naturalis ratio subserviat fidei"). —*S. Th.* I, 2, 2, *ad* 2: "Faith presupposes natural knowledge, in the same way as grace does nature, and as a perfection presupposes something capable of

138 A Consistent Ethic of Life

being perfected" ("sic enim fides præsupponit cognitionem naturalem, sicut gratia naturam, et ut perfectio perfectibile").

28. *S. Th.*, I-II, 112, 1, *in c.* ("donum ...gratiæ excedit omnem facultatem naturæ creatæ."); cf. *S. Th.* I-II, [114, 2, *in c.*, and 5, *in c.*. Note, too, the clarity and ardor with which Aquinas draws his conclusion in S. Th. I-II,] 113, 9, *ad* 2: "The goodness involved in the grace of one person is greater than the natural goodness involved in the whole universe" ("bonum gratiæ unius majus est quam bonum naturæ totius universi").

29. Joseph Cardinal Bernardin, "A Consistent Ethic of Life: An American-Catholic Dialogue," Gannon Lecture, Fordham University, December 6, 1983, p. 10.

30. Incidentally, let me add that I am of the opinion that this imbalance is not limited to the United States bishops, or to Catholic teaching in the area of life ethics. Vatican II's Decree on the Training of Priests *Optatam totius* (16) implies that all of Catholic moral theology suffers from this imbalance, and lays down that it "must be renewed by means of a more lively contact with the Mystery of Christ and the history of salvation." While remaining scholarly, it should, "better sustained by the teaching of Holy Scripture, illumine the high calling of the faithful in Christ, and their obligation, in charity, to bear fruit for the life of the world."

31. Gal 1, 4; cf. the expression "this world": Rom 12, 2; cf. 1 Jn 2, 15.

32. This is a well-known Pauline theme: Gal 5, 1; 1 Cor 8, 9; 9, 19; cf. Rom 8, 15. Note, however, the related theme in 1 Pet 2, 16.

33. Cf. Jn 3, 17; 6, 37-39. The same theme in Joseph Cardinal Bernardin's address to the National Consultation on Obscenity, Pornography, and Indecency, Cincinnati, Ohio, September 6, 1984, p. 28.

34. 1 Cor 15, 55.

35. Mt 5, 39. 44-45. 48; cf. Lk 6, 36; Rom 12, 19-21 —Here lie the Christian roots, I submit, of two important points made by Fr. Richard McCormick: his criticism of "the dominance of independence in Western (especially American) thought" and "the interventionist mentality" (Richard A. McCormick, S.J., *The Consistent Ethic of Life: Is There an Historical Soft Underbelly?*, pp. 106-108). Catholic ethics should not be afraid to fundamentally question the predominance of the technological imperative in modern medicine. To a Christian, physiological death is not the ultimate power to be fought at all costs, nor is aggressive medical care, whether to keep physiological life going or to terminate it, the only "real" care. Ernest Becker's *The Denial of Death* (New York, Free Press, 1973) remains a valuable analysis of this issue.

36. Cf. 1 Pet 2, 20-24; Jn 15, 13; Rom 5, 6-8; 1 Pet 3, 15- 22.

37. This idea could perhaps lead to a resolution of the question whether the Church's magisterium can ever infallibly teach natural-law moral norms. In my construction, any such claim to infallibility would be *indirect. Directly,* the magisterium is competent in matters of Christian faith. If, in the light of faith-convictions capable of being infallibly taught, the Catholic magisterium should discern compelling natural-law arguments supporting those same convictions, we might perhaps speak of infallibly taught natural-law norms. On this issue, cf. Francis A. Sullivan, *Magisterium,* New York—Ramsey, Paulist Press, 1983, pp. 136-152.

38. Cf. Joseph Cardinal Bernardin, "A Consistent Ethic of Life: An American-Catholic Dialogue," Gannon Lecture, Fordham University, December 6, 1983, p. 7: "In an age when we *can* do almost anything, how do we decide what we *ought* to do? The even more demanding question is: In a time when we can do anything technologically, how do we decide morally what we *never should do?*" Cf. also *The Consistent Ethic of Life: The Challenge and the Witness of Catholic Health Care,* Catholic Medical Center, Jamaica, NY, May 18, 1986, p. 69 and *passim; The Consistent Ethic of Life and Health Care Systems,* Foster McGaw Triennial Conference, [Loyola University, Chicago], May 8, 1985, *passim.*

39. As in the case of the State's right to administer capital punishment: Joseph Cardinal Bernardin, "The Death Penalty in Our Time," Criminal Court of Cook County, May 14, 1985, pp. 61.

40. Joseph Cardinal Bernardin, "A Consistent Ethic of Life: Continuing the Dialogue," William Wade Lecture, St. Louis University, March 2, 1986, p. 19.

41. Joseph Cardinal Bernardin, Address at Seattle University, March 2, 1986, 77.

42. Cf. Richard McCormick's worry about the lack of the Catholic Church's credibility on this issue (*The Consistent Ethic of Life: Is There an Historical Soft Underbelly?*, p. 107-108).

43. One example was the public announcement of Cardinal Law of Boston to the effect that free medical and psychological help would be available at St. Margaret's Hospital in Dorchester, Massachusetts, to any pregnant woman to help her carry her child to term, in a case in which she should not want, for whatever reason, to take responsibility for it. This is entirely in continuity with the tradition mentioned by Cardinal Bernardin, in his address "The Face of Poverty Today: A Challenge for the Church," The Catholic University of America, January 17, 1985, p. 41. —Could it be that there is room for a renewed call for almsgiving in the Catholic Church—now significantly composed of middle-class and upper-middle class citizens—to support these institutions in an era when the State seems reluctant to use its taxing power responsibility on behalf of the poor and the marginal?

44. Cf. Richard A. McCormick, S.J., *The Consistent Ethic of Life: Is There and Historical Soft Underbelly?*, p. 107-108.

45. Joseph Cardinal Bernardin, "Linkage and the Logic of the Abortion Debate," Right to Life Convention, Kansas City, Missouri, June 7, 1984, p. 25.

46. Joseph Cardinal Bernardin, "The Face of Poverty Today: A Challenge for the Church," The Catholic University of America, January 17, 1985, p. 42.

47. Cf. Ernest L. Fortin, "The New Rights Theory and the Natural Law," *The Review of Politics* 44 (1982) 590-612, esp. 601-602. For other examples, cf. F. J. van Beeck, *Catholic Identity After Vatican II—Three Types of Faith in the One Church*, Chicago, Loyola University Press, 1985, 28-29.

48. Cf. *The Mystery of the Supernatural*, Rosemary Sheed, Trans. New York, Herder and Herder, 1967, esp. 181-216.

49. Richard A. McCormick, S.J., *The Consistent Ethic of Life: Is There an Historical Soft Underbelly?*, (97-104). Let me suggest that the absolute normativeness of the biologically given plays a disproportionate role, too, in theories put forward by some Catholic experts in medical ethics.

The Consistent Ethic—A Philosophical Critique

John Finnis
University College, Oxford

Preliminary Clarifications

The phrase "the consistent ethic of life" is a name, not a thesis. Philosophical reflections seek first the propositions which the phrase's author[1] intends, and which must be borne in mind when studying the discourses in which he uses or recalls it.

In speaking of "a consistent ethic of life," Cardinal Bernardin calls for such an ethic to be *developed* or *constructed*.[2] But he speaks as a bishop. Thus he presupposes, with his hearers, that Catholic moral teaching is, already, *consistent*—contains no contradictions or arbitrary truncations. And he presupposes, too, that Catholic teaching includes, already, at least the essential moral principles and norms applicable to, and linking the elements of, the whole spectrum of issues he has mentioned: genetics, abortion, war, capital punishment, euthanasia, pornography, hunger, homelessness, unemployment, education...[3] Indeed, none of his discourses suggests a need for any new moral norm, and all assume and imply the following proposition—the first of three which I shall formulate as articulating the essence of Cardinal Bernardin's call:

> CEP1: Individual Catholics must seek a self-consistent and positive acceptance of the whole framework of linked values, principles, rules, and applications in Catholic teaching over the whole spectrum of linked human life issues, old and new.

Thus: "The consequence of a consistent ethic is to bring under review the position of every group in the church which sees the moral meaning in one place but not the other. The ethic cuts two ways, not one: It challenges pro-life groups and it challenges justice and peace groups"[4]—and, of course, each of their individual members.

But if there is already, in essentials, a Catholic ethic to be found and lived consistently by every Catholic, what is still "needed"? What is still to be "developed" or "constructed"?

Cardinal Bernardin's answer is clear: What must be developed are "our ways of thinking, our attitudes, our pastoral response."[5] These must be *made* consistent, not with the facile "consistency" of those who commit themselves to nothing, but with the active concern of all those committed to the well-being, life, and dignity of others. If *our* ways of thinking, attitudes, and activities are thus made consistently responsive to those goods, then we (believers) may hope for the development of "an attitude or atmosphere in society" at large, a social ethos which is the precondition for any successful, nationwide defense and promotion of those goods.[6] So, Cardinal Bernardin says: "The purpose of proposing a consistent ethic of life is to argue that success on any one of the issues threatening life requires a concern for the broader attitude in society about respect for life. Attitude is the place to root an ethic of life, because, ultimately, it is society's attitude—whether of respect or non-respect—that determines its policies and practices."[7]

Hence, a second proposition named by "the consistent ethic of life"—

> CEP2: Catholics have a responsibility to foster in themselves, and thereby in their fellow-citizens, an ethos of respect for human life in all its forms and stages, and a readiness to promote the dignity

and quality of life of every person across the whole spectrum of
threats to life, dignity, and quality of life.

The link between CEP1 and CEP2 is made clear by Cardinal Bernardin:
Catholics cannot adequately fulfill the responsibility identified in CEP2
unless they share a common judgment about what the ethical requirement
that human lives be respected implies for such great issues of national
policy as abortion, capital punishment and nuclear deterrence and war.[8]
But this Catholic consensus can scarcely arise unless Catholics individually each seek what CEP1 calls for: consistency in their individual thinking
and attitudes concerning human life.

A third proposition conveyed by Cardinal Bernardin's discourses about
the consistent ethic is related to the very fact of his making those discourses as a bishop and indeed as the chairman of the U.S. Bishops' Committee
for Pro-Life Activities. But he does not leave it merely to inference. Instead, it is a theme of the discourses that a Catholic bishop has, as such,
responsibilities in relation to the fulfilment by society and individuals of
their affirmative responsibilities identified in CEP1 and CEP2. Indeed, "the
consistent ethic challenges bishops to shape a comprehensive social agenda."[9] So we can articulate—

> CEP3: To foster the desired consensus amongst Catholics and
> thus the desired ethos in society at large, Catholic bishops should
> publicly commend not only the principles of Catholic teaching on
> the whole spectrum of "life" and "quality of life" issues, but also
> policies which appropriately apply those principles right across
> that spectrum.

Later I shall disengage and discuss other positions mentioned or implied
in Cardinal Bernardin's discourses on these themes. But these three
primary formulations will provide the structure of my paper: CEP1 is the
theme of Part I, CEP2 of Part II, and CEP3 of Part III.

Three further preliminary observations.

First: It would be rash for a foreigner to try to assess the impact of Cardinal Bernardin's discourses on the public ethos in the United States or the
thought and morale of America's Catholics. Nothing I shall say will imply
any such assessment.

Second: However, I do not doubt the prediction that the non-Catholic
public will, in some measure, be favorably impressed by seeing that the

concern of Catholics is limited *neither* to one or two issues given an emphasis so exclusive as to appear eccentric and sectarian, *nor* to issues which, according to the believers' varying predilictions, seem selected to fit all too smoothly into the platforms of one or another political party.

Third: CEP1 and CEP2 can be understood as stating propositions which should, I believe, be accepted, and accepted as important. Thus far, at least, an episcopal call for a consistent ethic of life is surely fitting. But, CEP3 seems to me open to doubt, so far as it states and argues for an episcopal *obligation* to promote "prudential" judgments in national politics, a course with side-effects quite adverse to the fulfilment of a bishop's undoubted responsibilities.

More generally, the discourses in which the consistent ethic has been promoted seem open to helpful clarification. Even in relation to CEP1 and CEP2, the discourses *can* be understood or misunderstood as conveying questionable or mistaken propositions. So, too, can those two formulations: CEP1 can be misunderstood as suggesting that the relevant moral norms are constructed by a Church which shapes rules it judges will best promote human life or well-being in the long-run; CEP2 can be read as proposing an impossibly wide range of affirmative individual or group responsibilities, and an impossible search for the "best policy" to fulfill them.

The following reflections, then, are offered in the hope that they may serve not only the good ends which Cardinal Bernardin's discourses so clearly identify and so vigorously pursue, but also the philosophical precision which Christian teaching, like Christian theology, has always sought.

I
Which Consistent Ethic?

The consistent ethic is presented by Cardinal Bernardin as "primarily a theological concept, derived from biblical and ecclesial tradition about the sacredness of human life, about our responsibilities to protect, defend, nurture and enhance this gift of God."[10] "(B)ehind the consistent ethic" stand certain themes: "the theological assertion that the human person is made in the image and likeness of God, the philosophical affirmation of the dignity of the person and the political principle that society and state exist to serve the person."[11] My philosophical reflections will range over all these sources and themes, using the freedom of the philosopher to seek the concepts and premises required to give sense and justification to the relevant biblical, ecclesial, theological and political affirmations.

My first reflection, then, is that some of the conceptual resources required for a consistent ethic acceptable to Catholics are omitted from the foregoing list of "themes," and are generally overlooked in the fifteen discourses I have seen. The seamless garment explicitly in the discourses is not big enough to clothe the Christian. Moreover, if seamless, it has gaps and loose ends which, left unstitched, could expose the Body of Christ to "every wind of doctrine...".

The duty which CEP1 urges, to find and hold a consistent ethic of life, its protection and promotion (including its promotion by provision of life's basic necessities), has a basis which everyone will agree to: love of neighbor. Christian morality's primary principle is "Love your neighbor as yourself" (understood within the frame of "Love God above all things" and "Seek first the Kingdom").[12] And that principle is, I suggest, the true seamless garment not to be divided by impious, uncomprehending or self-interested hands.

Philosophically, that first principle of morality can be formulated more abstrusely: One ought to choose and otherwise will those and only those possibilities whose willing is *compatible with integral human fulfillment*, i.e. with the good of all persons and communities, conceived not as a goal attainable by some world-wide billion-year plan but as a guiding ideal which inspires and rectifies practical thinking by the general principles and more specific norms it implies.[13]

For, of course, this first moral principle in both its biblical and its more philosophical articulations needs specification. The principle's implications for human choice among the various basic human goods—life, knowledge, friendship, etc.—need to be identified. Love of neighbor needs to get down to cases.

Some of the necessary specifications no one wants to argue against. The Golden Rule as Jesus stated or restated it[14] is one such specification—highly general, no doubt, but still an implication of the first principle and potent in its own implications for moral reasoning; a will marked by egoism or partiality does not love or respect neighbor as such and cannot be open to integral human fulfillment.[15] Derived, in turn, from the Golden

Rule of fairness are such more specific but still general norms of common morality and common law as "equality before the law" or "equal protection of the law," and such fully specific moral judgments as: Jill who wants her husband Jack to be faithful acts unfairly in sleeping with Sam.

But Jesus and St. Paul stressed the *breadth* of morality's seamlessness: Love fulfils *all* the commandments[16]—all the key moral norms. And in the constant traditional understanding, some of the commandments go beyond the demands of fairness. "Thou shalt not commit adultry," for instance, is read as absolutely exceptionless, even though adultery committed by a couple who find it mutually agreeable to have an "open marriage" is not unfair. Now, right here, we find a serious problem for Catholics who want to identify (as CEP1 bids) a consistent ethic of life. Does "Thou shalt not kill" state (or imply) a moral absolute, or not?[17]

Published theological statements on this have been guarded; prudent contemporary theologians avoid listing kinds of cases in which they might or might not approve killing the innocent. Even so, a significant number of significant theologians publicly suggest that killing (in a full sense, direct, intentional, of innocents...) is sometimes justified.[18] Popular opinions among Catholics today (clergy, catechists, and others) are not so guarded; the principle that killing is justified when it is the "lesser evil" finds wide acceptance and is resorted to across a spectrum of cases—e.g., abortion when the mother's life or health is seriously jeopardized, or in cases of rape or incest, or of probably defective child, or multiple pregnancy (quintuplets etc.), and perhaps in other cases such as pregnancies amongst young girls and middle-aged women, or generally in cases where it seems to them that contraception was justified or required for "responsibility" but a contraceptive failed or, alas, wasn't used.

Two "consistent ethics" of killing are held before every individual Catholic who tries to follow CEP1's injuction to identify and live a consistent ethic of life. There is the seamless garment one finds in the *New York Times* or the *Washington Post* (or, in London, in *The Guardian* or *The Sunday Times*); wide sectors of Catholic opinion are picking it up, trying it for fit, and finding it rather comfortable, at least when worn conservatively. And there is the seamless garment one finds in the teaching proposed or approved by John Paul II, in continuity with the Catholic tradition.[19]

Cardinal Bernardin's discourses leave careful readers in no doubt which of these two contradictory "consistent ethics" of killing he proposes. The discourses insist upon the absolute character of the "basic moral principle that the direct killing of the innocent is always wrong."[20] As the Pastoral Letter on War and Peace over whose preparation he presided states: "the lives of innocent persons may never be taken directly, regardless of the purpose alleged for doing so," and "*no* end can justify means evil in themselves, such as the executing of hostages or the targeting of non-combatants."[21]

Still, I have already suggested that Cardinal Bernardin's discourses do not deploy all the resources available to him as a Catholic bishop for illuminating the sense and the strength of the tradition which he wishes to uphold. Now I should add that some features of his exposition of the moral norm on killing are likely to confuse Catholics who look for guidance in clarifying the issues in dispute between the two competing "consistent ethics." My purpose in commenting on these features will not be to lay out any full-dress argument on any of them, as I and others have laid out the relevant arguments elsewhere. I shall attempt no more than a *clarification* of the issues. Success in this attempt might be of some help to Cardinal Bernardin in his own project: upholding and passing on the constant and very firm moral teaching which should guide the faithful in their response to CEP1, and thus shaping the Catholic consensus needed to promote the social ethos called for by CEP2.

Let me take a representative passage in which the issues seem to me misstated:

> Precisely because life is sacred, the taking of even one life is a momentous event. Traditional Catholic teaching has allowed the taking of human life in particular situations by way of exception—for example, in self-defense and capital punishment. In recent decades, however, the presumptions against taking human life have been strengthened and the exceptions made ever more restrictive.[22]

The traditional teaching, however, has a form and logic different from that suggested by this passage. It is not that killing is a bad thing, to cause which is *generally* wrong but in exceptional cases right; nor that there is a desirable presumption that the exceptions be limited, and tightened whenever possible—a presumption which is, however, "overridden"[23] in at least two types of case. Rather, the traditional interpretation of "Thou shalt not kill" is: The direct killing of the innocent is always wrong, except when divinely authorized in particular cases (e.g. Abraham and Isaac).

The traditionally stated exception just mentioned is, of course, a theological issue not relevant to the issues raised by Cardinal Bernardin; so I shall here set it to one side.[24]

Nor will I dwell here on the concept of *innocent*. As used in this context, it refers to persons *not* within one of the two classes whose killing is justifiable according to the traditional common morality: those guilty of capital crimes and those engaged in forcible violation of society's just social order. The sources of this concept of innocence have been analysed in our recent book on nuclear deterrence.[25] But the clarification needed in the context of the "consistent ethic of life" can better begin with the traditional teaching's concept of *direct* or *intentional* killing.

Why "Directness" in Killing Matters

The idea of direct killing is that one intends the death. In indirect killing, though one's behavior brings about the death, and one foresees that, and accepts it, one does not intend it. And one intends the death when it is either the end *or a means* which one adopts (whether gladly, indifferently, or reluctantly) by one's *choice*. Popes who use the term "direct" to enunciate the moral norm about killing, e.g. Pius XII, Paul VI and John Paul II, have many times explained the term thus: "either as an end in itself, or as a means of attaining another end."[26]

But some say that this distinction—between direct and indirect, i.e. between the intended and the merely accepted, i.e. between end or means and side-effect—is a scholastic artefact, not essential to Christian teaching. Others add that the artefact was crafted as a device for lightening the otherwise intolerable burden of moral absolutes, and for achieving objectives more frankly acknowledged by a moral theory which looks always to the "lesser evil" and the "proportionate good."[27]

Both these claims seriously mistake the sense, force, and justification of the norm in its traditional understanding, and of the distinction which the norm embodies.[28]

The use of the distinction begins in Scripture: Wilful murder, punishable by death, is distinguished in the Pentateuch from unpremeditated manslaughter and accidental killing, whose perpetrators find asylum in a city of refuge (Exod. 21:12-14; Num. 35:16-23; Deut. 19:4-6 and 11).

But much more important, I believe, for the clarification of the morality of killing have been Christian reflections on God's will, reflections made directly relevant to ethics by the fundamental principle of Christian anthropology: that human beings are created in the image of God. The relevant Christian understanding is expressed in a canon of the Council of Trent:

> If anyone says that it is not in man's power to make his ways evil, but that God performs the evil works just as he performs the good, not only permissively but also properly and per se...: *anathema sit.*[29]

Trent here speaks of God's relation to the sinful human will. But no adequate Christian understanding of creation, of providence, or of predestination, can do without the distinction, in God's willing, between direct and permissive willing.[30] The same understanding is decisive for Christian anthropology and ethics because human beings face the same problem (and not merely because of sin): In making choices, one brings about bad side-effects, including side-effects which one can confidently predict. And from the outset, Christians have understood that Jesus did not choose to kill himself, did not choose to be killed, but did (as the Second Eucharistic Prayer puts it) "freely accept" his death as a foreseen effect of his own choice to remain faithful to his mission. In the Christian understanding, God cannot directly will what is bad; to do so would be inconsistent with his holiness. Jesus as man, then, cannot either. Nor may those who follow him.

Why Choices to Kill Innocents Are Always Wrong

We are now nearing the foundations of the traditional doctrine on killing. The wrongness of killing the innocent is not just that they get dead—a "bad thing to happen," a "sad state of affairs," or even (in Cardinal Bernardin's above-quoted words) "a momentous event".[31] Nor is it even that their being dead at our hands is unfair to them (as it very often is). Christian morality is more in the heart than in the results; one's intention is morally more basic and important than any performance or behavior by which that intention is carried out.[32] Any performance—i.e. any outward action, considered as the execution of a choice—has its primary moral significance from the act of the will (the choice or intention of means or end) which it embodies and carries out, or on which it depends in some other way. Directly killing the innocent—i.e. carrying out a choice (intention), to kill the innocent—is excluded from Christian life precisely because it is straightforwardly a choice against human life.

Given the Christian understanding of the significance of choice and action, the traditional norm thus follows from the first principle of Christian ethics: love of neighbor. For human life is intrinsic, not extrinsic, to the human person. A choice against human life is thus a choice against the person: anti-life, therefore anti-person. It is thus incompatible with love of the person, i.e. with that first principle of Christian and rational ethics.

The link I am tracing between the first principle and the specific norm against killing is—like the Golden Rule—an intermediate principle of wider application: One may never choose to destroy any *basic* human good—any intrinsic aspect of *personal* well-being—for the sake of any ulterior good, however important. "Evil" (e.g. destruction or damaging of a basic human good) "may not be done" (willed, intended, chosen as means) "for the sake of good."[33]

Reflection on the foregoing clarification of the traditional norm should not omit its tight relationship to the Christian understanding of *free choice* (a reality which philosophy vindicates against denials, but which pre- and post-Christian philosophies more or less fail to grasp). In Christian understanding, human choices are not merely events or states of affairs like the events and states of affairs which they initiate and bring about. They have a twofold further significance.

First, they *last*, beyond the behavior which executes them, until, if ever, one changes one's mind. Choices thus can last into eternity, and they can be understood as Vatican II (building on St. Paul) does in *Gaudium et Spes* 38-39, as contributing here on earth the material of the heavenly Kingdom. The "material" of the Kingdom includes persons, with the moral selves they have shaped by their choices.[34]

For, second, choices *reflexively* shape the character, the personality, the soul of the one who chooses.[35] The reality of these reflexive consequences is easily illustrated. Over the past decades, we have so often seen how someone who decides to resolve *one particular* moral issue in a certain way becomes a "different person"—one who resolves whole ranges of moral issues differently, and who adopts new attitudes to the human body, the course of history, the nature of salvation and human destiny, the proper conduct of scholarly controversy...

Here, then, is a dimension of consistency in ethics which should not be overlooked. And reflexive consequences like these are similarly strikingly manifest in the life of whole societies such as yours or mine. Societies, like individuals, can of course live with a large measure of inconsistency and intellectually incoherent compromise. Still, the adoption of an approach—

constitutional, statutory, administrative, judicial, or in folkway—to one social problem suggests, provokes or even demands, and certainly often
meets with, the adoption of similar approaches to other problems, if only
for the sake of consistency. (My colleague Ronald Dworkin has illuminat-
ingly studied some of the dimensions of this rational pressure for consistency, under the name "integrity.")[36] Thus the social consequences of the
social adoption of a solution—any solution—in a "conflict situation" include indefinitely ramifying reflexive changes in the character of the
people, their stance in the international arena, the content of their laws and
institutions, their education of their young...

A special and contemporary challenge has made more evident than ever
before, perhaps, the significance of these reflexive dimensions of individual and social choice for an understanding of the bases of the traditional distinction between direct and indirect. That distinction, we can now
see, is integral to the Christian understanding of divine and human nature:
What is directly willed (intended) is *adopted*—however reluctantly or disapprovingly—and embraced by and *integrated into* the will. What is not
chosen as end or means, but merely permitted (accepted) as a foreseen
result of one's behavior, is not.[37] The challenge I refer to can be labelled
"proportionalism." I shall explain what I understand by that term. Here it is
enough to note that theologians who embrace a proportionalist ethical
methodology suggest that we could, in an authentically Christian way, re-
read and re-think the tradition so as to dispense with the direct-indirect distinction (at least in relation to all the norms relevant to the consistent ethic
of life).[38]

The Proportionalist Challenge

The "proportionalist" or (the names matter little) "consequentialist"
proposal is this. In situations of morally significant choice, the overall net
pre-moral human value or disvalue involved in and resulting from the
various alternatives available for choice can be rationally assessed, prior to
moral judgment. Choice intended to, say, destroy human life can sometimes be thus identified as the choice of the greater net value or lesser net
disvalue.

Discussing that claim, chapter IX of *Nuclear Deterrence, Morality and
Realism* (1987) shows with some fresh arguments and illustrations (which
I shall here not even summarise) that the commensuration of goods and
bads which would be needed so to guide morally significant choice is not

merely impracticable but logically impossible.[39] Where commensuration is possible, morally significant choice is out of the question.

As common speech suggests, of course, *many sorts of commensuration of goods and bads are possible*. That chapter lists many senses in which one thing or state of affairs can be said to be "better" or "worse" than another—many intelligible and coherent senses of "greater good" and "lesser evil," and of "proportionate good" (e.g. as used in traditional formulations of the "principle of double effect," rightly understood).[40] *None* of them, we there show, is what proportionalists need; none is rationally based on the sort of overall, *pre-moral* commensuration, *capable of rationally guiding morally significant choices*, which is required by the proportionalist or consequentialist proposal. As meant by proportionalists, the proposal to guide morally significant choice by identifying the "lesser evil" or the "greater good" is like other plausible-sounding but incoherent proposals, e.g. to identify the largest natural number, or to prove any point provided it is the most obvious one.[41]

The *reflexivity of choice* which I discussed above is worth recalling in this context. It creates one of the many dimensions of incommensurability which render incoherent the proposal to guide choice by identifying greater and lesser proportions of pre-moral human goods and bads.[42] How could one conceivably assess the overall net pre-moral value and disvalue of the more or less comprehensive changes of attitude—or, similarly but even more extensively, of social ethos and practice—which so often result from a single choice? Some secular consequentialist philosophers have felt obliged to admit that, by seeking to settle a specific problem of choice by attending to anticipated proportions of pre-moral goods and bads, one becomes a different sort of person—one who stands ready to sacrifice personal commitments and stable identity, for the sake of achieving "greater good" or preventing "lesser evil." Indeed, such philosophers[43] sometimes feel obliged to concede that this reflexive consequence of adopting proportionalism might make that adoption the greater evil! But we should not seek this concession; we should be content, instead, with the more accurate reflection: This sort of consequence simply cannot be commensurated with the other consequences of one's particular choices. Instead of re-arguing these points, elaborately argued elsewhere, I simply suggest that one consider an example of a type of morally significant choice: abortion. Even in the rather narrow range of cases in which some Catholic theologians will allow direct abortion as "the lesser evil," the commensurations they suggest or assume are grossly impressionistic and manifestly deniable. Partly, because one cannot foresee the future. But above all, because one cannot know, compare and commensurate the everlasting realities with which one is dealing when one decides to blot out that individual human being. The goods at stake, in that individual—not to mention in his or her mother (as mother, and as the chooser) and in all who must choose to adopt or reject this choice to kill—are goods not adequately distinct from persons. And so the shortest reply to the proportionalist challenge is: *Persons* cannot be weighed and balanced.[44]

Persons Include Embryonic Human Individuals

Some, of course, object that the unborn are not persons, at least not at the early stages. But these "early stages" are stages in the life of biologically living, human individuals. Nobody can demonstrate, and the Catholic Church has never asserted, that these youngest of human individuals are always certainly persons. But the Church does teach that they should be presumed to be. And rightly. For what can we point to as common to all whom we consider persons, other than that they are living human individuals? Thus it is manifestly arbitrary to deny that some or (as in US law's contemporary denial) all of the unborn living human individuals are persons, or to be treated as persons. The denial is plainly motivated by the desire to allow them to be disposed of or used as material for destructive experiments or other useful exploitation.

But are there not *bona fide* objections based on twinning and on the non-immediate development of neural organs and capacities? These objections seem to appeal to elements of the tradition—notably to St. Thomas's doctrine of matter and form, and his conception of the successively vegetative, animal and intelligent stages in human generation. (They pass over in silence the Church's unfailing teaching, unchallenged by St. Thomas, that killing at any stage of human generation is gravely wrongful.)

Such an appeal to Aquinas's opinions about human generation is misconceived. It overlooks their strict dependence on empirically false biology. What Aquinas thought he knew about human generation was this. The formative principle is male semem, *neither organic nor living*, and generation proceeds by sudden (*subito*) generations *and corruptions*: Semen corrupts into bloody matter with a plant's life and soul, which perishes and is replaced by animal life and soul, which perishes and is replaced by human life informed by the sensitive and intellectual human soul.[45]

Had Aquinas known about the *organic life* which organizes the one billion items of molecular information in the one-cell conceptus with a *self-*

directing dynamic integration which will remain continuously and identifiably identical until death perhaps ninety years later, he would I believe have concurred with most of his followers (and almost everyone else) since the eighteenth century: The fertilized human ovum is specifically human; indeed, the youngest human embryo has already a body which in its already specified (but quite undeveloped) capacities is apt for understanding, knowing and choosing; he or she already has the biological capacity appropriate to supporting (given only metabolic transformations of air, water and other sustenance) specifically human operations such as self-consciousness, rationality and choice.

Similarly, objections about twinning (and about the assumed possibility of human mosaics) misconceive the biological facts. Biologically, one always finds just individuals. If these split, or combine to form a mosaic, one then simply finds one or more different individuals.

Such replies to the objections do not demonstrate that the fertilized human ovum is a person. They show that there is no factual gound whatever for denying that it is a person. Thus, since one picks out human persons in other cases by picking out living human individuals, one must presume that the youngest of living human individuals are persons, too; to presume otherwise is just arbitrary discrimination.

Capital Punishment and Just War

An issue which I set aside in beginning these clarifications now returns in the shape of an obvious objection to their strategy. How can the traditional allowance for killing the innocent—by capital punishment, and in just war—be other than a proportionalist "exception," a permission to adopt an anti-life will when that is the "lesser evil," i.e. is necessary to preserve a greater good, the common good?

Scripture and Church teaching give no support to that reading, though it may perhaps find some support in some preconciliar theologians (who did not contemplate the proportionalist challenge). Rather, capital punishment and war are envisaged in the sources as *authorised* by God because doing *justice* to one who has violated or is violating, the community's order of reciprocal rights and duties, the just order willed by God; in the Old Testament there seems also to be the further dimension of purifying God's holy community from the corruption of evil.

Reflecting on the proportionalist challenge, and on the fundamental structure of a rational (and of a Christian) ethics, I and others have offered (in chapter XI of *Nuclear Deterrence, Morality and Realism*) a philosophical account which excludes *all* choices to kill—but which shows the justifiability of all, or nearly all, the types of death-dealing action which the tradition clearly allowed in order to protect the rights of the innocent.

We begin from the simplest case, self-defense. Even in the tradition, that is not an accepted "exception" to the norm excluding choices to kill. (Here, then, is another amendment I propose to the text from Cardinal Bernardin quoted above at note 21.) Following Aquinas's classic account of lethal self-defense—an account which entirely excludes any intent to kill one's assailant—we show that self-defensive behavior, known to be likely to bring about the assailant's death, need involve no choice to kill but only accepting that death as a side-effect.[46] Provided that that acceptance of the side-effect is consistent with *other* moral principles (such as fairness)—if you like, is morally "proportionate"—the choice to use these lethal means of self-defense is fully justifiable.[47]

The analysis of individual self-defense is then expanded to the context of social defense, as in war against internal or external assailants. Here, too, our account is anticipated by certain theologians in the tradition; their accounts of just killing in war require, like ours, that military action be always directed toward stopping the enemy's unjust use of force, not toward killing even those who are bringing that force to bear—and whose deaths must never be more than a side effect.[48]

Arguably, even capital punishment could be included within this form of justification for death-dealing behavior. Aquinas, for one, did not think so: "It is not right to intend harm to anyone except in the manner of punishment, for the sake of justice."[49] My two co-authors of *Nuclear Deterrence, Morality and Realism* judge that capital punishment involves choosing to destroy or damage a basic human good, bodily life, and thus cannot be justified; it is a choice of a bad means to a good end (retributive justice). I am inclined to think that the intentions of a public official seeking to restore the violated order of justice have a unique structure; the death of someone capitally punished is not an end in itself, but neither need it be regarded as a means to an ulterior end, since it can be intended precisely as *itself* a good, namely the good of restoring the order of justice.[50] Clearly, the act of capital punishment calls for further analysis in the light of a fully adequate theory of human action.

In sum, chapter XI of our book shows that the lines drawn by the norm identified in our philosophical account—forbidding every choice to kill (every direct killing)—are very close to those drawn by the traditional norm against killing the innocent. Someone who agreed that human life is a basic good of the person, and that evil (e.g. destruction of a basic good of a person) may not be done for the sake of good, but who lacked an analytic apparatus explicitly distinguishing what is chosen as means from what is accepted as side-effect, could hardly express the implication of those agreed principles more accurately than by saying: "Killing the innocent, except by accident, is always wrong."

Developing the Tradition Consistently

True, our philosophical account differs somewhat from traditional morality at its present stage of development. But the difference runs with the grain of the tradition's development. I would not say what Cardinal Bernardin says in the quoted text, that presumptions against taking human life have been "strengthened" and the restrictions "made" more restrictive. These formulations can suggest the position that moral teaching is a matter of prudent law-*making*, establishing moral norms fashioned or "honed" for proportionately best consequences.[51] (Cardinal Bernardin's discourse at Seattle University identifies this position about the *source* of specific moral norms, apparently in order to reject it, but fails to disentangle it from the position which he does clearly argue against and reject, viz. that the *content* of the moral norm about killing includes proportionalist exceptions.)[52]

The moral teaching which shapes the traditional ethic of life is not a law-making but an identification, ever more adequate, of *truths* about human good and human action—about the *intrinsic* demands of love or respect for persons. So I would say that the tradition is developing by penetrating ever more deeply to the full impications of its underlying principles and presuppositions—those I have here been seeking to indicate.

Perhaps the pace of the tradition's development has been quickening, or will quicken, in response to the challenge of proportionalism. It is easy to underestimate how radical that challenge is. If one adopts proportionalism only as a limiting strategy to deal with "conflict situations" within a substantially traditional ethic, one will not notice how drastically it departs from the Christian conception of divine providence and human responsibility: God knows what is for the best but we do not. But if one adopts proportionalism at all, by what principle does one limit it? After two decades of theological debate, no coherent limiting principle has emerged;

nor will one ever be found, for none is consistent with proportionalism's master principle.[53]

If on the other hand, with some theologians, one abandons the attempt to limit that master principle, one falls into a *reductio ad absurdum*. For, given the Christian doctrine of providence, one should then accept the following as a moral principle: "If in doubt about what is right, *choose whatever you are inclined towards*! (For if you accomplish what you attempt, you can be certain that on the whole it was for the best, since it must fit into the plan of providence.)"

Moral absolutes, of the specific kind unfailingly taught in the tradition and rejected by proportionalism, fit the Christian conception of our subordinate human role as workers in the diving plan, who share in the eternal law without having it all laid out before us. In that conception (elaborated in the final chapter of *Nuclear Deterrence, Morality and Realism*), such dependence on a providence truly shared but only partially understood is accepted as the real matrix in which one's choosing and action have their most important significance: not as bringing about the this-worldly results one hopes for, truly important though thay may be (if they occur at all), but as preparing material for the Kingdom, especially people and their own moral selves as shaped by their moral choices.

The difference between traditional and proportionalist ethics goes, however, much wider. On the traditional approach, Christians identified their affirmative responsibilities—what works of mercy to do—by considering their vocational commitments, their opportunities to bear witness, and so forth. A Carmelite in her cloister did not need to feel guilt about not being an activist for poor women in the ghetto, but prayed for them, lived simply, perhaps shared with them excess donations she received.

But once one adopts proportionalism, it seems that one should consider everything one could do, what results one could hope for, and what will be the results of not doing all that one *could* do—and then seek to achieve the results embodying greatest overall good. Of course, no one really takes this seriously and consistently: Who tells an American couple to forget *whose* children are the ones going to college and whose are the ones starving in Africa (though the cost of a year in college might keep a multitude of starving children alive that year)?

Here, as in attempts to identify or establish a stable limiting norm about killing, acceptance of the proportionalist method destroys but cannot build;

the method yields nothing but mere rationalizations for doing what is chosen on some other ground—feelings, social conventions, etc., or a residual, inconsistent acknowledgement of the principles, norms and counsels taught in the tradition.[54]

In short: One's whole ethic of life will be different if one approaches it consistently in a traditional way with moral absolutes and affirmative responsibilities specified by diverse vocations, or if one approaches it consistently in a proportionalistic way, trying to weigh and measure. The latter approach yields no substantive, consistent ethic, but generates an unbounded number of ethics each shaped according to the varying feelings, the degrees of respect for traditional or cultural norms, and the hunches of their authors and adherents. No compromise which admits a proportionalistic component into the traditional ethic can be anything other than internally inconsistent; elaborated consistently, it must tend to dissolve (in the minds of its exponents) whatever moral norms conflict with the surrounding culture. It, too, yields a consistent ethic only in that negative sense.

So one might rephrase the heading of this Part. The contest is not, strictly speaking, between two "consistent ethics," but between two consistent ethical approaches only one of which could yield (as it does) a consistent ethic. Yet contest there is, and any attempt to promote or fulfill CEP1 must face and resolve it.

II
Implications for Social Action

I now turn to a question raised by CEP2: Should a Catholic be concerned to promote particular social/political policies across the whole range of issues mentioned in Cardinal Bernardin's discourses?

The text on which I shall focus in this Part is particularly well-known; the Cardinal has re-affirmed it in the face of criticism. I shall argue that, read in its more obvious sense, it is open to justified criticism. It is:

> Those who defend the right to life of the weakest among us must be *equally visible* in support of the quality of life of the powerless among us... (e.g.) the hungry and the homeless... Such *a quality of*

life posture translates into specific political and economic positions on tax policy, employment generation, welfare policy, nutrition and feeding programs, and health care. Consistency means we cannot have it both ways: We cannot urge a compassionate society and vigorous public policy to protect the rights of the unborn and then argue that compassion and significant public programs on behalf of the needy undermine the moral fiber of the society or are beyond the proper scope of governmental responsibility.[55]

To simplify my discussion, I shall focus on just two of the many issues there mentioned by Cardinal Bernardin: (i) *infanticide*, and (ii) *feeding the hungry*. And I shall focus on those questions of social policy or action which involve *the law* (whether as prohibiting or exempting conduct or as authorizing expenditures and administrative procedures). These simplifications are to be kept in mind throughout.

In their fundamental logical structure, infanticide and feeding the hungry are representative, both of the Cardinal's spectrum of life and dignity issues, and of the further dimensions of that truly seamless garment, love of neighbor as oneself, for the sake of God and his Kingdom (philosophically speaking: of a will for integral human fulfillment). Infanticide is the subject of a moral absolute, applicable always and everywhere to everyone. Feeding the hungry is the subject of a grave affirmative responsiblity, whose implications for particular individuals depend upon their other responsibilities.

Even before we explore the difference between moral absolutes and conditioned affirmative responsibilities—a difference which the discourses advert to[56] but do not explore—it is evident, I suggest, that the text I have quoted needs a clarification or amendment. No individual (or group) need, or even could reasonably, be "equally visible" in support of the consistent ethic's requirements in each and every one of the relevant issues. People do *and should* have different commitments and responsibilites. A conscientious Congressman should not be expected to be a right-to-life activist; he should vote consistenly with the norm excluding any intent to kill the innocent, and he should work for less unjust laws and policies; he might focus his high-visibility activities on welfare reform or some other just policy. A person deep into the picketing of abortion clinics and baby-starving maternity wards (and perhaps in-and-out of jail) should not be expected to be knowledgeable about and working at welfare reform.

Cardinal Bernardin has in fact made this point: The consistent ethic does not mean that everyone must do everything.

> There are limits of time, energy and competency. There is a shape to every individual vocation. People must specialize; groups must focus their energies. The consistent ethic does not deny this.[57]

So the phrase "those who...", in the earlier-quoted text, must have been used in a sense which many hearers and readers will, I think, have misunderstood: *That community* (e.g. the Church) *which* opposes infanticide must also, as a community, be equally visible in support of the hungry and homeless... Even with this clarification, the statement seems rather imprecise: Even in a community rich in diverse talents and charisms, *equality of visibility* seems scarcely the relevant measure of fulfillment of very diverse responsibilities—some absolute, some affirmative, and all arising in ever-shifting contexts of urgency.

But perhaps I have been pressing this fragment of the text too hard. So I turn to the main questions of this Part.

Infanticide

My first question is: What social policy should Catholics support in relation to the *law of infanticide*? Should the intentional killing of a child, by "act" or "omission," whatever the circumstances, be prohibited and punishable as a crime?

Throughout the civilized world, now as in Aquinas's day,[58] the criminal law of homicide closely follows, "translates," indeed transcribes the community's common morality. Each community tries to identify what forms of killing and of death-dealing behavior or omission are *morally wrongful,* and then declares those forms of conduct unlawful and criminal.[59] Despite the severe strains introduced into the common moral-legal tradition by social acceptance of Dresden, Hiroshima and Nagasaki, and of abortion, the Anglo-American law of homicide remains essentially consistent with the common law and Christian morality's absolute exclusion of killing the innocent.[60]

This virtual coicidence of moral law and state/national law in relation to the definition and prohibition of homicides (including infanticide) is to be expected and supported. The fundamental moral principle of love of neighbor has its most immediate political application through the mediation of the Golden Rule, the rule of fairness which yields the fundamental political and constitutional principles: equal dignity of persons, equality before the law, equal entitlement to the law's protection. The first condition of fair human inter-relationships is that one's own life and death be not at the disposal of another's choice. Hence the law of homicide should conform to morality's exclusion of all choices to kill any human being. The legal rule's most immediate source is the principle of equal dignity; the moral norm's most immediate source is the sanctity of life as a basic human good never in any instance to be destroyed as an end or as a means. But the two sources coincide in their implications.

How different from the ancient world! How different, too, from the new world which consistent utilitarians, and other consistent consequentialists and proportionalists, envisage and promote! Those are ethico-legal univer- ses in which there is no (or no consistent) acknowledgement of human bodily life's sanctity—the more than instrumental significance of that life as an intrinsic and basic human good,[61] and its immunity in every instance from any choice to destroy it as end or as means. Nor do they acknowledge the equal dignity of every human person: Those who lack "quality of life" to some level selected by others, and some of those whose existence is thought likely to lower the quality of life of another, are removed from the protection of the law's prohibition.[62] They are deemed "better off," or even just "better," *dead*; the deliberate bringing about of their death is declared to be a "necessity" or at least "the lesser of evils." Those in power are thus permitted—sometimes at their own free initiative, sometimes only after legal formalities—to kill those who are thus under their dominion.

(In periods when a culture, or an individual, is in transition from the ethic and law consistently founded on love of neighbor and equal dignity to the ethic and law founded on "balancing of values" by those in power, the fact of transition may be veiled—diaphonously—by a requirement that the choice to kill be carried out only by "omissions," "letting die," with- holding of sustenance...[63]. Consistent value-balancers regard such veils with understandable contempt.)[64]

In short: Those who wish to make exceptions to the law of infanticide accept that they must argue, or assume, that deliberately killing some human beings is *morally* justified. They rightly acknowledge that this is no place for a gap between law and morality. The implications of love of neighbor, as understood in Catholic morality, make clear (I have sug- gested) why such a gap, here, would be deeply unjust, and why both morality and the law must absolutely exlude the killing of babies as of other human persons.

Thus my question about the social policy that Catholics should support in relation to infanticide has a single, straightforward answer.

More generally, the moral absolutes of the tradition have a number of direct "translations" into social policies which in the strictest sense *apply*—are *deducible* from—the absolute moral norm. So, for example, the Pastoral Letter on War and Peace (1983) rightly judged that the absolute norm, "the lives of innocent persons may never be taken directly" (para, 104), *does* translate directly into such applications, or norms of "policy," as: "It is not morally acceptable to intend to kill the innocent as part of a strategy of deterring nuclear war" (para. 178).

But how far, if at all, are such translations, or applications *stricto sensu*, available in relation to the affirmative moral norm, "Feed the hungry"?

"Feed the Hungry"

This norm, like the norm against infanticide, is an implication of love of neighbor via the Golden Rule: Since one wants the means of sustenance for oneself, one must feed the hungry when and in the way that one's other responsibilities fairly allow. Since people's other responsibilities vary widely with their commitments and opportunities, the responsibility articulated by the norm "Feed the hungry..." will be fulfilled by a vast variety of individual and social acts at various levels. It will be violated by various forms of unfairness.

Some of these violations are quite straightforwardly identifiable, and straightforwardly translatable into law. Failures to feed the hungry can be omissions chosen in order to hasten death, and thus violations of the ethico-legal absolute exluding killings—itself, as we have seen, a norm articulating the requirements not only of the sanctity of life but also of fairness. Or such failures to feed can be negligence which unfairly flouts all accepted standards of responsibility of parents or guardians (including the standards of care which those parents or guardians expect from their own medical and other attendants).

Another of the many forms of unfairness emerges from Cardinal Bernardin's reference (at the end of the quoted text) to those who resist state-funded welfare on the score that it undermines society's moral fiber. What undercuts their argument is not some proportionalist computation that the undermining of moral fiber is disproportionate to, outweighed by, the survival or health of the need. It is that those who make the argument make it with a biased selectivity. They support constitutional, economic, educational and other social policies which also result in, or risk, undermining the moral fiber of some or many of those affected by them—undermining it by materialism, consumerism, indulgence in frivolity and baseness, indifference to the responsibilities which go with rights and advantages, and other immoralities commonly accompanying prosperity.

The demands of fairness, then, are one main respect in which the consistent ethic's consistency indeed "means we cannot have it both ways."

But how far does this mean that a fair "quality of life posture *translates* into specific political and economic positions..."?

From Consistent Ethic to Specific Policies

The suggestion is ambiguous. In many issues and contexts, a fair respect for the basic needs of one's fellow citizens, one's fellow human beings, entails that there be *some* specific measures to meet those needs, yet fails to identify (leaves underdetermined) *which* specific measures. In these many instances, the moral norm does not "translate" into "specific political and economic positions." Instead it requires that individuals, groups, and political communities *choose* from among various possible appropriate measures (and nothing can be chosen without being fully specific).[65]

There are many morally significant criteria for detecting *inappropriateness* in proposals for such choice. But these criteria cannot be expected to identify as inappropriate all proposals save one policy, uniquely appropriate to the issue in question. There can be few if any issues or contexts in relation to which there is only one right answer to the questions how "best," i.e. how *rightly*, to fulfill such affirmative responsibilities as "Feed the hungry."

The Pastoral Letter of 18 November 1986, *Economic Justice for All*, puts a similar point thus—

> the movement from principle to policy is complex and difficult and... although moral values are essential in determining public policies, they do not determine specific solutions. (para, 134).[66]

That statement needs a little clarification. Its context concerns affirmative social and individual responsibilities, not moral absolutes. The denial, "Moral values do not determine specific solutions," should read as meaning: Moral norms articulating affirmative responsibilities such as "Feed the hungry" do not entail uniquely correct specific "solutions," though they enable many possible public policies to be identified as incorrect, i.e. unjust or in some other way immoral. Read in this sense, the Pastoral Letter seems to be correct in denying that the quality of life posture "translates" into *specific* political and economic positions.

Now this has some implications often overlooked. I shall identify two.

Rightful Opposition Between Adherents to the Consistent Ethic

Even with (an impossible) unanimity on the facts and likely consequences, it is possible for some members of our society to oppose, *rightly*, social programs which other members *rightly* propose and support in fulfillment of an affirmative norm such as "Feed the hungry."

I take as my first premise a judgment of the Pastoral Letter *Economic Justice for All*, para. 185: The disparities of wealth and income in the United States are such to be "unacceptable... inequities," offensive to justice. I take (not from the Pastoral Letter) one further premise: It is now politically impossible, and no substantial U.S. political party now proposes, to reduce those disparities to the extent required by justice.

Consider now a welfare program to feed the hungry, to be funded (a) by taxation on income, sales/purchases, etc., and (b) by reducing the funds which might otherwise have gone to housing, education, health care and pensions for all the relatively poor (above as well as below the "hungry-poverty" line).

The burden of such a program upon those who are just above the hungry-poverty line is inequitable, relative to the burden on the very rich who after paying their taxes retain an inequitably high level of income of wealth. And the burden of such a program upon those who are just above the hungry-poverty line is inequitable, relative to the burden on the very rich who after paying their taxes retain an inequitably high level of income and wealth. And the burden on those just above the hungry-poverty line makes it more difficult, if not impossible, for them to fulfill their serious affirmative responsibilities for the education and health of their children.

In such a situation, those hungry-poor who live responsibly, and who need the welfare program, can rightly support it. Yet those only a little better-off (who may be very numerous) may rightly *oppose* the program. In doing so, they need not be manifesting a wrongful indifference to the needs of the worst-off. They need only be manifesting a rightful concern to fulfil their own responsibilities to their children, and expressing a rightful judgment that a prior responsbility for funding the relief of the worst-off falls, in justice, on those who are, inequitably, very rich.

For the program is both really just and really unjust; its justice is only relative.

(As for the very rich, they are in a moral perplexity by reason of the prior injustice of their position. They cannot oppose the program without compounding their injustice to the worst-off, nor support it without compounding their injustice to the not quite so badly off. *This* program, with its attendant injustice, would not have been needed if they had not been hanging on to their inequitable advantages.)

Legislators as such, finally, whether personally poor or rich, can rightly either support or oppose the just/unjust program, for the competing good reasons I have mentioned. But all legislators have a serious responsibility not so to act as to leave the worst-off starving. For, since everyone would rather accept many unfair deprivations than starve, it is grossly unfair for anyone specifically responsible for the public good to accord to *per se* reasonable protest against the starvation-preventing program's unfair features an ultimate practical priority over preventing starvation.

This analysis could of course be refined. But it may already suggest one of the serious problems inherent in asserting, without some clarifying distinctions, that

> CEP3:...Catholic bishops should publicly commend not only the principles of Catholic teaching on the whole spectrum of "life" and "quality of life" issues, but *also policies* which appropriately apply those principles right across that spectrum.

All who express or insinuate support for a specific welfare program—except perhaps legislators at the decisive moment of voting—not only express *acceptance* (I do not say "approval") of the serious injustices involved in carrying out that program, in our inequitable societies. They also become open to the charge of preferring the imposition of those particular injustices to lending active support for alternative specific welfare programs which would involve neither those nor, perhaps, any other injustices.

Such a charge might be resisted by arguing that support for those alternatives is futile—the rich are not going to allow their privileges to be taken from them. This sort of defense may suffice for the politician. But if tried by the preacher it is considerably less convincing, in so far as it depends on contestable assessments of probabilility, and an overtly pessimistic attitude to the leaven of the gospel. Those among the preacher's flock who suffer the injustices involved in the program he supports may well hear the defense with skepticism, in more sense than one. (More about the preacher's predicament in Part III.)

Now to a second implication of the difference in "applicability" between moral absolutes and affirmative responsibilities.

A Litmus Test Available to Voters

Single-issue voting is absurd, but in considering how to choose among candidates for high political office it is reasonable to give their views on infanticide a very different weight from their views on various public programs for feeding the hungry.

Single-issue voting for candidates makes no sense, strictly speaking. For our constitutional systems require us to vote, not for programs (responses to "issues"), but for people to hold office. Candidates who profess to hold the view one favors on one's preferred "single issue" may in fact not hold it, or may be unable ever to act on it, and/or may hold views one reasonably deplores on other issues, including important issues one has not even envisaged.

What one reasonably desires, then, are candidates who have ability and good character—who will try to act on what they publicly profess, and who will respond with justice to the whole range of issues (including unforeseen issues) which will fall within their authority during their tenure of office. *Character*, after all, is the foundation and substance of that attitude or ethos which Cardinal Bernardin's discourses invoke as a primary concern (see CEP2).

So it is reasonable for a voter to use candidates' discoverable convictions about (or "positions on") infanticide as *a litmus test of bad character*, to give little or no weight to their preferences among possible policies regarding feeding the hungry, and (subject to exceptions) to vote accordingly.

For since the social and legal application of the moral truth about infanticide is quite straightforward, those who are willing to relax the legal prohibition of infanticide show themselves to have very bad character, at least so far as justice is concerned.[67] Those who oppose particular policy approaches toward feeding the hungry may be unjust. But usually that is not so clear. (An exception would be any who admit indifference to the hungry, let alone any who propose their elimination by starvation.) For the opposition to particular programs may be motivated by preference for alternative programs, or different methods of funding, or for policies which would more or less rapidly and more or less completely shift the undoubted responsibility for feeding the hungry back to the neighborhood and family communities (where, in many societies, it rests to this day), leaving the organs of the national community with, in this field, only the most strictly subsidiary function.

I do not insinuate any preference for the last-mentioned view. But I do say that a candidate who preferred it might well be of good character, in relation to all the norms of, say, Catholic social teaching. Such a candidate might well hold a truly consistent ethic of life—an ethic which not only applies absolute moral and legal norms protecting innocent life from assault and intentional neglect, but also extends to all the many "quality of life" issues Cardinal Bernardin has mentioned (and to all the other aspects of justice), and requires a sincere recognition of the relevant affirmative norms and responsibilities.

Two Footnotes.

What I say about infanticide as a litmus test of politically relevant bad character applies also, it seems to me, to abortion. To an educated person, the sort who seeks high office in our societies, abortion is not more obscure an issue of justice than infanticide. (The countless protestations to the contrary, the endlessly shifty rationalizations for killing children while unborn, the market for "probable opinions" of theologians and philosophers, are signs of pervasive bad conscience, of that *mauvaise foi* for which Christian doctrine has another name.)

The same is true of abortion funding, though here there may be more room for a kind of self-deception whose implications for character are more difficult to assess.[68] A politician who supports the provision of public funds for abortion, as a means of alleviating poverty or disparity of "opportunity" between rich and poor, violates the absolute norm which excludes intending to kill the innocent.[69] Those who thus choose to fund abortions, whether or not with feelings of disapproval and repugnance—"We're personally opposed but..."—*personally will,* i.e. choose as a means, *that abortions be done,* with public funds. They act as prime contractors, procurers, in arranging for the disposal of unborn children presented (for destruction) to the health- care providers whose destruction-services are secured by the government's prior undertaking that *these* services will be paid for when performed. In a consistent ethic of life, as in common and Christian morality, the moral absolute excluding killing obviously excludes the procuring of killings, and—being itself an implication of love of neighbor"—conditions the fulfillment of one's serious responsibilities to diminish poverty and the unfair balance of opportunities between rich and poor.

In short, though single-issue voting, strictly speaking, makes no sense, one may reasonably vote according to this rule of thumb: Willingness, however reluctant, to relax the legal prohibition on infanticide, or to support the judicial permission of abortion as a means of securing "privacy" or maternal health or "fairness to the poor," or to promote the public funding of abortions for any such end, or as a means of securing or retaining public office lest worse people be elected, is sufficient manifestation of unsuitability for high office; few of the politically relevant positions on poverty and welfare are such a manifestation.

Of course, sometimes one may vote for a candidate who manifests this sort of bad character. But only as a way of doing what one can to prevent the election of a candidate who also manifests relevantly bad character and who has some other or wider unsuitability for public office. And sometimes one may find the test unusable because one has insufficient evidence to discover the truth about what the candidates are willing to do if elected.

III
An Obligation of Bishops?

The discourses distinguish between "moral principles" and "the application of these principles to particular policies"—more briefly, between "principles" and "specific solutions," "specific political and economic policies," "particular strategies," "policy proposals," "policy conclusions" or "policy judgments."[70] They state that Catholic bishops, though speaking with "a different authority" when they do so, offer "policy conclusions" in order to foster public debate, to "give a sense of how the moral principles take shape in the concrete situations our society faces," and "to stimulate the public argument."[71] The discourses recall with approval a distinction drawn in the Pastoral Letter on War and Peace (paras. 9-10), between "universally binding moral principles" and "applications of these principles," applications which involve "prudential judgments...based on specific circumstances which can change or which can be interpreted differently by people of good will." The Letter adds that "the moral judgments that we [the U.S. Catholic bishops] make in specific cases" are "not binding in conscience."

All this calls for clarification. Being universals, the absolute moral norms can be called principles. Their direct application does call for judgment (sometimes so straightforward that errors in application are almost inconceivable), but not for any additional *moral* deliberation or judgment. No further moral norms or responsibilities can require or authorize any choice other than: not to do what the moral absolute identifies as morally unacceptable.

It seems incautious, therefore, to speak as if a teacher whose mandate is authoritatively to identify and propose universal (general) moral principles cannot authoritatively apply the moral absolutes to particular policies. If the particular policy is overtly or obviously inconsistent with a moral absolute, it can and should be condemned by those who have authority to propose that principle.[72] When, however, a public policy is open to interpretation, to differing characterizations, then a judgment on it will carry the full authority of a teacher of moral truth only if expressed hypothetically: "*If* this policy requires or authorizes any person to attack non-combatants either as an end or as a means, then it must not be proposed, supported or implemented, even if the consequences of not supporting or implementing it seem likely or humanly-speaking certain to be very bad..."

So it is not universally true that the immediate applications of moral principles call for "prudential judgment," unless "prudential judgment" includes the simple and straightforward application of moral absolutes to instances falling under them. But the virtue of prudence is indeed fully engaged when the "application" is of affirmative norms, and the fulfillment is of affirmative responsibilities.

For no affirmative norm can be applied without considering and assessing other *moral* norms, including the very specific norms which apply to some individuals, groups, or political communities but not to others, because of differences in their respective commitments, formal and informal. (I have already said something about such commitments in the constitutional, legal or political sphere, when discussing the dimension of consistency called by some communal "integrity.") Every choice has bad side-effects, and the range and content of one's moral responsibility to avoid, prevent or minimize those side-effects depend upon one's situation, one's opportunities and alternative options, and one's vocation with its responsibilities. Assessing all this well is the role of prudence, the intellectual disposition to make uprightly reasonable choices.

Now CEP3, as implicitly deployed in Cardinal Bernardin's discourses, seems to propose that Catholic bishops have an obligation to be ready to make, regularly and frequently, prudential judgments of the following form: It is appropriate for me as a Catholic bishop to fulfill my affirmative responsibilities as teacher and pastor by making a particular public statement intended to affect the national political debate on a specific "policy issue" (say, a welfare program to feed the hungry, or house the homeless).

Now, both episcopal affirmative responsibilities and civic affirmative responsibilities are undoubtedly serious. But the decision to be an actor in national political life, and to urge fellow-believers to be actors, promoting or lending direct support to specific proposals for national policy, is a decision likely to have some notable bad side-effects which I shall shortly sketch. If, however, the making of such decisions is an episcopal *obligation,* then accepting those side-effects will in many cases be obligatory, since not to make the decision will also have bad side-effects. If, on the other hand, the making of such decisions is not within the obligations of a bishop as bishop, then acceptance of the side-effects of making them should be assessed rather differently by episcopal prudence.

What, then, are the bad side-effects I have in mind?

The episcopal office carries the responsibility of catechizing believers about their duties as Christians, and primary among those duties is the affirmative responsibility to find and accept a personal vocation which, in all its richness and complexity, will shape a life by faith, hope and love. Now the vocation of most Christians, while not negating their responsibilities as citizens, will be far removed from involvement in national or state political life. Yet contemporary secular humanism insistently teaches that the most truly significant arena, "where the action is," is the arena of "world history" or "national life," where great worldly power is exercised. Christianity seems to teach otherwise—that the kingdom it hopes for is built up, through faith and good works in this life, in *mystery*, and as really by the faith and good choices of those who are utterly marginal to the transactions of "world history." Can one confidently affirm that in contemporary Western societies Christian believers are receiving from their bishops a catechesis which challenges the secular humanist assumption, and effectively communicates that faith should shape every believer's vocation however far most elements of that vocation may be removed from publicity and "public life"?

Again, episcopal office includes the responsibility of calling non-believers to conversion. Among those needing conversion are the non-believers who hold or seek political office. If bishops, in the interests of political relevance and of "being taken seriously by important people," were to base their public pronouncements on some kind of groundrule excluding from serious attention any "impracticable" or "other-worldly" option—such as unilaterally ending nuclear deterrence, or taking from the wealthy *all* the property they do not administer in accord with the Christian conception of property as social responsibility—they would be passing over an opportunity to preach the Gospel, in its prophetic integrity and its unembarrassed denunciation of clear and sure evils, to many who might otherwise have heard its radical challenge.[73]

Again, episcopal office now disqualifies its holders from actually exercising any high political responsibility and participating directly in the actual choice of national or state policies. And their own responsibilities prevent bishops acquiring the detailed knowledge of options, opportunities, costs and other realities which is needed and often possessed by those who do make and execute high political decisions. In both these ways, bishops are prevented from making *truly prudential* judgments about the political community's fulfillment of its affirmative responsibilities. For prudence, strictly speaking, is wisdom in *choosing,* and only those whose position requires them to choose are well placed to have the appropriate knowledge of the options. Insofar as actual decision-makers are wicked people and/or unbelievers, they are unlikely to be impressed either by the authority or by the wisdom of episcopal pronouncements on matters of state. Where, however, they are believers, they are likely to be distressed by the authority just in so far as their own prudent judgment, made in accordance with Christian teaching, differs from that of their bishops.[74]

Finally, as I argued in Part II, support for specific policies for fulfilling affirmative social responsibilities in an unjust society involves material cooperation in moral evil. What sort of material cooperation in evil is appropriate is properly judged by those who, each in their own specific situation and vocation, must choose. What is appropriate for one believer may be inappropriate for another, given differences of role and responsibility. Most believers are likely to be confused, and find the truth of their faith somehow obscured, when a bishop takes stands which involve him in approving material cooperation in evil, and in taking sides with some believers against others on matters which the faith itself leaves open.

My purpose in sketching these bad side-effects is not to argue that American bishops have erred in prudential judgment, or that their choices have been more liable to create these effects than the comparable choices of popes or of bishops in other places. The prudential judgment in question can be made only by Catholic bishops. And many popes and bishops, for many years, have judged it good to accept these side-effects (assuming they were aware of them), in the interests of good causes, which have varied, in detail, from time to time and place to place.

Several good causes are proposed in Cardinal Bernardin's discourses: the stimulation of public debate, for the sake, in turn, of developing consensus among Catholics and thus promoting a life-respecting and life-enhancing ethos in society at large (CEP1 and CEP2).

But are these truly good causes sufficient to justify the position that Catholic bishops have an obligation to promote, in the public forum, specific policies for fulfilling non-absolute, affirmative social responsibilities? Or is the promoting of such policies rather something which a bishop *may* do, if and when in his prudent judgment doing so will achieve some good for the sake of which he is prepared to accept bad side-effects such as I have indicated?

Philosophical reflections can do no more than pose the question. But they can extend to one final observation.

Suppose that bishops made the prudential judgment and decision *not* to "shape a comprehensive social agenda"[75]—i.e. *not* to accept, save in exceptional cases, the bad side-effects of participation in political debates, or the contest of candidates, about specific policies on the national issues listed in Cardinal Bernardin's discourses: Such a decision would not imply that the many Catholic lay people have erred, who have regarded such participation as squarely within their own personal competence and vocation in faith—and thus as among *their* affirmative obligations—and who in many cases have sought to work together, giving joint and public witness to that faith in doing so.

Notes*

1. Cardinal Joseph Bernardin, in the discourses listed below. The phrase has, however, an episcopal pre-history in e.g. Archbishop Medeiros's 1971 address, "A Call to a Consistent Ethic of Life and the Law," *Pilot*, 10 July 1971, 7, noted in Richard A. McCormick SJ, *Notes on Moral Theology 1965 through 1980* (University Press of America, Washington DC, 1981), 399. Cardinal Bernardin's discourses are cited herein by number, as follows; page numbers in ( ) refer to this volume.

> 1: Fordham University (Gannon Lecture), 6 December 1983, *Origins* 13 (1983) 491-4; (1-11).

> 2: University of Chicago, 16 January 1984, *Origins* 13 (1984) 566-9

> 3: St. Louis University (Wade Lecture), 11 March 1984, 33 *Origins* 13 (1984) 705-9; (12-19).

> 4: Kansas City (National Right to Life Convention), 7 June 1984, *Origins* 14 (1984) 120-2; (20-26).

> 5: Cincinnati (National Consultation on Obscenity, Pornography and Indecency), 6 September 1984; (27-35).

> 6: Georgetown University, 25 October 1984, *Origins* 14 (1984) 321-8

> 7: Report to U.S. bishops on Committee for Pro-Life Activities, 14 November 1984, *Origins* 14 (1984) 397-8

> 8: Catholic University of America, 17 January 1985; (36-48)

> 9: University of Missouri, 7 March 1985, *Origins* 14 (1985) 759-61

> 10: Loyola University, Chicago, 8 May 1985, *Origins* 15 (1985) 36-40; (49-58).

> 11: Criminal Court of Cook County (Criminal Law Committee), 14 May 1985; (59-65).

> 12: University of Notre Dame, 1 October 1985, *Origins* 14 (1985) 306-8

> 13: Seattle University, 2 March 1985, *Origins* 15 (1986) 655-8; (77-85).

> 14: Catholic Medical Center, Jamaica, New York, 18 May 1986; (66-76).

> 15: University of Portland, Oregon, 4 October 1986, *Origins* 16 (1986) 345-50; (86-94).

2. See, e.g. 9:759. Such an ethic is "needed": 1:493(7); 3:707(14).

*All materials in brackets [ ] were added after the Symposium.

3. Sometimes this pre-supposition surfaces, more or less clearly: e.g. 10:40(58) on the framework for moral analysis provided by the consistent ethic of life which is "primarily a theological concept, derived from biblical and ecclesial tradition."

4. 13:657(83).

5. 15:347(88).

6. 1:493(9), see also 2:568-9 on "setting an atmosphere" in society; 3:708(17) on a "systemic vision of life" which "seeks to expand the moral imagination of a society"; 4:122(25) on "the need to cultivate within society an attitude of respect for life" and to "build a network of mutual concern for defense of life"; 5:11(34) on the "comprehensive moral vision which the consistent ethic of life promotes"; 6:325 on the "posture" to be developed in the "analytical setting" of the seamless garment; and 6:326 on the effort "to 'see' the helpless among us"; 8:4(39) on the need to "make space for the faces of the poor...in the public agenda"; 9:761 on creating "space in the public debate"; 10:38(52) on "quality-of-life posture"; 11:3(61) on the need to respond to "all the moments, places or conditions which either threaten the sanctity of life or cultivate an attitude of disrespect for it"; 13:656(77ff)) and 658(77ff) on developing a "moral vision," and 657(77ff) on the consistent ethic's "function...to gather a constituency" against certain social forces; 15:348(86) on the desperate need for a "societal attitude or climate that will sustain a consistent defense and promotion of life," given that it is attitude that determines social policies and practices.

7. See 11:10(65); 14:5(69).

8. On the urgent desirability of Catholic consensus on these issues, see 1:493-4(10); 13:656-8(77ff).

9. 13: 658(77ff). See also, e.g., 6:327; 8:12(47).

10. 14:16(76); see also 10:40(58).

11. 15:348(91).

12. E.g. Matt. 19:19; 22:39, 6:33.

13. For much fuller discussion of the ground, sense, and force of the first moral principle, see Finnis, Boyle and Grisez, *Nuclear Deterrence, Morality and Realism* (Oxford University Press, Oxford and New York, 1987), 282-4; Grisez, Boyle, and Finnis, "Practical Principles, Moral Truth, and Ultimate Ends," *American J. Jurisprudence* 32 (1987), secs. VII-VIII.

14. "Treat others the way you would have them treat you": Matt. 7:12; Lk. 6:31.

15. For a clarification of this intuitively obvious relationship between the first moral principle and the Golden Rule, see Finnis, Boyle and Grisez, *Nuclear Deterrence,* 285. On other intermediate principles such as this, see ibid., 287-7; Grisez, *Christian Moral Principles* (Franciscan Herald P., Chicago, 1984), chs. 8, 10; Finnis, *Fundamentals of Ethics* (Georgetown U.P., Washington DC, 1983, 1986), 68-76.

16. Cf. Gal. 5:14; Rom. 13:9; Matt. 22:39-40.

17. Throughout, I mean by "(moral) absolutes" specific, exceptionless moral norms which exclude types of act described or describable without evaluative terms and without reference to further circumstances and motives falling outside the description: e.g. "Adultery (sexual intercourse with one not one's spouse) is always wrong." This is the sense in which the term "absolute" is used in Cardinal Bernardin's discourses, too: e.g. 13:656(77ff). [Like the rest of Catholic moral doctrine, the teaching that some specific but universal norms are absolute is proposed and transmitted on the basis not of some natural law philosophy but of the sources mentioned in the teaching's recent magisterial reaffirmation (in the post- Synodal Apostolic Exhortation *Reconciliatio et Paenitentia* (1984) para. 17): "there exist acts which, *per se* and in themselves, independently of circumstances, are always seriously wrong by reason of their

object... This doctrine, based on the Decalogue and on the preaching of the Old Testament, and assimilated into the *kerygma* of the Apostles and belonging to the earliest teaching of the Church, and constantly reaffirmed by her to this day...".]

18. See, e.g., Richard A. McCormick SJ in McCormick and Ramsey, *Doing Evil to Achieve Good: Moral Choice in Conflict Situations* (Loyola U.P., Chicago, 1978), 261-3; id., *Health and Medicine in the Catholic Tradition: Tradition in Transition* (Crossroads, New York, 1984), 131-2; Josef Fuchs SJ, *Christian Faith in a Secular Arena* (Georgetown U.P., Washington DC, 1984), 82-4; id., "Christian Faith and the Disposing of Human Life," *Theological Studies* 46 (1985) 664 at 678-9, 681-2. I believe that Charles E. Curran was correct in stating, already in 1973, that "there is a sizable and growing number of Catholic theologians who do disagree with some aspects of the officially proposed Catholic teaching that direct abortion from the time of conception is always wrong": Curran, *New Perspectives in Moral Theology* (Fides, Notre Dame, Ind., 1974), 193; for Curran's own view, then, that abortion is justifiable in certain cases of grave harm (including psychological harm) to the mother, and of rape, see ibid., 191-2. I believe that the 97 clerical, religious, and other signatories of the "Catholic Statement on Pluralism and Abortion" in the *New York Times,* 7 October 1984 (reprinted *New York Times,* 2 March 1986, E-24) were correct in stating that "A large number of Catholic theologians hold that even direct abortion, though tragic, can sometimes be a moral choice."

19. [No more than Vatican II or Trent or the Popes does Cardinal Bernardin propose a teaching such as "Directly killing the innocent is always wrong" for acceptance as being the "conclusion" of the "deductive systematic method" of some natural law theory or social ethics. *No* part of the Catholic ethic has been authoritatively proposed in such a fashion. An old-fashioned consensus of theologians like Francis Huerth SJ or Gerald Kelly SJ explained Catholic moral teachings with bad philosophical arguments; the philosophical arguments deployed against those teachings by new-style moral theologians like Scholz, Schueller, Fuchs, Knauer, Janssens, *et al.*, are at least as bad as their predecessors'. Yet the teachings remain matter for a non-fallacious philosophical reflection, which not only defends them against ungrounded criticisms but also could make them more accessible and fruitful.]

20. 4:121(23); also 1:493(8) ("the principle which prohibits the directly intended taking of innocent human life" as "always wrong"); 3:708(16) ("the prohibition against direct attacks on innocent life"; "this principle is...central to the Catholic moral vision"); 13:657(77ff) (the "absolute prohibition" "against the intentional killing of the innocent").

21. United States Catholic Conference, *The Challenge of Peace: God's Promise and Our Response* (1983), paras 104, 105 (emphasis added); see also paras. 148, 332.

22. 15:347(89); see also 10:37(51); 14:3(68).

23. See 13:656(81).

24. [Note that I say the "traditionally stated exception." On a more adequate account of moral absolutes, which Aquinas *sometimes* uses, cases such as Abraham and Isaac, even using the mediaeval exegesis, are *not* to be considered as "exceptions" to or "dispensations" from the moral absolutes of the Decalogue, but are rather cases in which God so changed the usual conditions in which the relevant act was chosen that the choice fell outside the moral absolute against killing, which is thus truly *exceptionless.* See the comprehensive explanation in Patrick Lee. "Permanence of the Ten Commandments: St. Thomas and His Modern Commentators," *Theol. St.* 42 (1981) 422-443. There is here no question, as Walter gratuitously asserts, of "requir[ing] the divine to intervene and direct personal conscience" in order to remedy some unspecified essential lack in creation.]

25. Finnis, Boyle and Grisez, *Nuclear Deterrence,* 87-8.

26. Thus Pius XII, Address to the Italian Catholic Union of Midwives, 29 October 1951, 43 *AAS* (1951) 838-9: "...no man, ...no...'indication'...can show or give a valid juridical title for *direct* deliberate disposition concerning an innocent human life—which is to say, a disposition that aims at its destruction either as an end in itself, or as a means of attaining another

end that is perhaps in no way illicit in itself... for example, to save the life of the mother... a most noble end...". The equivalence, in this context, of "direct" and "as an end or as a means" is clearly stated in Pius XII, Discourse to the St. Luke Medical-Biological Union, 12 November 1944 (*Discorsi e Radiomessagi* VI (1944-45) 191-2, cited in Paul VI, *Humanae Vitae*, note 14, and in the Congregation for the Doctrine of the Faith, *Declaration on Procured Abortion*, 18 November 1974, 66 *AAS* (1974) 735, para. 7 at note 15 ("Pius XII clearly excluded all direct abortion, that is, abortion which is either an end or a means"); also in S.C.D.F., *Donum Vitae*, 22 February 1987, at note 20. The phrase "directly intended," sometimes used by Cardinal Bernardin [e.g. 1:493(8)], is an uneasy combination of two traditional ways of speaking.

27. E.g. McCormick in McCormick and Ramsey, *Doing Evil to Achieve Good*, 255; id., *Notes on Moral Theology 1965-1980*, 506; Fuchs, *Christian Ethics in a Secular Arena*, 79. [McCormick's paper says that any rule or principle using the term "direct" is "not clear in one of its most relevant and urgent terms; for Germain Grisez's understanding is certainly not that of popes and theologians who appealed to the rule." But if one referred to Grisez's writings since 1966, one would see that he understands "directly willed" in just the terms I mentioned: intended as an end or chosen as a means. There are cases where it's not easy to say whether some occurrence or state of affairs is included within the means, and where Grisez has suggested (for the reflection, not the practical guidance, of Christians) one or two applications of the term "means" marginally different from those proposed by the Holy Office and the pre-Vatican II *consensus theologorum*. But in most of its applications, the term "means," and thus the term "direct," remain all too clear for the comfort of those who dislike their implications. As with the letter "a," or the color orange, or the term *human*, there are marginal cases where we're not sure whether to apply the term or not, but the concept of the letter "a," or of the color orange, or of humanity, remains in each case clear and in many central cases indisputable in its application; such terms are fit for use in definitive teaching, as when the Church teaches that Christ died for all humankind although one might legitimately wonder whether monsters or day-old embryos fall within the reference of the term "humankind."]

28. For a much fuller philosophical exposition, see Finnis, Boyle and Grisez, *Nuclear Deterrence*, 288-91; Finnis, "The Act of the Person" in [Proceedings of the Congress of Moral Theology, Rome, 1986 (forthcoming)], sec. IV and V (the latter section includes a detailed critique of the positions of Bruno Schueller and Richard McCormick which deny the *per se* moral significance of this distinction).

29. Decree on Justification, canon 6, DS 1556. [Walter thinks it curious that I omitted the last words of the canon; but they add nothing relevant here, and their omission conceals nothing— it is obvious that Trent is here concerned with God's responsibility for sin ("man's power to make his ways evil"). See further notes 31 and 38.]

30. [This is one of the passages which Walter cites to illustrate his astonishing thesis that I presuppose a priority of will over intellect. Such a priority is inconceivable, in my view, since the *will* manifested in upright intentions is nothing other than a pursuit of what *intellect* identifies as reasonable. In none of the passages mentioned by Walter is there any question of the relationship between intellect and will. See further note 39.]

31. [On God's foresight and permission of evils he does not per se intend or will, see Aquinas, *de Veritate* 5, 4 ad 11; *ST* I, 19, 9 ad 3; 49, 2c; I-II, 39, 2 ad 3; 79, 1-4. (The "direct"-"indirect" *terminology*, in the sense used by the modern magisterium, emerges long after Aquinas, who conveys it with terms such as *per se* as opposed to *per accidens, praeter intentionem*, etc.) Behind Aquinas lie Augustine and John Damascene. [Walter thinks that *ST* I, 19, 9c establishes that Aquinas thought "God wills (*vult*) the evil of natural defect...". My reason for citing here the ad 3 to that article was precisely to indicate to careful readers that a reading such as Walter's of the body of the article utterly falsifies Aquinas' thought; for in the ad 3 Aquinas adds two essential precisions, (i) that the *only* sense in which God wills natural defect is that he *wills to permit them*, and (ii) that God does *not* choose even non-moral evils whether as ends *or as means* (not even "for the sake of the preservation of the natural order"), but only *permits* them by a *providentia concessionis*. See generally Lee, "Permanence of the Ten Commandments...", *Theol. St.* 42 (1981) 422 at 435-6.] [Walter also here claims that "throughout the *Summa*" the meaning of *per se* is "for the sake of itself" as opposed to "for the sake of something else." This too is a very serious mistake: start the very long list of

counterexamples with II- II, 64, 8c where what is willed or intended *per se* (i.e. either as end or as means) is contrasted with what is willed or intended *per accidens* or *casualiter*.]

32. If one says:

"When human life is considered 'cheap' or easily expendable in one area, eventually nothing is held as sacred and all lives are in jeopardy." (15:348(89)) one will—*unless one differentiates between event/happening and human choice/doing*—be met with the thought that since we tolerate many deaths for the sake of rapid to-ing and fro-ing on our roads (and do little to eliminate infant mortality in Africa), we cannot consistently regard human life as sacred and therefore can, in consistency, choose to kill for the sake of alleviating misery or poverty or discrimination between rich and poor or whatever other value is felt to be at least as weighty as rapid transit.

33. [In the most comprehensive misunderstanding of my ethical theory which I have ever encountered, Walter attributes to me a thesis which I have regularly denied and which has no even remote counterpart in my writings. According to this thesis, I assume (without proof or argument) that the basic human goods are moral goods; or alternatively, I attribute a moral significance to them because I "identify the creative and moral aspects of God's will vis-á-vis the basic human goods" and so assume that "the mere fact of [the basic goods'] existence as such must also constitute the moral will of God for humanity." Walter repeats this claim again and again, but it is sheer invention; in my fundamental ethical work, *Natural Law and Natural Rights* (Oxford U.P., Oxford and New York, 1980), I regularly repeat and adopt Aquinas' position that the will of God for creatures (including humankind) cannot be discovered by reasoning and so (I say) cannot be appealed to in any philosophical argument about basic goods, or about the moral significance of those goods (which in themselves are not "moral goods": pp. 59, 101) as that significance is rationally expressed in the requirements of practical reasonableness, and the specific moral norms (pp. 49, 130, 403-4). So too, here, the clarification of the norm against choosing to kill the innocent makes no appeal, however covert, to the will of God, creative or moral.]

34. [Note the word "includes." Contrary to Walter's assertion I never "define" the material of the Kingdom and never claim that it is moral selves that "make up" that material. As the texts cited in the next note make clear, the point *for which* one acts uprightly is *not* the shaping of one's moral self which might endure into the Kingdom, but the this-worldly realization or protection of human goods in persons (e.g. "what actions do to and for people in conflict situations"). What the proportionalists overlook, however, is that the *effect* of such choices includes the reflexive effects on the character of the chooser, effects which are real (even when the hoped- for this-worldly effects of the choice fail to be realized), and potentially everlasting, and incapable of being commensurated in the way that any non-irrationalist proportionalism requires. As Vatican II states (*GS* 39), The material and growth of the Kingdom, "must be carefully distinguished from earthly progress," notwithstanding the Christian ethic's vital concern for such progress.]

35. See Grisez, *Christian Moral Principles*, 50-9; Karol Wojtyla, *The Acting Person* (Reidel, Dordrecht, 1979), 149-52; Finnis, *Fundamentals of Ethics*, 136-42.

36. Dworkin, *Law's Empire* (Harvard U.P., 1989), chs. 6-7.

37. [See also the excellent account by Joseph Boyle, "The Principle of Double Effect: Good Actions Entangled in Evil," in Donald G. McCarthy (ed.), *Moral Theology Today: Certitudes and Doubts* (Pope John Center, Saint Louis, Missouri, 1984), 250-251. The interpretation of this passage offered by McCormick is simply confused, and impossible.]

38. For, e.g. Richard A. McCormick's rejection of the moral relevance of the traditional distinction in all cases of causing "non-moral evil," see McCormick and Ramsey, *Doing Evil to Achieve Good*, 254-65. As McCormick admits and explains (258-9), this makes it difficult to understand why the same direct-indirect distinction is vital in the case—where both he and Bruno Schüeller wished to retain it—of inducing another to act wrongfully. [Walter, in speaking of "Finnis' allegations," simply overlooked this note, and further seems to have overlooked the pages I here cite, in which McCormick with commendable frankness lays bare the

fragility of Schueller's position which he had summarized on the page cited by Walter; what McCormick is rightly observing is that proportionalists lack any *reason* to preserve the direct-indirect distinction in relation to moral evil. The point has been noticed by many secular philosophers, e.g. Samuel Scheffler, *The Rejection of Consequentialism* (Clarendon Press, Oxford, 1982), ch.4 and works there cited. Consider the case where one can confidently judge that, by inducing someone to commit adultery (or a murder) with full freedom and deliberation, one will prevent a number of murders.]

39. See also Finnis, *Fundamentals of Ethics,* 80-120. [The arguments of those pages, and of the chapter from *Nuclear Deterrence, Morality and Realism* cited in the text, establish the irrationalism implicit in Walter's assertion that moral good can be "discerned" "after all the various goods (non-moral values) and evils (non-moral disvalues) are assessed." No rational justification for, or even explanation of, such "discernment" can be offered; and what is freely asserted is freely denied, as we illustrate at great length in relation to the rival "discernments" of the risks and benefits of nuclear deterrence. There is no question of my "distrusting" human reason or intellect or believing that "reason cannot... make reasonable distinctions where they exist" (I simply deny, with reasons, possibility of making rationally the distinctions which the proportionalists claim to "discern" without reasons); nor am I interested in "erecting moral absolutes in reason's place to guard against the uncertainties and potential abuses of human moral discernment and judgment"— which is precisely the task explicitly undertaken by McCormick and other proportionalists: see note 51 below.]

40. The Pastoral Letter, *The Challenge of Peace* explains the proper sense of "proportionate" and "disproportionate," with helpful philosophical precision (after affirming a principle—"no end can justify means evil in themselves, such as the executing of hostages"—which in proportionalist thought is false or devoid of relevant meaning):

> "even if the means adopted is not evil in itself, it is necessary to take into account the probable harms that will result from using it *and the justice of accepting those harms.*" (para. 105, emphasis added).

The paragraph continues, very pertinently:

> "It is of the utmost importance, in assessing harms *and the justice of accepting them,* to think about the poor and the helpless, for they are usually the ones who have the least to gain and the most to lose when war's violence touches their lives." (para. 105, emphasis added)

41. [I of course do not assert, as Walter claims, that the latter two proposals are part of the proportionalist project; they are merely analogous instances of plausible-sounding incoherence, *like* proposals to identify the overall greater pre-moral good in situations of morally significant choice.]

42. Bartholomew M. Keily SJ, "The Impracticality of Proportionalism," *Gregorianum* 66 (1985) 655-86, rightly emphasizes proportionalism's failure to take coherently into account the reflexive or immanent consequences of human acts.

43. See, e.g., Scheffler, *The Rejection of Consequentialism,* 7-10, 41-70, attempting to accommodate the arguments in J.J.C. Smart and Bernard Williams, *Utilitarianism: For and Against* (Cambridge U.P., Cambridge and New York, 1973), 116-7; Williams, *Moral Luck* (Cambridge and New York, 1981), 40-53; cf. also Derek Parfit, *Reasons and Persons* (Clarendon P., Oxford and New York, 1984), 24-8, 42-3.

44. [To understand *choice* is also to understand the acting *persons* who constitute themselves most fundamentally through their free choice in serious issues. Underlying the difference between the consistent Catholic ethic and the consequentialist or proportionalist transformations of it are differences in conceptions of the person—just as the difference between the Catholic ethics of sex-life and proposed transformations of that ethic is traceable not to any contrast between "nature" and "person" but to contrasting conceptions of the person. Thus the foundational consideration in the CDF's March 1987 Instruction on AIH and husband-wife IVF is not at all what McCormick's paper asserts. For that foundational consideration con-

cerns not biological facticity, nor an "intention of nature" forbidding the separation of unitive and procreative, but a conception of the dignity of the person, that is of the child as "equal in personal dignity to those who give him life" and therefore as "not to be desired or conceived as a product," not to be *made* as *object*, in that relationship of domination which necessarily exists between *maker* and *made* and which is "per se contrary to the dignity and equality that must be common to parents and children": *Donum vitae* (1987) II.B.4-5. The human and personal good being defended by the Catholic teaching against manufacturing babies is that basic good of inter*personal* harmony which is the ground and substance of justice, friendship, and charity, and the root of the consistent ethic. This is one of the respects in which Catholic teaching on sex-life ethics has appropriated more and more deeply its understanding of the absolutes entrusted to it by the New Testament and the tradition, by a fifty-year development involving collaborative discussion going far beyond past statements and earlier *consensus theologorum*—a course of development which is, *pace* McCormick, even more "biblical, communal, dynamic, personal" than the development of Catholic *social doctrine* (as, *pace* McCormick, it's called in all the relevant Vatican II documents and very many magisterial statements, not to mention Puebla itself, down to today).]

45. *ScG* II, 89; *ST* I, 118, 2; *de Pot.* 3, 9 & 12.

46. *ST* II-II, 64, 7c: "it is wrongful for one human being to intend to kill another, for the sake of defending himself." Cf. note 49 below. See also Grisez, "Toward a Consistent Natural-Law Ethics of Killing," *Am. J. Juris.* 15 (1970) 64 at 73-9; Finnis, *Fundamentals of Ethics*, 131.

47. [Thus Scholz and McCormick are simply mistaken to treat the fleeing horseman's trampling of the blind and crippled as a *means* to his escape. That trampling in no way assists his purpose, is no part of his proposal—it succeeds totally even if the hooves miss every one of these potential victims. What he cannot do—and this is the source of Scholz's confusion—is *ignore* the effects he's accepting by choosing to flee down this occupied road. The distinction between object and side-effects, between choice and acceptance, is not a carte blanche; there remains the question posed in the manualists' ambiguous work "proportionality," as in the fourth of their fourfold set of conditions of legitimate "double effect." The question they were posing amounts to this. *Granted* that what is not chosen, but merely accepted, falls outside the principle that evil may not be done for the sake of good—more broadly, the principle that one must never *choose* to destroy, damage or impede any instantiation of any basic good of any human person—still there remain all the other relevant moral principles derivable from the first principle of love: e.g. the principle of fairness, or the principle that one should carry out one's commitments, and so forth. So, *if* we revolt at the horseman's act, it is because we regard it as deeply unfair to those whom he allows to be subordinated to a self-interested purpose of escape. (Here Fr van Beeck's proposed norm, "No self-serving killing, has its place, *alongside* the norm against direct killing.) The scenario is not, however, described with enough precision to know whether or not the horseman's purpose is self-interested, his action with its side-effects unfair, or our appropriate reaction one of revulsion. One thing is clear: the question is not decided by showing that what was done and accepted was done and accepted with reluctance. All manner of wickedness is done with reluctance, in that emotional sense "unwillingly" and even "disapprovingly"—but yet with full reflection and freedom, by the free choices which constitute the human *heart* with which Christian morality is through and through concerned. (One chooses to perform abortions, reluctantly and disapprovingly, because that is the only way to become a successful obstetrician and gynaecologist these days...)]

48. Augustine Regan CSsR, "The Worth of Human Life," *Studia Moralia* 6 (1968) 207-77 at 241-2; id. *Thou Shalt Not Kill* (Mercier, Dublin, 1979), 77-9, argues that this restriction is implicit in the main Christian just-war tradition as it emerged once an essentially punitive conception of the justice of war began to break down with the rise of nation states in the sixteenth century.

49. *ST* II-II, 65, 2c; see also I-II, 95, 2c. In II-II, 64, 7c he allows the rightness of a public official intending harm (to kill) by way of suppressing activity which, if completed, would be worthy of punishment; cf. 64, 2 ad 3 (note the objection to which this is a reply); 65, 2c; *in II Sent.*, dist. 42, q. 1, a.2c. He does not adequately show that it is acceptable for such an official, for justice's sake, to have an intention different from private citizens' intention in legitimately

defending themselves, viz. to repel the unjust attack by all necessary means, even means foreseeably certain to cause death (in which case the killing is a side-effect of the morally significant choice).

50. McCormick, "Notes on Moral Theology: 1984," *Theol. St.* 46 (1985) at 52 n.4, says of this retributive notion of punishment, as advanced in my *Fundamentals of Ethics,* 128-35: "One must ask whether such a notion makes any Christian sense." He omits to mention that the notion is not peculiar to me but (as I showed, ibid., p. 135) is the notion advanced by St. Thomas (*ST* I-II, 87, 6c; *S.c.G.* III, c. 140, para.5; c. 146, para.1), a moralist whom McCormick frequently invokes as a sound embodiment of Christian sense. Pius XII judged this retributive conception to be, indeed, *the* Christian conception of just punishment: Discourse to the Sixth Congress of Penal Law, *AAS* 45 (1953) 739ff.

51. See, e.g., J. Bryan Hehir in Gessert and Hehir, *The New Nuclear Debate* (Council on Religion and International Affairs, New York, 1976), 48-9, 92. More elaborately, Richard A. McCormick has argued that the norm prohibiting direct killing of non-combatants in warfare is "a law established on the presumption of common and universal danger," viz. the danger arising from "human failure, inconstancy, and frailty, and our uncertainty with regard to long-term effects." See McCormick and Ramsey, *Doing Evil to Achieve Good* (1978), 44-5; see also 227, 232, 251-3, 261 on our, or the Church's, "adoption" of a hierarchy of values, as the basis for "exception-making." On this "teleological character of exception-making," see also McCormick, "Notes on Moral Theology: 1984" 46 *Theol. St.* (1985) at 51, 54.

52. See 13:656-7(80). Certain of the Cardinal's formulations of the issue can, moreover, arouse rather than allay misunderstanding: e.g. "Nor can we allow the moral principle protecting innocent life be subordinated to other claims *because the consequences of such a process would not be confined to abortion.*" 6:325, emphasis added.

53. For a critical examination of one influential theologian's attempt to find a limiting principle, see my *Fundamentals of Ethics,* 99-104; Grisez, *Christian Moral Principles,* 161-4.

54. On the inevitable reduction of proportionalism to rationalization, see Finnis, *Fundamentals of Ethics,* 94-105.

55. 1:493(8-9) (emphasis added); re-affirmed in 13:657(77ff); see also 10:38(52); 14:6(69-70).

56. Cardinal Bernardin has alluded to this distinction, but only in rather generic terms. He has repeated that "a consistent ethic of life does not equate the problem of taking life (e.g. through abortion and war) with the problem of promoting human dignity (through humane programs of nutrition, health care and housing)" (3:707(15); also 13:657(77ff)). And he has stressed the "analogical" character of the consistent ethic, and its irreducibility to a single type of problem (2:568; 5:707(17-18); 10:37(51); 15:348(81))).

57. 13:657(83).

58. See *ST* I-II, 95, 2c.

59. An exception now relates to the act of suicide (as distinct from assisting another to commit suicide), which can be regarded as having no *necessary* direct implications for justice (fairness). In other respects, the dominant trend of modern American and English legal thought and policy is tightening the coextensiveness of the legal and moral judgment on homicide. Where nineteenth and early twentieth century law defined as murderous *any* death-causing act done in the course of committing felony, and in other circumstances allowed juries to find intention on the basis that a *reasonable* man would have *foreseen* death as a consequence of his actions, the modern law tends more and more to reject these divergences from the moral conception of murder, i.e. of intentionally causing death. The process of assimilating the law of murder to the ethics of murder is not quite complete, insofar as, e.g., *foresight* of the likelihood of causing grievous bodily harm (short of death), is treated as an "intent" sufficient to sustain a charge of murder.

60. Thus our law continues to accept not only that consequentialist rationalizations of choices to kill give no moral ground for admitting such choices, but also that human acts must be analyzed in much the same way as I sketched in Part I. Indeed, such an act analysis—identifying ends and means in proposals adopted for choice, and distinguishing both ends and means from side-effects foreseen and caused but not part of the proposal adopted by choice—gives an unsurpassedly adequate theoretical account and explanation of almost all the actual decisions of Anglo-American courts concerning intention and *mens rea* in homicide, though not yet of all decisions nor of the terminology used and accounts offered by many judges and legislators. Similarly, the law accepts what a sound analysis of intention proposes, in relation to omissions, namely that one who has an affirmative responsibility such as feeding the hungry *can* choose to make non-fulfillment of that responsibility a *means* of killing by omission, in which case the violation of the moral and legal absolute forbidding intentional killing of innocents.

61. See, e.g. Joseph Fletcher, *Morals and Medicine* (Beacon, Boston, 1960), 211: "...the body and its members, our organs and their functions—all of these *things* are a part of what is over against us...". For reflections on the influence of such dualism amongst certain influential Catholics, see Grisez, *Christian Moral Principles*, 198 with n. 42 thereto. For philosophical critique, see ibid., 137-8; Germain Grisez and Joseph Boyle, *Life and Death with Liberty and Justice: A Contribution to the Euthanasia Debate* (Notre Dame U.P., 1979), 372-8; Finnis, Boyle and Grisez, *Nuclear Deterrence*, 304-9.

62. See the citations to, and quotations from Glanville Williams, Joseph Fletcher, Michael Tooley, and H. Tristram Engelhardt Jr., in Grisez and Boyle, *Life and Death with Liberty and Justice*, 218-220, 488-9. See further, e.g., Jonathan Glover, *Causing Deaths and Saving Lives* (Penguin, Harmondsworth, 1977), 154-69; Peter Singer, *Practical Ethics* (Cambridge and New York, 1979); Michael Tooley, *Abortion and Infanticide* (Oxford U.P., Oxford and New York, 1983); John Harris, *The Value of Life: An Introduction to Medical Ethics [Routledge and Kegan Paul, London and Boston, 1985]*, chs. 1, 2, 4, 5.

63. See, e.g. the testimony of eminent and influential English and Scottish physicians at the trial of *Regina* v. *Arthur* (November 1981), quoted in Linacre Centre Report, *Euthanasia and Clinical Practice* (Linacre Centre, London, 1982), 86-7. Cf. also Richard A. McCormick SJ, "To Save or Let Die: The Dilemma of Modern Medicine," *J. Am. Med. Ass.* 229 (1974) 172 at 175; A. R. Jonsen, SJ, and others, "Critical Issues in Newborn Intensive Care: A Conference Report and Policy Proposal," *Pediatrics* 55 (1975) 756 at 760-62; McCormick, "A Proposal of 'Quality of Life' Criteria for Sustaining Life," *Hospital Progress*, 56 (September 1975) 79.

64. E.g. Harris, *The Value of Life*, 29-47.

65. The classic exposition of this matter remains Aquinas, *ST* I-II, 95, 2 on *determinations* (as contrasted with quasi- deductive applications) of natural law; see also 99, 3 ad 2; 100, 3 ad 2; Finnis, *Natural Law and Natural Rights* (Oxford U. P., Oxford and New York, 1980, 1986), 281-90, 294-5; "The Authority of Law in the Predicament of Contemporary Social Theory," *Notre Dame J. Law, Ethics and Public Policy* 1 (1984) 115-37; "On 'The Critical Legal Studies Movement'," *American J. Jurisprudence* 30 (1985) 21-42.

66. The passage continues: "They [moral values] must interact with empirical data, with historical, social, and political realities, and with competing demands on limited resources. The soundness of our prudential judgments depends not only on the moral force of our principles, but also on the accuracy of our information and the validity of our assumptions." One must add that prudential judgments can be sound without being correct (or incorrect); for many of the necessary "assumptions" relate to future consequences which are simply indeterminate and unknowable, not least because they involve the future free choices of many people. Thus there can be, and often are, alternative and *competing* sound prudential judgments on one and the same issue.

67. Their ultimate personal culpability is another matter, which their fellow citizens cannot reasonably be concerned to assess.

68. For a discussion showing the complexity of an accurate analysis of ends, means, and side-effects in some voting-situations, see Finnis, Boyle and Grisez, *Nuclear Deterrence*, 344-7, 357-62.

69. Cf. Richard A. McCormick, SJ, "Medicaid and Abortion," *Theol. St.* 45 (1984) 715 at 716-17. Germain Grisez, "Public Funding of Abortion: A Reply to Richard A. McCormick, S.J.," *Homiletic and Pastoral Review* 85.9 (June 1985) 32, 45-51, carefully demonstrates the point made above.

70. See e.g. 1:493(8); 6:327; 8:12(43); 14;6(70).

71. See 8:12. Cf., similarly, *Economic Justice for All*, para. 20: "we feel obliged to teach by example how Christians can undertake concrete analysis and make specific judgments on economic issues."

72. This seems at least implicitly suggested by Cardinal Bernardin, when he says that the Pastoral Letter's "most stringent [and] binding" conclusions is that "directly intended attack [] on civilian centers is always wrong," and that this "conclusion" or "principle" has two "implications" or "extensions": "such attacks would be wrong even if our cities had been hit first," and "anyone asked to execute such attacks should refuse the orders" [1:493(8)].

73. It is alleged that the Ad Hoc Committee which drafted the Pastoral Letter on War and Peace adopted as a "firm groundrule" that "it would not, under any circumstances, support unilateral nuclear disarmament": Jim Castelli, *The Bishops and the Bomb* (Doubleday, New York, 1983), 79. The book making this allegation is not fully reliable. I do not suggest that the motives of such a decision, if it were made or proposed, were anything other than a sincere belief that unilateral renunciation of nuclear deterrence is not morally justifiable. The eventual Pastoral Letter asserts (para. 333) that "surrender" is an "indefensible choice"; I do not deny that unilateral renunciation of nuclear deterrence would be tantamount to surrender, but I can discover no argument in the Letter which even attempts to justify the claim that unilateral renunciation is an indefensible choice. I am also among the many readers of the Letter who find it lacking any coherent argument for its apparent conclusions that the retention of a nuclear deterrent which includes (like all existing and foreseeable Western deterrents) proposals for counter-value retaliation can be a morally defensible choice.

74. The difficulties confronting a bishop in assessing specific policies for discharging complex sets of affirmative responsibilities are illustrated by the multiple mistakes made by the U.S. bishops in assessing U.S. nuclear deterrent policies in relation to the straightforward moral absolute which they called "discrimination" (and which they stated with precision and force). They failed to describe actual U.S. nuclear policy; they failed to attend to official and unofficial strategic writings which stress the need for a deterrent to include threats and plans to destroy cities as such for intra-war deterrence and for final retaliation; through inattention to the historical use and thus the meaning of the relevant formulae, they misinterpreted certain ambiguous formulae put before them by government officials intent on influencing their Letter; they confused targeting policy with strategic intent. (See Finnis, Boyle & Grisez, *Nuclear Deterrence*, 18-28, 36-8, 160-1, 172-4.) These are all the mistakes of *outsiders*. Truly prudential judgments are the judgments of insiders.

75. 13:658(83). See text at note 9 above.

Response to John C. Finnis: A Theological Critique

James J. Walter

Professor Finnis has organized Cardinal Bernardin's speeches on "the consistent ethic of life" around three distinct propositions. Though I will disagree later that "the consistent ethic" is fundamentally propositional in nature, nevertheless I will accept Finnis' structure to organize the first part of my response to his paper. In this first part I will offer a brief analysis of what I take to be Finnis' theological position on crucial issues, e.g., theology of creation and divine providence, that undergird and guide his rejection of proportionalism. By comparing his theological position on these issues with those of some proportionalists, I will indicate at a few selected points where Finnis appears to have fundamentally misrepresented the basic thrust of the proportionalist methodology. In the second part I will offer what I think Cardinal Bernardin intends by his "consistent ethic of life."

Part I:
An Analysis of Finnis' Position on
Proportionalism

It is hardly an overstatement to say that Finnis devotes a significant portion of his paper to a vigorous criticism of the proportionalist methodology. In fact, his entire analysis of CEP1 is taken up both with this discussion and his belief that the proportionalist method will severely hamper, or possibly destroy, Cardinal Bernardin's successful promotion of CEP1. (157) He notes that his "philosophical reflections will range" over the issues with "the freedom of the philosopher" (144) to offer "a clarification of the issues" (146) in order to provide Cardinal Bernardin with "the philosophical precision which Christian teaching, like Christian theology, has always sought." (143) Though it will be impossible to analyze all the allegations which Finnis has brought against proportionalists in this short space, I would argue that: his "freedom" has perhaps been too expansive in interpreting the texts he has used; his "clarifications" have really obscured the basic intent of the proportionalist methodology; and Finnis' "philosophical precision" has not always been accurate in providing Cardinal Bernardin with what proportionalists have in fact argued.

It may be helpful at the start simply to list the allegations which Finnis brings against proportionalism and its proponents. There are twenty-three in all: (1) Proportionalism (P) has re-read (150) and has watered-down the traditional understanding of direct-indirect for its own purposes (147), has denied the *per se* moral significance of the distinction (174, note 26), and thus has dispensed with the distiction (150); (2) P is anti-love because it makes choices against the basic goods of persons (149); (3) P is anti-persons because it weighs and balances persons by weighing and balancing the basic goods which are "not adequately distinct from persons" (152); (4) P is anti-life in its permission to kill directly the innocent (153); (5) P is anti-sanctity because it does not acknowledge human bodily life's sanctity (160); (6) by adopting a "quality of life" position (160) P does not acknowledge the equal dignity of every human person; (7) P is really consequentialism (150, 151, 152 160); (8) P is impracticable and impossible as a methodology because it attempts to commensurate "goods and bads which would be needed so to guide morally significant choice" (150); (9) P denies any relevant meaning to the phrase "no end can justify means evil in themselves" (177, note 40); (10) P is incoherent in that it seeks "to identify the largest natural number, or to prove any point provided it is the most obvious one" (151); (11) P is "grossly impressionistic and manifestly deniable" (151); (12) P is a radical challenge to and departure from the Catholic tradition's emphasis on God's providence (155); (13) P chooses whatever the individual is inclined toward and then indentifies this choice with God's providence (156); (14) P is concerned more with bringing about "this worldly results" than with depending on God's providence (156); (15) P seems to destroy the 'tradition's understanding of vocational life in its activism (156-157); (16) P's "method destroys but cannot build" (156); (17) P's method "yields nothing but mere rationalizations for doing what is chosen on some other ground—feelings, social conventions, etc." (157); (18) P is "inconsistent in its acknowledgment of the principles, norms and counsels taught in the tradition" (157); (19) P "generates an unbounded number of ethics" (157); (20) P "must dissolve whatever moral norms (of the tradition which) conflict with the surrounding culture" (157); (21) P is a form of "bad faith" (*mauvaise foi*) (166); (22) P promotes "bad character" in the way that it decides specific issues on abortion and its public funding (167); and thus (23) P is inconsistent with Cardinal Bernardin's CEP1 (157).

This is a formidable list, indeed! To respond to each one of these allegations would almost require the rewriting of the hundreds of pages that have been authored by proportionalists over the past two decades.[1] My intent here is not to defend proportionalism; rather it is to show on a few selected issues where Finnis has in fact misrepresented the theory on the basis of his own underlying theology.

Finnis' deontological normative theory, in which he grounds negative moral absolutes and from which he derives the first principle of morality, is clearly formulated, in part at least, on the basis of his adoption of a certain theology of creation and view of God's will and divine providence. In this view, the will of God as creator has established certain basic human goods which are definitive of human well-being, e.g., life, knowledge, friendship, etc. and which cannot be adequately distinguished from persons. (152) *God's moral will* can be discovered in the appreciation of and respect for these basic goods. In this regard, the creative and moral aspects of God's will appear to be identical. In other words, to discover God's *creative* will in these basic human goods is to discover God's *moral* will for human behavior. Divine providence, which is ultimately mysterious in that it is not all laid out before us (156), seeks the realization and protection of these basic created goods in the form of the eternal law. Whenever evil is done, which Finnis defines as the "destruction or damaging of a basic good of a person" (149 & 155), God's moral will can only by inclined permissively, that is, God never directly wills (*per se* or intends as an end or as a means) the destruction of created goods (including the innocent) for some other purpose but only permits (indirect), albeit with foresight, the evil associated with the divine or human action.

At this point, the implications of Finnis' position for human action become apparent. Our role is to place ourselves in the matrix of divine providence (156) in order to discover the *moral* will of God *in the created order* (the creative will of God). When we discover one of the basic human goods, we must, like the moral will of God, seek to protect it. If, however, our actions involve a destruction or damaging of one or other of these goods, then, like God's moral will, we can only permit the evil and not intend it either as an end or as a means. Moral absolutes, deontologically formulated, stand as human formulations of God's creative and moral will. These moral absolutes can involve some limited exceptions, but *all* the exceptions can only be authorized by God (146 & 153).

The authorization of the exceptions in this view is based on two theological beliefs: one is epistemological in nature, and the other is concerned with God's agency in the world. The first can be stated in Finnis' own words as "God knows what is for the best but we do not" (155), and the second entails the view that God, as lord over life and death, has reserved strictly to divine agency alone the authorization to kill the innocent. The latter position on divine agency not only construes creation as lacking something essential for its own self-realization and thus requires the divine to intervene and direct personal conscience,[2] but it also views the divine anthropomorphically as an agent *in the world* rather than *transcendent* to it.[3] In sum, if we violate the moral absolute of directly killing the innocent, we not only usurp divine providence in claiming to know what is best but also act from a defect of a right (*ex defectu juris in agente*).

If we look briefly at the theological views of those who have formulated the proportionalist methodology, we can bring into focus why Finnis would reject proportionalism and also how he has misrepresented some of its positions.

First, proportionalists reject Finnis' identification of the creative and moral aspects of God's will vis-á-vis the basic goods. The creative aspect of God's will may very well have willed certain basic goods to exist for the well-being of humanity, but to hold that the mere fact of their existence as such must also constitute the moral will of God for humanity is an unproven assertion. For example, God has evidently willed in creation that certain physical structures should exist for the transmission of life, but it cannot be assumed that the divine moral will necessarily and in every respect is revealed in those structures as such. Proportionalists are aware that Aquinas can define the natural moral law as a law of reason, and thus in one place in his *Summa* he can state quite clearly that "moral ends are accidental to a natural thing, and conversely the relation of a natural end to morality is accidental,"[4] and then later he can maintain that at the level of the natural law where animals and humans share the same basic tendencies God's *moral will* is revealed in the physical tendencies placed in both *at creation*.[5] The historical reasons why Aquinas held to two opposing views on the natural moral law do not concern us here, but what is important is that proportionalists have sought to correct this deficiency in Aquinas' theory.

The second point is that proportionalists understand the will's relation to evil quite differently from Finnis. To begin with, one must properly and clearly distinguish the will's relation toward non-moral evil and its relation toward moral evil. The texts of the tradition from which Finnis quotes, especially those of Aquinas and the Council of Trent, prohibit the willing *per se* of *moral* evil or *sin*. Two examples will serve to make my point that Finnis does not properly distinguish the two kinds of evil.

First, the quotation from Trent in Finnis' text curiously omits the final phrase of canon 6, viz., "so that Judas' betrayal no less that Paul's vocation was God's own work." Besides the fact that one should be careful in using a canon from a Council without also exegeting its historical context and doctrinal intent, it is surely the case that Trent considered such an act of betrayal on Judas' part as *sinful*, and thus God's will could have only permitted this! Second, Finnis quotes from Aquinas' *Summa*, I, q. 19, art. 9, but his references is to Aquinas' reply to the third objection, which is primarily concerned with refuting the erroneous position that God wills that evil should exist. However, in the body of this same article Aquinas clearly states that God wills (*vult*) the evil of natural defect, which is non-moral evil, for the purpose of preserving the natural order, but God in no way wills the evil of sin (*malum culpae*).[6]

Neither I nor any other proportionalist can see here how God's *moral* will is only disposed indirectly (in Finnis' sense) or permissively vis-à-vis non-moral evil (natural defect). The real issue, which Finnis seems to miss, is that God does not intend the evil of natural defect for the sake of itself (the meaning of *per se* for Aquinas throughout the *Summa*) but for the sake of something else (*propter aliud*) which is good, viz., that the natural order be preserved. The point is that the divine will, at least as far as Aquinas could surmise, can be disposed such that it chooses *non-moral* evil *as a means* in itself but not for the sake of itself, but God cannot intend *moral* evil (sin) either as a means or as an end. But because Finnis seems to have identified the creative and moral aspects of God's will as far as the basic human goods are concerned, he appears to believe that these goods are *moral* in themselves. Thus any action against them which is intended either as a means or as an end must entail that the agent's will adopt, embrace and integrate into itself [150] the *moral* evil of the destruction of a *moral* good. But this is a *petitio principii*; it begs the question because it assumes without any proof or argument that these goods are *moral* (in themselves because basic. One could still consider these goods basic without elevating them to the status of *moral*) goods. Thus, one could recognize that their importance for human well-being is more fundamental than other are, but they remain in themselves created goods like all other created realities, and as such they are non-moral.

If Finnis could cogently argue his point on the *moral* nature of the basic human goods, and thus why the creative and moral aspects of God's will are identical vis-à-vis *these certain* created goods *but not others*, then he might be correct in some of his allegations against proportionalism. His begging of this very important question has led him, though, to misrepresent what the proportionalists have really said.

Proportionalists do *not* allow the intending of a *moral* evil either as an end or as a means, but only allow an agent to permit such evil. As such, they do admit *in fact* the *moral* relevance of the traditional distinction between direct and indirect vis-à-vis moral evil, contrary to Finnis' allegations.[7] However, because they make a fundamental distinction between moral and non-moral evils, and because they do not grant that Finnis' basic human goods are *moral* goods in themselves, they argue that it is possible to intend a non-moral evil *in se sed non propter se*, i.e. in itself but not for the sake of itself. In other words, agents can intend the damaging of a created good (non-moral evil) *as a means* as long as this evil is proportionate to the value represented in the end, which is willed in and for the sake of itself. For proportionalists, it is only after all the various goods (non-moral values) and evil (non-moral disvalues) are assessed that the *moral* good can be discerned. This discernment, contrary to Finnis' allegations, is not the simple summing up of some natural number [150-151] or merely "the overall net pre-moral human value or disvalue involved in and resulting from the various alternatives available for choice." [150]

Finnis' theological position on the issues of moral epistemology, especially on the trustworthiness of human moral judgment, and eschatology (the relation between our human future and the Absolute future) also lie behind his rejection of the proportionalist methodology. In analyzing his position on these issues I will note briefly where Finnis again misstates what proportionalists have held.

Two anthropological presuppositions seem to control Finnis' position on moral epistemology. First, he clearly places Christians in a "subordinate human role as workers in the divine plan, who share in the eternal law without having it all laid before us." [156] The second presupposition entails giving a priority to the will over the intellect. This priority is evident at various places in his critique of proportionalism. Philosophically, he formulates the first principle of morality as "One ought to choose and otherwise will those and only those possibilities whose willing is *compatible with integral human fulfillment*." [144] He interprets Jesus' statement on the love of neighbor as oneself in terms of the *will* freed of egoism. [144] He claims that "Christian morality is more in the heart than in the results; one's intention (which emanates from the will) is morally more basic and important than any performance or behavior by which that intention is carried out." [148] And finally, his entire analysis of the distinction between direct and indirect revolves around the freedom of the will and the necessity of the human will to refrain from adopting, embracing and integrating evil into itself.

I would suggest that Finnis gives little weight to human reason's ability to discern the morally good, and this position on moral epistemology is not only compatible with but also one of the key sources of his deontological formulation of moral absolutes at the level of normative theory. By locating and emphasizing "the real matrix in which one's choosing and action have their most important significance" [156] in divine providence whereby "God knows what is for the best but we do not" [155], one must necessarily place human reason and moral judgment in subordinate roles. Because Finnis has identified the creative and moral aspects of God's will vis-à-vis the basic human goods, the role of reason with respect to these goods is simply to acknowledge and appreciate their presence as the moral will of God. As such, the central issues for Finnis become the role of the *will* and its posture toward these basic (moral) goods.

One does not have to stretch the imagination too far to see the philosophical influence of Kant's emphasis on the purity of the human will and some form of his categorical imperative behind Finnis's first moral principle. Also, one does not have to probe too extensively to grasp how far Finnis' formulation of this principle of morality is from Aquinas' principle of "good is to be done and pursued, evil is to be avoided" (*bonum est faciendum et prosequendum, malum est vitandum*) and his confidence in human reason and its ability to discover the morally good in light of this fundamental principle.

Furthermore, one of the many reasons why Finnis rejects the proportionalist methodology is because he can find no coherent limiting principle for its application. [155] In essence, Finnis seems to believe that reason cannot discover plateaus, i.e., make reasonable distinctions, where they exist but will wind up sliding down the slippery slope toward a *reductio ad absurdum* by choosing whatever one is inclined towards. [156] Finnis would erect moral absolutes in reason's place to guard against the uncertainties and potential abuses of human moral discernment and judgment. Finally, the necessary intervention of divine agency to establish exceptions by dispensation to these absolutes indicates that redeemed creation as a whole and human reason in particular both lack sufficient resources to discern the morally good in specific, though limited, situations. In sum, if the *morally* good is determined by God, either through the divine will in the creation of basic human goods or through divine dispensation, then human reason is relegated to a truly subordinate role, and the key issue becomes the probity of the human will.

Finnis' position on Christian eschatology is also quite consistent with his anthropological presuppositions, moral epistemology and deontology. There are two explicit references to the "heavenly Kingdom" in his text [149 & 156], and both speak of the necessity to prepare "material" for this kingdom. Two questions arise: what is this "material" to which Finnis refers?, and what is its relation to God's absolute future (kingdom)?

In answering the first question, it is important to note that in both places where Finnis speaks of "material" he frames the issue in terms of human moral choice as an *act of the will*. He claims that choices (acts of the will) last beyond the behavior which executes them, and they last into eternity. [149] In one place, he states that "[T]he 'material' of the Kingdom includes persons, with the moral selves they have shaped by their choices" [149], and in the other place he defines "material" as "especially people and their own moral selves as shaped by their moral choices." [156] I would suggest that Finnis understands the "material" for the kingdom as the moral character which agents have reflexively shaped through the probity of their wills (choices) in relation to the basic human goods. In other words, fidelity of the human will to God's creative will is the "stuff" from which the kingdom is primarily built. As such, placing a prime emphasis on "this-worldly results" [156] or on the fruits of action (values realized) as the "material" for the kingdom is deprecated, if not rejected.

If my answer to the first question above is correct, we have some insight into how Finnis views the relation of the human future to the Absolute future of God's kingdom. If it is moral selves which have been reflexively shaped by proper choice that make up the "material" for the kingdom, then what is " carried over" into the kingdom is primarily moral selves properly formed in fidelity. But what about the fruits of our *actions* that have realized concrete *values* for others in our existence now? Do not these values (fruits of our actions) also perdure into the kingdom? Finnis cites *Gaudium et Spes* nos. 38-39 in making his point that it is moral selves which last into the kingdom, but the text of this document makes it clear that "charity and its fruits endure" and that "the expectation of a new earth must not weaken but rather stimulate our concern for cultivating this one."[8] Contrary to Finnis' interpretation of these passages, I do not see the texts restricting the "material" for the kingdom primarily to the building up of moral character, as important as this is. The realization of truly human values through our actions (fruits of charity) *also* perdure into the kingdom, and this, it seems to me, is the import of the Council's emphasis on cultivating and taking seriously our existence as we now know it. If I am correct in my interpretation, then, besides his emphasis on the goodness of the will, Finnis needs to pay much greater attention to what actions do to and for people in conflict situations.

I am aware, of course, that to interpret the text of *Gaudium et Spes* in this way I have possibly opened the door to Finnis' criticism that proportionalism is consequentialistic, hopes for "a goal attainable by some worldwide billion-year plan" [144], etc. But I don't think that the door is really opened here. I would suggest that what generates these remarks, in part, on Finnis' side of the door is: (1) his distrust of human reason's ability to discern the *morally* good among all the non-moral values and disvalues and (2) his eschatology, which at once accords scant attention to the importance of actions and their consequences now and for the kingdom and construes this life as being more discontinuous than continuous with life in the kingdom.[9] In sum, I would suggest that many of Finnis' allegations, which in my mind are really misrepresentations of the fundamental intent and substance of proportionalism, can be traced back to his beliefs that are at variance with those held by proportionalists on these and other important theological issues.

Part II:
An Analysis of Cardinal Bernardin's "Consistent Ethic of Life"

Finnis has described Cardinal Bernardin's "consistent ethic of life" as "a *name*, not a thesis." [140] He then proffers that the essence of Bernardin's call for a consistent ethic in his speeches[10] can be formulated into three distinct propositions. I would like to argue briefly in this part that what Bernardin intends by his consistent ethic is not a name, a thesis or a set of propositions; rather he is proposing a moral stance that is at once comprehensive, analogical, and dialogical.

Simply defined, a moral stance is a coherent and consistent combinations of normative value judgments about the world, God and self.[11] Like all stances, Cardinal Bernardin's consistent ethic of life structures one's fundamental understanding of moral experience, serves as a critique of others' interpretations of moral reality, and becomes a source of ethical criteria to evaluate particular actions and social policies.[12] Though a stance is always logically prior to systematic reflection on specific issues, nonetheless it seeks such reflection by its very nature. Because a stance is the foundation of or matrix within which moral imperatives are discovered and ultimately justified, the validity of the imperatives rests on the validity of the stance. Thus, if a stance lacks comprehensiveness, coherence or authenticity, then so do the moral imperatives which have been discerned from within the stance.

Bernard Lonergan has made use of horizon analysis to clarify the nature and importance of a moral stance. Horizons can be understood literally as the line where earth meets the sky and where they limit our field of vision. In this ocular model, horizons change when we move from one position to another. If we move from an ocular to a disclosure model of conceiving horizon, we can grasp that there are also horizons to our knowledge and desires, and they too can change on the basis of what we care to know and love.[13] When we use a disclosure model of horizon as a way of understanding stance, we see that all stances imply two necessary poles: a subject pole and an object pole. A moral stance is formed through the interaction between a subject pole, which involves the existential questions of the agent about his/her commitments, attitudes, lived values, actions and social policies, on the one hand, and an object pole, which involves the range of data or "world" that comes into view for the agent to interpret, judge and act on, on the other. In essence, the interaction between these two referents fashions how we look on reality, and it structures our understandings and judgments about the world, God and self.[14]

Allow me now to apply this interpretation of moral stance to Cardinal Bernardin's consistent ethic. Bernardin most often describes what he means by a "consistent ethic of life" by reference to a "vision"[15] or a "framework."[16] These words render in another way what I have called moral stance or horizon. The vision or framework (stance) which he seeks to articulate is comprehensive in scope,[17] consistent in application,[18] analogical in character,[19] and dialogical in its culture and social policy.[20] Each of these descriptions of his vision is important in itself to understand and appreciate.

The vision which Bernardin proposes is comprehensive in that it refuses to leave out any life issue that affects persons. At the subject pole where one's attitudes and commitments come into view, he is committed to a full range of issues where human life and dignity are at stake, and these commitments and attitudes are nourished and informed by various theological themes.[21] Though he argues that these themes are specifically grounded in the New Testament, he believes that neither the themes nor the content generated from the themes are unique to the Christian stance.[22] By arguing in principle that the themes and content are not specific to Christians, Bernardin is able, at the level of his vision (stance), to dialogue with others in society who are not Christian. At the object pole where the range of data or "world" come into view, Bernardin's consistent ethic of life is comprehensive in that the vision encompasses all the particular issues from womb to tomb. Put negatively, his moral stance refuses to exclude any issue that threatens the dignity of the human person, and he employs this vision to criticize other groups whose stance is narrowed by commitment to one specific issue, e.g., abortion.

On almost every page of his speeches, Cardinal Bernardin calls for a consistency in attitude and in the use and application of certain moral principles. Though I will assess neither the adequacy nor the validity of these moral principles here, what is important for my purposes is to indicate how the consistency he calls for is part of his moral vision. Of course, any particular moral stance can be inconsistent, and to that extent it is incoherent, and possibly even inauthentic. People can hold to one thing, yet incoherently do something else that is inconsistent with their basic attitudes and commitments. Likewise, individuals and whole communities can commit themselves to certain moral principles to inform and direct their behavior, but then they can be highly selective and serendipitous in the application of these principles. One of the hallmarks of an *adequate* vision of moral experience is its ability to tie together attitude and doing, commitment and application. It seems to me that it is this adequacy that Bernardin seeks to achieve in his emphasis on consistency. He will use consistency not only to assess the adequacy of others' stances but also the adequacy of various social attitudes and policies.

The moral stance of Cardinal Bernardin is also analogical in character because it seeks to view issues which are not identical but which have some common characteristics.[23] Though he insists that each issue along the spectrum of life concerns must be considered on its own merits, he believes this should not dull our vision to the possible connections among these distinct concerns. A stance that is analogical, then, approaches the interpretation of moral experience with an eye to possible similarities; it refuses to look on our moral lives as disparate and unconnected. The radical existentialist or situationist's vision is inspired by the novelty of the individual and the particular. As such, their vision is committed to seeing only the disconnections within moral experience and the uniqueness of each moral issue. Bernardin's stance is quite different from this situationist view, and it is quite different from other stances, not as radical in their claim to particularity, that are narrowed by a desire to concentrate on the importance of a single issue at the expense of seeing connections to other issues. By paying attention to and focusing on the links that exist among a variety of issues, Cardinal Bernardin's stance can allow him to dialogue and form coalitions with others along a whole spectrum of concerns.

I indicated earlier that a moral stance is logically prior to systematic reflection but that it ultimately seeks that kind of reflection. When the contents of a stance are thematized, the attitudes and commitments embodied in that vision make their way into and influence systematic reflection on moral experience. Bernardin is certainly correct in describing his consistent ethic as a way (I would say "heuristic device") of defining the problems that confront human dignity.[24] This is precisely what a stance is and does. But he also claims that the consistent ethic is systematic.[25] He links this term to the nature of Catholic theology, which is the systematic reflection on religious-moral experience. As a reflective discipline, theology has the task of drawing out the meaning of each moral principle and the relationships among them,[26] and it refuses to look at and treat moral issues in an *ad hoc* fashion.[27] I would argue, though, that not all theologies can accomplish what Bernardin seeks. Some types of theology that have a narrow stance which lies behind them will not in fact look at and treat moral issues in any other way than *ad hoc*. Because a moral stance is not only the foundation of systematic reflection but also of the moral imperative discoverable by that reflection, the adequacy of a theology will depend upon the comprehensiveness and authenticity of the stance which gives rise to that discipline.

Notes

1. The best collection of essays on proportionalism is *Readings in Moral Theology No. 1: Moral Norms and Catholic Tradition*, eds, Charles E. Curran and Richard A. McCormick, S.J. (New York: Paulist Press, 1979). For my own analysis of the definition, structural criteria and epistemology of the proportionalist methodology, see James J. Walter, "Proportionate Reason and Its Three Levels of Inquiry: Structuring the Ongoing Debate," *Louvain Studies* 10 (Spring, 1984), pp. 30-40.

2. See Josef Fuchs, *Christian Ethics in a Secular Arena* (Washington, D.C.: Georgetown University Press, 1984), p. 102.

3. See Richard A. McCormick's essay in this symposium, "The Consistent Ethic of Life: Is There an Historical Soft Underbelly?," 96-97.

4. "Fines autem morales accidunt rei naturali; et e converso ratio naturalis finis accidit morali." ST I-II, q. 1, art. 3, ad 3. ("Now moral ends are accidental to a natural thing, and conversely the relation of a natural end to morality is accidental.")

5. ST I-II, q. 94, art. 2. For an analysis of Aquinas' position, see Louis Janssens, *Mariage et Fécondité: De Casti Connubii à Gaudium et Spes* (Paris: Editions J. Duculot, S.A., Gembloux, 1967), pp. 42-61.

6. "Unde malum culpae, quod privat ordinem ad bonum divinum, Deus nullo modo vult. Sed malum naturalis defectus, vel malum poenae vult, volendo aliquod bonum, cui coniungitur tale malum: sicut, volendo iustitiam, vult poenam; et volendo ordinem naturae servari, vult quaedam naturaliter corrumpi." ST I, q. 19, art. 9. ("Hence the evil of fault [sin], which is the privation of order towards the divine good, God in no way wills. But the evil of natural defect, or the evil of punishment He does will; by willing the good to which such evil is joined: thus, in willing justice He wills punishment; and in willing the natural order to be preserved, He wills some things to be naturally corrupted.")

7. For example, see Richard A. McCormick's analysis of Bruno Schüller's position on the principle of double effect where McCormick states, "Since this is so, the principle of double effect (involving a distinction between intending and permitting) has a legitimate place where actions inducing others to wrongdoing are concerned." Richard McCormick and Paul Ramsey, eds., *Doing Evil to Achieve Good: Moral Choice in Conflict Situations* (Chicago: Loyola University Press, 1978), p. 256.

8. *Pastoral Constitution on the Church in the Modern World (Gaudium et Spes)* in *The Documents of Vatican II*, ed. Walter M. Abbott (New York: Association Press, 1966), no. 39.

9. It is not unusual to find deontologists holding to a view of eschatology which emphasizes the discontinuities between our existence now and the kingdom. See Charles E. Curran's analysis of Paul Ramsey's eschatology in Curran's *Politics, Medicine, & Christian Ethics* (Philadelphia: Fortress Press, 1973), pp. 173-182.

10. Cardinal Bernardin's speeches are cited by number, as follows; page numbers refer to this volume:

    1: Fordham University (Gannon Lecture)

2: St. Louis University (William Wade Lecture Series)

3: Kansas City, Missouri (Right-to-Life Convention)

4: Cincinnati, Ohio (National Consultation on Obscenity)

5: The Catholic University of America

6: Foster McGaw Triennial Conference

7: Address to Criminal Law Committee (Cook County)

8: Catholic Medical Center (Jamaica, New York)

9: Seattle University

10: Portland, Oregon (Consistent Ethic of Life Conference)

11. Stephen Happel and James J. Walter, *Conversion and Discipleship: A Christian Foundation for Ethics and Doctrine* (Philadelphia: Fortress, 1986), p. 206.

12. Charles E. Curran, *Directions in Fundamental Moral Theology* (Notre Dame, IN: University of Notre Dame Press, 1985), p. 6.

13. Happel and Walter, *Conversion and Discipleship,* p. 15.

14. *Ibid,.* p. 206.

15. For examples where Bernardin describes the consistent ethic as a "vision," see 1:10, 2:13, 4:34, 9:79, 9:85 and 10:91.

16. For examples of the consistent ethic as a "framework," see 6:58, 9:85, and 10:88.

17. For examples, see 8:76 and 10:87.

18. Almost every page of Cardinal Bernardin's speeches makes reference to the necessity for "consistency" in the ethic that he proposes.

19. For example, see 9:79, 9:80, and 10:90.

20. Though Bernardin does not use the word "dialogical" to describe his stance, this word certainly renders his intent to "cast our case in broadly defined terms, in a way which elicits support from others." For examples, see 3:22 and 10:94-95. In addition, Bernardin's constant reference to culture and what is going on in culture not only indicates that cultural facts are relevant to his analysis but also clearly manifests his desire to dialogue with various groups within culture.

21. 6:58 and 7:63. One of the theological themes which reappears is an "option for the poor." On this theme, see 5:40, 5:47, 6:57, and 8:70.

22. 7:63, 9:78 and 10:91.

23. 9:80. Though the analogical character of Bernardin's vision is present, albeit implicitly, throughout all his speeches, he begins to make explicit reference to it only in his later talks.

24. For example, see 2:13-14. Bernardin also uses his vision as a way (heuristic device) for testing public policies, party platforms, and candidates. See, 2:17-18, 9:84, and 10:94-95.

25. 9:79, 9:83-84, and 10:89.

26. 10:90.

27. 10:90.

The Consistent Ethic of Life: A Protestant Perspective

I appreciate the accuracy of the title assigned me, "A Protestant Perspective." I attempt to provide *a* Protestant perspective, finally my own thought informed by both Protestant and other traditions.

Cardinal Bernardin's addresses are given in a directness and simplicity that masks sophisticated technical background and deep erudition. As one studies them signals come to mind: writings he does not cite, historical background he does not specifically allude to, implications of assertions one knows would be developed more if he did not perceive himself to be primarily a pastor but rather a moral theologian or social ethician.

The challenge of the consistent ethic of life is clear and itself answers to some traditional questions Protestants used to ask about Catholic ethics, e.g. if one is against abortion is there not also an equal obligation to promote social policies and social structures which sustain the lives one insists have a right? Or if one is against abortion, should one not also reconsider the tradition in relation to capital punishment? We know why that analogy has always been deemed inadequate; the fetal life is not in any sense an unjust aggressor as is the criminal.

196

Striving for consistency, or at least more coherence, is certainly commendable. And if one studies the scores of pronouncements about scores of particular moral issues made by Protestant denominations and ecumenical agencies one finds that the authors have grasped for various sorts of arguments, used various sorts of evidences, and have not thought through anything as coherent as is the consistent ethic of life. Any data or argument that seem to provide some backing or warrant for a moral intuition or a sense of moral indignation have too often, in Protestant ecclesiastical morality, seemed sufficient.

Alternative Ways to Respond as a Protestant

In papers of this sort, I line out various ways one *could* respond to the material under analysis in order to show that what I finally do is not the only possible thing to do, and in order to set what I do in a wider context of discussions.

Different approaches to ethics, and especially to medical ethics, raise issues of ecumenical relations between Roman Catholics and Protestants. It is probably easier, in the long run, to come to some general agreement about the relation between the doctrines of justification and sanctification, or even about the presence of Christ in the Eucharist than it is to come to agreement on some divisive moral issues. But, I take it, it is no easier for Protestants to agree with each other on some moral issues than it is for them to agree with some Roman Catholics.

Thus it would be instructive to address the consistent ethic of life by adopting the perspectives of various representative Protestant theologians who have written on matters addressed by Cardinal Bernardin. Such an approach would not only highlight certain general differences between Protestant ethics and Roman Catholic tradition, but also highlight differences among Protestants. One can begin with particular moral judgments by both Catholics and Protestants and move to examine the moral theories that frame them, and to the vindicating theological affirmations that finally back them. Or one can take the reverse course, i.e. examine the fundamental theological affirmations and their different authorizations and move from these to look at moral theories and at particular judgments.

For example, it would be instructive to compare the sections on "Respect for Life" and "The Protection of Life" in the *Church Dogmatics* of that most biblical and Protestant of twentieth century theologians, Karl Barth, with the consistent ethic of life. Backed by a theology of grace revealed in the biblical material interpreted as the election of all humanity in Christ, Barth's fundamental moral principle (though he does not call it that) is, "Thou mayest live." The moral theory is very different, and is backed by a different theology from Cardinal Bernardin's. Barth attacks the casuistic tradition because in it we humans become the determiners of life and death. In so doing we usurp the divine prerogative, namely that it is God alone who is to determine life and death. But since we are responsible to God to act in obedience and to endorse, witness to, and attest to God's grace, a kind of "practical casuistry " is required. But finally we are to hear the command of God which is always a particular command in the particular events in which we participate.

But does a different theology and different moral theory lead to a great difference on issues Cardinal Bernardin has addressed? In spite of Barth's heroic efforts to preserve the freedom of God, i.e. not to bind God to our moral reasoning, his reflections which are to help us hear the command of God come very close to the consistent ethic of life. A command of God is a gracious command. Abortion is a sin; the divine Yes to life is a No to abortion. But it is a forgivable sin, and seems to be so particularly in cases of "life against life." On euthanasia the divine No seems even more absolute, but gets qualified in the light of the growing arrogance of medical technology which, by artificially extending life, might also be usurping the prerogatives of God. It is hard to attest to a gracious God by taking the life of a criminal, but Barth seems quite sure that in the event of committing treason against the state during wartime God might command it. Similarly on the question of war, the divine No is louder and clearer than the traditional just war theories made it, but there are occasions when it might be commanded by God.

Cardinal Bernardin does not take up the traditional limit question of tyrannicide. This is an interesting issue. Can one justify the assassination of a tyrant, a person made in the image of God, for the sake of the common good? One of the most interesting excursuses in Barth's "special ethics" deals with this. In the end he raises the probability that God did command the assassination of Hitler, but those who could have done it when it could have succeeded did not hear the command. I think that on social justice questions Barth could not have had much disagreement with Cardinal Bernardin.[1]

One could compare the writings of Paul Ramsey, Joseph Fletcher, and Helmut Thielicke with those of Barth and those of Cardinal Bernardin. In that way one could sort out the grounds of similarities and differences between them at various levels of moral discourse—precise and practical judgments about classes of actions, e.g. euthanasia, the moral theories that frame how practical choices are justified, and the larger vindicating theological affirmations that back both the form of the moral theory and the content of the moral choices. The result would be a useful agenda of the critical issues in Christian ethics, but, also, that is not the purpose of this occasion.[2]

I think, however, that the strong presumption in favor of the protection and promotion of human life the consistent ethic of life expounds find no significant dissent among contemporary Protestant theologians, and that the deepening and enlarging of the implications of that presumption which Cardinal Bernardin espouses not only corrects earlier Roman Catholic teachings on particular matters but Protestant ones as well. Protestant history, no less than Catholic, does not provide a morally commendable record in many cases. But the presumption rests on something deeper than theological traditions. It may rest on a primal moral intuition, a principle of natural law, expressed in the common teachings of most cultures. The issues are not whether the presumption is sound, but whether it is properly yielded in an exceptionless moral rule, or in judgments about the circumstances in which the presumption can be overridden, i.e. tragic choices.

Another way to address Cardinal Bernardin's writings that I only suggest is a kind of philosophical assessment of the moral theory that is partly explicated and partly implied. What kinds of arguments are made? Since moral philosophers have provided types of ethical theory it is customary, but I think not as fruitful as some others do, to ask whether the ethic is consistently deontic, teleological, consequentialist, or cathekontic (H. Richard Nieburh's ethics of response and responsibility). Other papers in this symposium address these matters. My observation is that from the perspective of such typologies we have quite mixed arguments in the Cardinal's speeches. But I think mixed arguments are defensible. Further, I have long been persuaded that the theological contexts for ethics, depending on how they are articulated, often reasonably support a framework of mixed arguments in ethics. Significant distinctions are made by Cardinal Bernardin. As in the Bishops' Letter on War and Peace, so in the materials here there are distinctions between the theological warrants for moral principles and the principles themselves, e.g. the doctrine of creation in the image of God warrants the sacredness of life; between principles and their applications; between forms of moral reasoning, e.g. analogical and more strictly deductive, etc.

One can wonder, however, whether a more comprehensively developed theology might not lead to some differences in both the ethical framework and in some of the particular moral judgments. My own response below will make a case that a difference in theological perspective alters other matters.

Finally, for this section I list randomly some interesting aspects of Cardinal Bernardin's work that call for wider and more systematic development from an academic point of view. He indicates that there is a Christian vision in his work; the relation between the vision and the more particular choices could be developed further. What does a particular vision do for a moral outlook? Does it order what is valued and disvalued? Does it determine what is included and excluded as relevant factors to be taken into account in moral prescriptions? Does it function to sustain certain attitudes toward life? Attitude is another term used. I think it is a very important term, and could be developed more in relation to traditional concerns for the moral virtues. It also could be developed more in relation to other pastoral activities of the Church. Is there a way in which liturgical life needs to be thought about as an instrument that shapes and sustains certain praiseworthy moral attitudes? Given the social fact that religious communities do not have the same significance for many people that they had in the past, what activities are required in parishes and congregations to shape and sustain such attitudes? In a society in which persons are subjected to very diverse symbols and visions of life, how is the Church to sustain those moral attitudes and values that it deems proper?

The strategic considerations that Cardinal Bernardin notes could be developed further in various directions. The double role of the Church—mercy and advocacy—implies a theology of the mission of the Church that has ramifications for both traditional doctrines such as ecclesiology and for internal practice in parishes. Issues of church and state, church and world, could be more deeply developed.

The responder, however, cannot take up all the interesting and important matters that come to mind in reading Cardinal Bernardin's speeches. Thus I shall focus on what I perceive to be a significant tension in the materials, and argue that if a different theology backed different weights to matters present in the speeches one might come to some different judgments.

One Protestant Response.

I begin with some terms that Cardinal Bernardin uses in several places. Human life is sacred and human life is social. Both of these terms are in one sense descriptive terms. Given the doctrine of the *imago dei*, it is reasonable to *describe* human life as sacred; given observations about the characteristics of human life in the world (characteristics long noted one way or another in both biblical and classical sources) it is reasonable to describe human life as social. But the first description yields and warrants a virtually deontic moral principle immediately: the sacredness of human life grounds and perhaps even logically entails a moral imperative: thou shalt not take human life or at least innocent human life. This imperative, I think, wavers a bit in Cardinal Bernardin's work between being exceptionless and being a very strong presumption.

I think that the description of human life as social does not, in these writings, yield or back anywhere near as strong statements of value or moral imperatives. To be sure, in a few places the traditional term "common good" is mentioned, but it does not function with the same importance as sacredness in the proposals and prescriptions. One can hypothetically suggest, at this point, that if the description of human life as social were taken with the same weight as the description of individual human life as sacred, and that if this description backs a concern for the common good, there might be more occasions that are admitted when the common good might override the presumption in favor of individual human life.

That hypothesis is hardly a Protestant point! Indeed, as I review the history of Christian moral teachings since the 16th century, it is the Catholic traditions, both Eastern and Roman, that have sustained a consciousness of the social nature of life and of the common good more than the Protestant—though there are exceptions in the Protestant tradition. Thomas Aquinas's arguments in favor of taking human life under certain circumstances invoke Aristotelian notions of the common good; if the health of the social body is threatened by a diseased organ in it, it is justifiable to excise the diseased organ. Or if the death of a person threatens the common good, that is the argument against that life being taken; this is one of the arguments against suicide. Of course, the tension I perceive in Cardinal Bernardin's work is present in Thomas Aquinas as well, and one trembles in the face of historic events in which the tension has been eliminated, i.e. all events in which what was judged to be the good of the community or the state has warranted the elimination of persons for that end.

It is difficult, if not impossible, to develop a neatly consistent ethic if more than one value or principle is introduced. Indeed, the only way to have a rigorously consistent ethic in which the application procedures are deductive logic is to have a single moral principle, or at least a single principle or value that in every circumstance *overrides* all other principles and values. If someone's definition of the common good were the single principle or value to prescribe courses of action that could easily lead to a totally instrumental view of human life, and any instrument that did not contribute to the common good could be eliminated. If the single principle is the sacredness of individual human life that could lead to a view in which all social considerations are instrumental to the preservation of individual life. The social would have no other value than to be in the service of individual life.[3]

Every ethic that is relatively systematic and coherent rests on some descriptive principle or principles. In Cardinal Bernardin's case they are those I stated above; human life is sacred and human life is social. In Karl Barth's case it might, too simply, be stated that human beings are created as *de jure* covenant partners of the gracious God. Descriptions can be relatively simple or quite complex. Again to assert something too simply, for Thomas Aquinas humans are created in the image of God, but they are also parts in the order of a larger whole in which the less perfect serves the more perfect and all serves the good of the whole. That larger whole implies relationship between individuals and other persons which are interdependent, and implies that the good of the larger whole is to be morally considered as well as the rights of individuals. For Alan Gewirth, humans are voluntary and purposive. To state more such descriptive principles would be redundant for my purpose.

If I am correct about the importance of the descriptive principles, then one of the crucial choices in any ethics is what is included in and excluded from the description, how elements of what is included are related to each other, and what inferences are to be drawn from it in the formulation of human values and moral prescriptions. The basic description I have used in my work is that human beings are participants in the patterns and processes of interdependence of life in the world. This accents what might be implied in Cardinal Bernardin's statement that human life is social and enlarges the context to include the world of nature. The relations are those of inter-dependence (something not stressed in his work). This requires that a wider context be taken into consideration than is often the case in coming to choices about particular issues. The values and their ordering that are backed by this description are consequently different. It has implications for aspects that Cardinal Bernardin notes, vision and attitudes, as well.

In theological ethics the description necessarily involves an interpreta-tion of God and God's relations to the creation and to human beings. Dif-ferences in theology make a difference in what is judged to be a sufficient description, and consequently a difference in ethics. If God is *agape*, and *agape* is revealed most clearly in the cross, and if *agape* warrants a prin-ciple of covenant fidelity between human persons, Paul Ramsey's ethics are theologically grounded and the grounding backs his inprincipalization of love. And if convenant fidelity is philosophically interpreted in basically deontic terms the dominant strand of Ramsey's ethics and his judgments about particular medical and other matters holds. If God is related to the world and human beings redemptively through the gospel, through God's mercy revealed in the cross, and creatively through the law, through the or-ders of creation in which all human activity occurs, as in Luther, the form and the content of ethics follows from this. In the orders of creation, the civil society, morality is governed by law and justice; in the lives of Chris-tians it is governed by love. If God relates to human beings in very person-like ways, by God speaking and humans hearing his commands, and if those commands are always the permission of God's grace so that we hear a "thou mayest live," and if God is free to command in particular cir-cumstances what his grace requires, both the form and content of Barth's ethics follow from the theology.

With these examples I hope I have established how an interpretation of God and God's relations to the creation and to human beings affect both the content and the form of ethics. The description is not merely one of human life—a statement of anthropology such as human beings are volun-tary and purposive. It is one of human life, and for fulsome theological ethics all of creation, in its relations to God.[4]

Cardinal Bernardin regularly says that he speaks as a pastor. He does not speak as systematic theologian. But both what he says and how he says it are theologically informed. The theology is not developed in his work; a role differentiation is implied. It is very risky to infer from his pastoral ad-dresses what their full theological backing is, but for purposes of discussion I take the risk. He states in a section on "The Role of the Church" it "must be shaped by the perspective of the Scriptures as they are read in the Catholic tradition."[5] I take it that this statement is accurate for the whole of his work, and not just his work on the role of the Church. He also speaks of the consistent ethic of life as a vision. What theological backing for these speeches can one reasonably infer? What specifications of the Christian vision can one reasonably draw? How do these affect Cardinal Bernardin's interpretation or construal of human life? How does that construal affect what is included and excluded from his interpretations of the salient features of the circumstances the consistent ethic of life addresses? How does that affect the order of human and moral values? These questions are easier to answer if one is analyzing a systematic comprehensive moral theology than the addresses of a pastor.

The critical descriptive statement, as I noted at the beginning of this section is that every human being is created in the image of God. This means that "every human life has transcendent value," is sacred.[6] Rhetorically, one can ask, would the ethic be different if it were added that every human being is a part of a larger whole, and is to serve the well-being of the whole? Would it be different if it were added that every human being is finite and thus limited in his or her capacities to know in every case what is truly the good, and to control the consequences of actions? Would it be different if it were added that all human beings are "fallen" and therefore that short of the eschaton human life is lived in conflicts and moral ambiguity? In a section, "The Theological Foundation: Systematic Defense of the Person," Cardinal Bernardin again affirms the doctrine of the *imago dei* and the social character of life, but the section deals more with the method and form of Catholic ethics, then with theology, *per se*.[7] In that address, as in others, it seems to me that the purpose of the social is to support the protection and promotion of individual life. Again rhetorically, would the ethic be different if the social called for more development of what it means for persons to live together in families, and therefore one ought to look at what contributes to the well-being not only of individuals but also the family? In a parallel fashion, the well-being of communities, the nation, the whole human family?

Cardinal Bernardin is very clear that the sacredness of life involves not only its protection, but also its promotion.[8] The restraining prohibition is not sufficient; to say that "thou shalt not take innocent life" requires that one also say, "thou shalt promote life" as well. This reminds the Protestant reader of the exposition of the Decalogue in both Luther and Calvin; in both cases the Reformers find an underlying principle beneath the prohibitions that required positive as well as prohibited actions. Or, to use the more dramatic language of Barth, God's "Yes" to humanity is the first word and requires activity that attests to it; God's "No" is in the service of God's "Yes." But, rhetorically again, what is the "life" that is to be promoted? Is it only in focus ultimately on the well-being of individuals because they are created in the image of God? If that is the case, are there not inexorable negative as well as positive outcomes for the "life" of families, communities, and even the natural world? Would a different theological backing, a different moral vision establish the grounds on which it could be argued that restraints on the promotion of aspects of human life are necessary for the well-being of families, communities, etc.?

One notes with interest that in none of the speeches does Cardinal Bernardin argue that the promotion of life requires the birth of as many human beings as biologically could be born. The concern for the "quality of life" is clear in his work; promotion of life includes actions to provide certain desirable qualities of life. But are there no circumstances in which the concern for desirable qualities of life can override individual human life—and perhaps even under a dire circumstance justify the tragic taking of innocent human life?

I return to the series of questions I raised before. The primary and almost exclusive theological backing for these speeches is that God created each human being in God's image. The vision is the consistent ethic of life which protects and promotes human life. The construal of human life is basically in terms of individuals and their transcendent value: the social concern is to protect and promote individual human life; the interdependence of human lives and of human life with the wider natural world is not given deep consideration. This construal makes individual human life its most salient aspect. Other aspects of life in the world are interpreted in the light of their negative and positive effects on the sanctity of individual life, for examples, modern technology, and cultural movements, or health care and economic reforms. The ordering of human values and moral principles follows from this as, I think, all of his addresses show.

In a sense this analysis is unfair to Cardinal Bernardin. There are grounds, other than technically theological and ethical, for what he has chosen to do. His addresses are to a wider American public as well as to the Church, and he seeks to have this moral vision taken into account in public debate, and to engage in public advocacy of its values. Thus the intended audience of the speeches to some extent determines what he does and does not develop. Also the times in which we live bring issues of the protection and promotion of individual human life into a particular focus: the threat of nuclear war, the presence of degrading poverty in the world, the growing technocratic dominance of our culture, the shifting ethos of our society away from the primary concern for life, and the perceived inconsistency between those who are, for example, anti-abortion but militarist or pro-abortion but peace advocates. He sees the church as teacher as well as advocate in the public arena, and his agenda is thus determined by the public agenda. All of these considerations can be adduced as justifications for the particular focus of the consistent ethic of life as he develops it in the light of the signs of our particular times.

Signals of a Protestant perspective that is in contrast with my depiction of Cardinal Bernardin's have already been sent in this paper. Whether it can fairly be called a Protestant perspective is a good question. It has received as sharp criticism from Protestants as it has from Catholics. I shall not fully develop that perspective here and certainly not embark in one more justification of it. I want it to have heuristic value here, to highlight by contrast what Cardinal Bernardin's speeches do not say. No reader will be persuaded to accept my perspective by what I say here, but some might be moved to reflect on whether points raised are not significant, they might be included in an expansion or revision of the moral vision under discussion at this symposium. My intention is not to be polemical, but ironically pedagogical.

The sharply controverted theology that I have proposed significantly qualifies precisely what I see as the anthropocentrism and ultimately the individualism in Cardinal Bernardin's speeches. The critique that I have developed obviously addresses what many persons see to be central in the Christian faith and tradition; it is not in any sense a critique aimed at Cardinal Bernardin or at any particular strand of the Christian tradition.

The basic structure of my perspective can be stated with much more verbal economy than I used in the two volumes of its presentation. God is interpreted as the ultimate power that is the source of all things, that sustains and governs all things, and that creates conditions of possibility for development of all things and is the final determiner of the destiny of all that is. The divine ordering of all things is through their patterns and processes of interdependence; human life participates in these patterns and processes. As close as I can come to stating the ultimate purposes of God is to express some sympathy for a statement one finds in Thomas Aquinas and in Jonathan Edwards to the effect that God created all things ultimately to God's own glory. I reiterate the anthropological principle which is critical for the ethics: Man (individual persons, communities, the species) is a participant in the patterns and processes of interdependence of life in the world. The central ethical statement is this: We are to seek to discern what God is enabling and requiring us to be and to do as participants in the patterns and processes of interdependence of life in the world. The "we" again refers to individuals, communities and the species. We, as participants, are to relate ourselves and all things in a manner appropriate to their relations to God. My argument is that ethics needs to be theocentric rather than anthropocentric: i.e. its norms should be based not upon what is good for man, but what is in the service of God. This does not mean that the human is without special value; it does mean that while God is the source of human good, God is not the guarantor of human good. What is good for man and what serves God are not mutually exclusive, but they are not necessarily the same either. The purposes of God are vaster than we perceive if our ethics has an anthropocentric and individualistic focus. God, rather than man, is the measure.

Relevant to this paper are several items yielded by this perspective. Individual, communities, the species and other things are described and interpreted in the context of larger wholes. Thus there is a greater value placed on the common good of larger wholes. Self-denial and even self-sacrifice can be required for the sake of a larger whole. Since God does not order the whole of the creation so that there is an automatic harmony between defensible values of parts and the good of the whole, moral ambiguity is a profound and continuing fact of human experience and in some situations genuinely tragic choices have to be made. For example, in a justifiable war for the sake of the common good of a nation military conscription subjects individuals to risk of individual life for the sake of a larger whole. The choice is tragic. In family the good of the whole, given the limitations not only of economic but other capacities, require that the justifiable well-being of each member cannot be fully promoted. Choices are ambiguous. Social policies which both Cardinal Bernardin and I would support require for the sake of distributive justice a taxation rate that limits our discretionary income, income which we might be motivated to allot to other socially worthy causes. The choice is not without ambiguity. I shall not give more examples here. I have elsewhere interpreted in some detail suicide, marriage and family, population and nutrition issues, and the allocation of biomedical research funding within this framework.

In contrast to Cardinal Bernardin's foundational statements there are two critical differences which, in a sense, reverberate through my approach to ethics. The doctrine of the *imago dei* is decentered and human life as social is developed differently and in a way that yields somewhat different ethical judgments. I have no desire to argue against his position or for my own at this point. But from my position I wish to make comments about what I would like to see more explicitly recognized in his work.

Certainly the major practical purpose of any pattern of ethical thought is to direct human action in such a way that some possible choices are eliminated, that moral ambiguity is mitigated, and tragic choices avoided. Within Roman Catholic moral theology the principle of double-effect comes to the fore in the recognition of potential moral ambiguity, and is an effort (in various ways in which it is used) to reasonably justify choices in which more than one value or principle is at stake. (I have no interest here in getting into issues debated about the principle of double effect in recent Roman Catholic literature). The perspective from which I work is also intended to reduce ambiguity, but it cannot reduce it to the extent that Cardinal Bernardin's consistent ethic of life does, and it forces the recognition of the sometimes tragic character of justifiable moral choices.

It is my conviction, however, that while the consistent ethic of life justifies commendable moral attitudes and backs commendable moral and public policy choices, its articulation tends to avoid stating the ambiguities that are often consequent to its application. The consequence of adhering resolutely to the consistent ethic of life can lead to the suffering of innocent persons and in some instances even to tragic outcomes for the sake of morality itself. The perspective from which I work does that as well. And it is that reality of moral life that I wish we could be all clear and forthright about.

There are many refined, technical procedures and details that all of us who are learned in moral theology and ethical theory can adduce in every ambiguous case that confronts us. I think we all need to be more forthright about the ambiguity that is a part of life because the well-being of individuals and the well-being of others including "larger wholes" is not harmonious. It may be in eschatological vision or it may be in some highly abstract ideal order, but it is not in many decisions about how human life is to be protected and promoted—not only life and death decisions but daily ones of no highly notable consequences. Whether we are directed by a consistent ethic of life or a significantly different one, recognition of ambiguous and sometimes tragic choices affects our attitudes and our actions. One says this to oneself as well as to others.

Notes

1. Karl Barth, *Church Dogmatics*, III/4, Edinburgh: T and T Clark, 1961, pp. 324-470.

2. My own efforts in this regard were published in *Protestant and Roman Catholic Ethics: Prospects for Rapprochement,* Chicago: University of Chicago Press, 1978.

3. There are cogent philosophical ethics which are based on a single principle, e.g. Alan Gewirth, *Reason and Morality,* Chicago: University of Chicago Press, 1978. His Principle of Generic Consistency is not purely formal; it has moral content. This rights based ethic gets worked out with reference to some of the issues Cardinal Bernardin has addressed to quite different conclusions, e.g. in Gewirth's discussion of abortion, p. 142.

4. This incidentally, is why I think that a number of currently influential Roman Catholic moral theologians who argue for autonomous ethics, i.e. ethics in which the agent is self-legislating, are theologically inadequate—but this is not the place to debate such an issue.

5. "The Face of Poverty Today: A Challenge for the Church," 17 January 1985, Catholic University of America, p. 36.

6. "The Consistent Ethic of Life: An American-Catholic Dialogue," Fordham University, 6 December 1983, p. 1.

7. "Address," Seattle University, 2 March 1986, p. 79.

8. Fordham Address, p. 9, and other places.

Response to James Gustafson, "The Consistent Life Ethic: A Protestant Response"

Lisa Sowle Cahill

I will introduce my essential response briefly, in three points, then develop these points further in relation to specific remarks of Prof. Gustafson.

1) I take Prof. Gustafson's *fundamental critique* of the "consistent life ethic" to be that it is with excessive—or at least misplaced—consistency that it holds up the sacredness of the individual. Indeed, this ethic consistently values the individual at the expense of the common good. More fundamentally, this ethic discounts the possibility that the interests of human persons and of the social whole or the whole of creation might not be mutually compatible. 2) Gustafson's *contribution as a Protestant* is to emphasize the ambiguity and even, as he insists, the "tragedy" of the moral life. Since the sixteenth century, the traditions of the Reformers have emphasized the radical effects of sin on the creation, and on humanity's

ability to know, choose, and accomplish what is right for human persons to do. Underlying and supplementing this Protestant contribution is Prof. Gustafson's own Reformed or Calvinistic heritage, which yields the comprehensive motif of God's sovereignty, and at least suggests the importance of experience as a resource for and criterion of religious moral claims. 3) The *insights which Catholicism can appropriate* from this Protestant critique are that the natural law method as empirically-grounded also must meet the test of concrete experience; that moral norms regarding personal rights and duties must be reconsidered in relation to the reality of human being as social, historical, and fallen; and that the reality of moral ambiguity should not be denied in favor of a false certitude or security. In other words, Gustafson challenges both the method and the conclusions of the consistent life ethic.

Critique

Gustafson's critique is advanced concisely toward the close of his remarks. He acknowledges that although he intends his own perspective to "reduce ambiguity," still "it cannot reduce it to the extent that Cardinal Bernardin's consistent life ethic does, and it forces the recognition of the sometimes tragic character of justifiable moral choices."[1] This "tragedy" infers preeminently an unavoidable incompatibility between the good of the created universe and of each and every individual who is a part of it. I shall return to this claim in a few moments. For now, it will suffice to draw attention to two of its key features: the assertions that, 1) the Cardinal's ethic denies real and irreducible ambiguity; and, 2) even ambiguous and tragic choices may be objectively justifiable (not just the products of limited knowledge or sinful will).

Gustafson's Contribution as "Protestant"

Gustafson's comparison of Barth and Bernardin is instructive. He dwells on the similarities in their respective uses of a general principle of respect for life, and compares some of the results for their substantive conclusions. Yet a still more basic and important difference lies in the model or framework each assumes to be adequate for understanding moral epistemology and moral agency. How do we *know* what is right? How do we *decide* what to do? The Catholic "natural law" model in general assumes that a reasonable and consistent order of moral values is apprehensible by the human intellect; a rightly knowing moral intelligence both is free to and is obligated to act on the values so known. Barth's ethics of the "command of God," on the other hand, drastically removes the prerogative of moral discernment from reason, and gives it to the obedient hearing of faith. Moral obligation arises not from the intrinsic marks and purposes of a shared human nature, but from the sovereignty of the divine will, indicated in—but not captured by—natural values and biblical imperatives. While the Catholic tradition prizes the universality and consistency in ethics which makes public moral discourse possible, Barth exhibits a tremendous reticence to bind the divine will to any human need for clarity and security. Gustafson presses the difference in viewpoint practically when he questions whether Barth's and Bernardin's shared presumption in favor of life should be articulated in terms of "an exceptionless moral rule," or in terms of "judgments about the circumstances in which the presumptions can be overridden, i.e. tragic choices."[2] To stress judgments rather than rules is to imply the constant engagement of personal evaluation in the determination of what is divinely willed on particular occasions. As a Protestant, Gustafson is challenging the classical metaphysical underpinnings of natural law ethics. He also appears to suggest that a revisionist natural law model which merely recognizes the historicity of human being and knowing would be insufficient from a Protestant Christian perspective. Through his use of Barth, he recommends for our consideration a model in which human moral agency responds to the constant commanding and calling of the Creator, a model of relationship and obedience, rather than of immutable order and natural rationality. Although Gustafson (as distinct from Barth) affirms that the participation of human beings "in the patterns and processes of interdependence of life in the world"[3] is a primary medium of moral knowledge, he seems to agree with Barth that these "patterns and processes" do not amount to an invariant ethics of nature.

A related and characteristically "Protestant" theme mentioned by Gustafson is the pervasiveness of sin in the creation, and its distorting effects on human intelligence and freedom. Sinfulness is added to finitude and limitation, and both are often given short shift in Catholic ethics. Natural law epistemology and anthropology are consequently overoptimistic about the potential of humanity to know and do what God wills. A more pessimistic view of humanity's natural moral capacities offers a larger point of entry for some of the "ambiguity" in moral choice which is a recurrent theme in Gustafson's paper. As I hear him, however (and as I have read other of his writings), the author of this paper is willing to go a crucial step further: "tragedy" can be the product not just of sin or failure, but of a basic incommensurability of the goods of individual creatures with one another, or with the divinely mandated relations of all things to one another in their relations to God. Gustafson is unwilling to grant that even a hypothetical "ideal metaphysical observer" could gaze upon a unified and prioritized system of natural realities and moral obligations in which every problem had its ideal solution (even granting, as Catholic tradition would, that the ideal can be impenetrable from the *de facto* vantage point of humanity's blurred moral vision). This is a major and radical point of difference which calls into question the very prospect of "consistency" in ethics, much more the assertion of absolute moral norms regarding individual rights.

Development of the Critique

In Cardinal Bernardin's writings, Prof. Gustafson discerns a "significant tension" between the affirmation that human life is sacred, and the affirmation that it is social.[4] The reference to life's sacredness is taken by Gustafson to imply the inviolability of the individual, while the reference to sociality is taken to imply the possible conflict of individual needs or rights with the goods of other human individuals and groups, or of entities within the natural universe, or even of creation as a whole.

Their major disagreement arises from the fact that Gustafson admits a radical inconsistency in the order of things between the "sacredness" of each human being and the coherence of the whole creation in relation to the sovereign God.[5] For Bernardin, as a Catholic natural law thinker, creation is an order whose orderliness can be known and must be acted upon. Sociality or interdependence will always include rather than preclude respect for individual life. For Gustafson, interdependence indicates a process of relating to other beings and to God which does not rule out conflict between anthropocentric interests and the interests of other creatures or of God's glory. These interests are not always to be settled in favor of humanity. A key statement is the following:

> My argument is that ethics needs to be theocentric rather than
> anthropocentric: i.e. its norms should be based not upon what is
> good for man, but what is in the service of God. This does not
> mean that the human is without special value; it does mean that
> while God is the source of human good, God is not the guarantor
> of human good.... The purposes of God are vaster than we per-
> ceive if our ethics has an anthropocentric and individualistic
> focus. God, rather than man, is the measure.[6]

Natural law ethics, of course, is deliberately, self-consciously, and consistently anthropocentric, and assumes metaphysical and moral orderliness as a basic premise.

One point on which I would have to disagree with Prof. Gustafson's interpretation of Bernardin is in the former's assertion that the theme of interdependence is "not stressed" in Bernardin's work.[7] I might even go so far as to suggest that it is precisely interdependence that is the motivating theme in the "consistent ethic of life." Bernardin draws connections among the dignity of persons; their rights to be social participants through access to such institutions as education, employment and health care, as well as to be protected from direct physical and moral assault; and the duties which both persons and sectors of society have toward other persons and groups. He also connects respect for life in each area to respect for life in all other areas, and encourages our culture to develop a vision of life which will enhance human dignity in every sphere, from abortion to nuclear conflict. Such a program is built precisely on an awareness of the interdependence of persons, both materially and morally.

In my estimation, the real issue separating Gustafson and Bernardin is not sociality versus individualism, but whether the moral demands of sociality can at least in principle be settled in a manner which still permits the absolute inviolability of certain rights or integrities of every individual, including the right to life. The tradition out of which Bernardin works is so committed to the proposition that social justice and individual rights can be reconciled, that it is willing to articulate the inviolability of those rights in the form of absolute moral prohibitions of certain specific incursions against them, such as the norms against abortion, euthanasia, and experimentation on embryos. Moreover, most proponents of this tradition are willing to assert that "just" social policy included protection of the whole spectrum of individual rights. Gustafson, on the other hand, thinks that a serious commitment to the common good as primary will involve us in *morally* "tragic" and "ambiguous" sacrifices regarding the valid rights of persons or groups—"*morally*" tragic because these sacrifices entail the undenied violation or at least subordination of some of the requirements of justice as equality.

Catholic ethics does not, of course, deny that good and bad are often mixed in moral choices. However, it would affirm that, at least in theory, it is possible to rank competing goods, among which some will even be "absolute." In consequence, an action which involves some bad results is still objectively and rather neatly justified if it has not sacrificed any higher values for lower ones, nor acted against an absolute value. *It is not acknowledged that any of the so-called "absolute" values can conflict so radically among themselves that a direct action against one or another will be morally required.* I take it that Gustafson's point—expanded in his two-volume work, *Ethics from a Theocentric Perspective*—is that moral experience does not bear out this confidence. This is a point with which many Catholics may agree existentially, but the traditional metaphysics and casuistry of Catholic moral theology militates against recognition of it. To reply effectively to Gustafson's charge, Cardinal Bernardin or the Catholic tradition in general will need to do more than simply *assert* the moral order of the universe, or to cling to confidence in order, rationality, and eventually human fulfillment because to do otherwise would be simply unthinkable. This tradition must confront seriously the prospect that the human experience of suffering, absurdity, and conflict simply do not bear out the tradition's claims. Of course, to rest confidence in a transcendent order guaranteeing the inviolability of every individual upon *faith* would undercut the very premise of shared human values upon which Bernardin mounted a public policy appeal in the first place. Moreover, Catholicism must confront seriously as well Gustafson's argument that a genuinely *theo*centric Christianity would not bear out such claims either.

Appropriation of Insights

Gustafson's trenchant charges of individualism and of suppression of the tragic come together as a broad critique of Catholicism's a priorism and superficial objectivism at the level of fundamental theology and metaphysics; of rationalism and deductivism at the level of epistemology; and of casuistry and absolutism at the level of normative judgments. I suspect that on the more basic points of ultimate metaphysical order Prof. Gustafson and Cardinal Bernardin will have to agree to disagree. But ambiguity and tragedy might be introduced into the Catholic moral theological vocabulary at least to the extent of appreciation of the finite and sinful conditions under which interpretation of the natural law proceeds. Indeed, I do not perceive Cardinal Bernardin as denying these conditions, even as conditions in which the *magisterium* itself operates. A challenge with which Gustafson leaves us, however, is to give the more ambiguous aspects of the consistent life ethic more explicit and indeed "consistent" recognition in the realm of the "personal" as well as of the "political." In calling for unity of the Catholic and the public moral visions across these spheres, Cardinal Bernardin may not have come to grips as directly as he needs with the fact that Catholicism's moral methodology and teaching style have been significantly different in these distinct but related areas of moral responsibility. Catholic "social" ethics allows for much more of the ambiguity of which Gustafson speaks than does Catholic "personal" ethics (e.g., sexual and medical ethics). It hardly needs to be noted that there would be many and varied political and ecclesial consequences of introducing a reexamination of "consistency" into the delineation of "personal" and "social" moral teaching. For a magisterial and pastoral Church representative to do so might with reason be considered imprudent. Yet if serious *theological* discussion of the "consistent life ethic" is to proceed, these fundamental questions cannot be avoided.

On a final note, I would like to turn a question to Prof. Gustafson. In his 1978 work, *Protestant and Roman Catholic Ethics: Prospects for Rapprochement* (Univ. of Chicago Press), Gustafson observed that any "fundamental convergence" between our two traditions "will occur only when there is more consensus on the basic outlook, principle, or metaphor that is appropriate to Christian theological ethics...." (p. 153). He has just now exhorted Cardinal Bernardin to improve his "consistent ethic of life"—in many respects representative of a typical Catholic outlook, advantages and disadvantages included—by giving up a little consistency and replacing it with some ambiguity. Ambiguity, as Professor Gustafson has just demonstrated so skillfully is a characteristically Protestant observation, if not principle. Does he think there is to be found another image or ideal which could replace that of consistency and serve as the emblem for an ethical point of view which would be not only more ecumenical, but also more true to experience, including its tragic elements? (The "seamless garment" metaphor served such a unifying function in the Cardinal's original quest for consistency.) At this re-visionist juncture, we no doubt all would like to discover an imagination-engaging metaphor to inspire a more unified Christian moral approach, and even enable Christians to join public debates. Is such an objective reasonable and desirable? Or is the ambiguity in moral experience unavoidably reflected at the levels of symbols, theory, and political discourse? Do different—even conflicting—religious and moral traditions have a function in representing this ambiguity? Is there a way in which to acknowledge ambiguity and pluralism both in moral theories and in concrete moral demands, without conceding a relativism of moral viewpoint which both Prof. Gustafson and Cardinal Bernardin would find objectionable?

Author's note: In the discussion following this response to Gustafson, the term "coherence" was suggested by Todd Whitmore, a doctoral student at the University of Chicago, as a possible replacement for "consistency." To speak of coherence would be to suggest that theological and ethical symbols and commitments should cohere internally with one another, and should cohere with human religious and moral experience. The term would help avoid the impression either that absolute moral consistency is possible at the experiential level, or that strict consistency is possible at the theoretical level among moral principles and norms, ethical evaluation, and systematic theological proposals. The term "coherence," however, is itself more a theoretical concept than an imaginative image. Thus it needs to be accompanied by an ecumenical image or symbol with roots in religious experience, Christian tradition or the bible. Possibilities might include "discipleship," "way of the Cross," "love of neighbor and enemy." In *Ethics from a Theocentric Perspective*, Gustafson has relied on John Calvin's religious theme of "piety"; on "participation" in the interdependence of relations in the world as a description of human moral agency; and on an ethical imperative derived from Calvin, H. Richard Niebuhr and other authors in the Reformed tradition, "to relate ourselves and other things appropriately to our relationship to God" (ETP II, 150). I suppose all these suggestions return us to a basic problematic: How are general or inconclusive themes, concepts, and metaphors to be interpreted specifically, to guide concrete moral behavior? Although there may be agreement about helpful metaphors, there may not be agreement about their precise interpretation. In addition, of course, certain themes and images tend to *favor* certain directions of development toward concrete ethics. So once again, we are confronted with what may be irreducible differences in perspective on the Christian moral life. At the very least, however, Gustafson's and Bernardin's perceptions of tragedy and ambiguity, on the one hand; and of the importance of social consensus and consistency, on the other, can serve as critical complements which work to keep one another honest.

Notes

1. Gustafson, "The Consistent Life Ethic: A Protestant Perspective," in this volume p. 208.

2. Ibid., p. 199

3. Ibid., p. 202.

4. Ibid., p. 201.

5. Ibid., p. 204-205.

6. Ibid., p. 207.

7. Ibid., p. 202.

The Consistent Ethic: Public Policy Implications

J. Bryan Hehir, Th.D.

There are several perspectives from which the Consistent Ethic can be examined. One of them is to evaluate it as a public policy or, more precisely, to examine it as a reponse to the public policy debate in the United States. Looked at in this fashion, the Consistent Ethic is understood as an attempt to provide a coherent framework and rationale for the public policy positions of the Catholic church.[1] Simultaneously it is an effort to engage the wider society in an assessment of this agenda and a comparison of the Consistent Ethic with other policy options in the public arena. One problem with taking this approach to the Consistent Ethic is that it risks reducing the entire enterprise to a tactic. There is, undoubtedly, a tactical dimension to the Consistent Ethic proposal, but it is not wholly tactical in its conception or consequences. In both the character of a Catholic social ethic and in the content of the specific positions of the Consistent Ethic, one can find the elements of the proposal; its tactical utility flows from its substantive foundation.

In this paper I will address the public policy implications of the Consistent Ethic by examining issues of its substantive moral content and its political consequences. The argument will involve three steps: (1) a commentary on the relationship of religion and politics as a setting for evaluating the Consistent Ethic; (2) an examination of the character of Catholic social ethics as a basis for the Consistent Ethic; and (3) an analysis of the political and policy implications of using the Consistent Ethic.

I. Religion and Politics: The Setting for the Consistent Ethic

The Consistent Ethic proposal originates in a specific religious community, but it is directed toward the political process. It seeks to contribute to and be judged by the wider political debate of a secular, pluralistic democracy. Looked at in this way, the Consistent Ethic is one strand in the increasingly visible and complicated intersection of religion and politics in the United States in the 1980's.[2]

The role of religion in the public life of the United States is not a new topic. The theme is continuous even if the role which religion has played on diverse issues and the visibility of the religion factor has varied over time.

The 1980s have evidenced a sharpening of the religion and politics debate; there is a new edge to the old question. There are differing explanations proposed for the new intensity of religion and politics. One view stresses the rise of new organizations in the religious community, particularly focusing upon the coalition of voices which form the "new religious right." Both Max Stackhouse and Richard J. Neuhaus stress the complexity of this phenomenon, analyzing the diverse origins, patterns of theological reflection and motivation which lie just below the surface of the coalition which is described as both new and right.[3] Nonetheless, the fact of the emergence of an organizational structure and an aggressive, religiously grounded position on a defined set of questions is offered as one explanation of the new saliency of religion and politics. A second explanation focuses upon personalities, defining the religion and politics intersection principally in terms of individuals who bring together the themes in sharp and often controversial ways. The personalities, unlike the organizations, move across the political spectrum in the views they espouse. The personalities are as different as Jerry Falwell, Jesse Jackson and John O'Connor.

It is undoubtedly the case that both new organizations and new individuals have contributed to the sharpening of the religion and politics encounter in the public mind and in the specific debates on some issues. But I would argue that it is precisely the nature of the issues which comprise the public policy agenda today, not organization or individuals, which provide a more satisfactory explanation of the religion and politics interaction in the 1980s. On a range of issues which have emerged in the 1970s and 1980s there is an irreducible moral dimension which has persisted as a major factor in the public policy debate. The argument here, of course, is not that the public agenda was devoid of serious normative concerns prior to the 1970s, but that the visibility and centrality of moral argument in the public debate has been much more prominent in the last 10-15 years. A catalyst for this theme was the 1973 Supreme Court decision on abortion, which thrust that issue into the center of American political life where it has remained through three presidential elections, through a host of legal challenges and legislative debates at the state and federal level about the funding of abortions and through the recent arguments about who should fill the Supreme Court vacancy. But the abortion example should not be seen in isolation; it is in fact one question, among others, which has catalyzed the political-moral debate. Just as the Court decided Roe vs Wade, the nation was profoundly divided by moral and political arguments about Vietnam. Partly as a consequence of the Vietnam debate, the Carter administration chose to put human rights at the center of its foreign policy, thus generating a substantial inquiry about the nature of human rights, their role in foreign policy and their relative weight versus other policy objectives.

In different ways the abortion case and the human rights policy illustrated how moral arguments became central to the empirical policy debate. The deep and persistent moral divisions on abortion have stymied the legislative process on a range of issues often not directly relevent to abortion at all. Failure to find a moral consensus for public policy on abortion has frustrated policy consensus on other "life issues" like the funding of genetic research or in-vitro fertilization. The human rights debate did not produce clear and decisive lines of moral difference like abortion, but a general degree of confusion about how best to proceed normatively and empirically on human rights cases. In both instances, however, the normative factor was directly tied to the capacity to shape a coherent, effective public policy.

This focus on issues rather than individuals or organizations recasts the religion and politics relationship. The issues raise the moral dimension of the policy debate directly. It is when the moral question is central that the religious communities are invited into or drawn into the policy debate as communities in possession of a moral tradition. It is the moral factor in the public argument today which catalyzes the religion and politics relationship.

It is possible to speak broadly of two major secular trends which create moral questions in the public debate directly relevant to the Consistent Ethic. The first is the impact of technology on political choice and public policy. In the last forty-five years this society has split the atom and cracked the genetic code. These discoveries symbolize the kinds of ethical issues which are found in the two major arguments of the 1980s: the ethics of nuclear strategy and the ethics of medical technology. The medical-moral questions have been part of the public policy process for the last twenty years, encompassing the "classical" issues of care for the terminally ill, transplants and experimentation as well as the contemporary questions which arise from new technologies, questions of genetic research, in-vitro fertilization, fetal experimentation and surrogacy. The medical-moral arguments are now carried on with significant inter-disciplinary collaboration, using a shared vocabulary and a well-defined agenda which is found in scholarly journals devoted to this topic. In a sense the medical-moral debates have become a model of how the society might address other issues of normative significance. Four national commissions have examined specific moral issues and made recommendations for public policy. No other topic of moral argument has been conducted in such a structured pattern either in the academic or the political communities.

The question of the ethics of nuclear strategy has been very visible in the public arena in the 1980s, but has as yet not produced a well structured interdisciplinary argument on the policy issues. The shift of the 1980s from previous decades is that interdisciplinary interest, expressed in the writings of individual ethicists and political and strategic thinkers, is higher. But the degree of interaction of ethicists and strategists does not approximate the collaboration in bioethics; nor has anything like the national commissions on ethics and medicine been approached in the strategic field. Given the public attention paid to the moral issues in the early 1980s, it seems surprising in retrospect that the Scowcroft Commission, which was charged with the assessment of the nature and future direction of American strategic forces, had no representation from the disciplines of theology or ethics. Such an omission in the medical field would be noted immediately.

Both fields, however, medicine and nuclear strategy share a common link to technology. In both areas of life the technological drive of the last forty years has produced questions which are qualitatively different than either medicine or military affairs previously confronted. The new questions are filled with technical complexity, but technical analysis does not exhaust their meaning or significance. First in the medical world and now in the strategic debate the moral issues have gained saliency with the professional community and with the wider public. Two pillars of the Consistent Ethic are the positions the bishops have taken on abortion and nuclear policy. The design of the Consistent Ethic is to recognize the differences in the nature of these two questions, the distinct theological and ethical foundations from which they are addressed, but to identify the empirical linkage of medical and military questions (in the sense of the technological revolution both face today) and then to highlight common moral principles which cut across both fields (e.g., defense of innocent life from direct attack).

The second secular trend which is addressed by the Consistent Ethic is the fact of interdependence. Papal and conciliar social teaching of the last twenty-five years have identified the increasing material interdependence of the world today as posing both a moral possibility and a moral problem. The *fact* of increasing interdependence means that peoples and nations regularly and systematically touch and shape each other's lives. The 1970s brought material interdependence home to U.S. citizens with the powerful example of the oil boycott imposed by the OPEC nations. In a manner almost unknown to this large and powerful nation Americans found their daily existence traumatized by decisions on the price and flow of oil in the Middle East. The experience produced several consequences, one of them being some reflection on how others experience the impact of interdependence when U.S. decisions (on food, interest rates and trade policy) are the determining factor. There is a moral possibility in the fact of material interdependence—it provides the basis for a more integrated international community. The moral problem of interdependence is whether the rules and relationships can be developed which prevent material interdependence from being used as a political or economic weapon, thereby turning the fact of material interdependence into a Hobbesian war of all against all. While the papal literature concentrates on interdependence and its consequences at the global level, the Consistent Ethic stresses both the domestic and international implications of interdependence. The politics of food vs oil, of trade policy and foreign aid are the stuff of global interdependence; moral choices surface in this multiplicity of "North-South" issues; but the domestic counterpart is visible in the politics and moral choices involved in the federal budget. Faced with a $200 billion deficit the United States faces new stringency in determining what it will spend and for whom. The annual budgetary process follows the logic of a zero-sum game when the choices are posed between defense spending and social spending. It is not a rhetorical device to say that one quickly faces choices between food stamps and missiles, between housing programs and SDI. It is easier to pose the problem than to address it adequately, but these kinds of choices embody the meaning of domestic interdependence. The Consistent Ethic met some of its strongest objections for attempting to relate the protection of human life from attack (war and abortion) and the promotion of human life through socio-economic programs. There are undoubtedly qualitative differences in the moral problems faced on these two fronts and decidely different empirical issues involved. But neither of these valid observations eliminates the fact that the budgetary choices made in our society do touch both of these issues (how we protect life and how we promote social welfare) and the way we choose engages the moral questions of interdependence.

The secular trends of rapid and extensive technological change as well as increasing material interdependence are long-term characteristics of our society. They have produced and will most likely continue to produce policy choices which have fundamental human consequences. In spite of the daunting technical complexity of these choices, it is reasonable to assume, based on the experience of the 1970s and 1980s, that policymakers and plain citizens will not be satisfied with confining the policy debate to its purely technical or empirical elements. The moral factors are so close to the core of the issues produced by technology and interdependence that they will surface or will be pulled to the surface for examination and analysis. While religious institutions have no corner on the market in these normative debates, both the traditions they possess and the constituencies they represent press them into the moral debate. The persistence of the religion-morality-politics themes which are guaranteed by the secular trends sketched here provides an open moment for the Consistent Ethic. It is a framework, not a detailed blueprint, for these issues. But its scope of issues, its attempt to relate empirical trends, moral principles and policy judgments and its interest in how distinct questions intersect, combine to give the Consistent Ethic a capacity for advancing the religion and politics argument.

II. The Consistent Ethic and the Character of Catholic Social Teaching

The open moment in the religion and politics relationship is an invitation to religious communities to share the resources of their moral vision with a society in search of wisdom about morality and public policy. Richard Neuhaus has argued two propositions convincingly: that religious values belong in the public life of the nation, but the religious communities must make a public case for their views, one which is not confined to credal convictions of a given religious community.[4] The Consistent Ethic proposal developed from a series of prior positions which the U.S. Catholic Bishops had taken in the public arena. It also derives from a wider Catholic social tradition which provides the structural ideas and the style of argument used in the Consistent Ethic. In this section, my purpose is to sketch elements of the Catholic social tradition which are foundational ideas for the Consistent Ethic.

Natural Law: The Consistent Ethic draws from both Catholic social ethics and Catholic medical ethics as it moves from abortion to warfare to civil and human rights issues. The theoretical framework which is the basis for both social and medical ethics in the Catholic tradition is the natural law ethic. As Ernst Troeltsch has illustrated the church moved early to the use of natural law categories drawn from classical philosophy to address a range of social questions for which the scriptures provide little specific moral guidance.[5] From Lactantius to Aquinas to the Spanish Scholastics and, preeminently in our day, to *Pacem in Terris* the Catholic social tradition has been shaped and structured in terms of natural law categories.[6] While Cardinal Bernardin's several lectures on the Consistent Ethic theme have not dealt explicitly with the ethical theory supporting it, both the purpose of the Consistent Ethic and its style of moral analysis place it solidly within the natural law tradition.

The Consistant Ethic has as its primary audience the Catholic community; it seeks to establish a framework of evaluation for a range of concerns which already engage the church but in a less than systematic fashion. But the Consistent Ethic is designed to reach beyond the ecclesial community; it must do this precisely because an effective engagement on the issues addressed must involve the wider society and influence the public agenda.

In Catholic social teaching the natural law has served two distinct funtions. The first, stressed by Troeltsch, has been to provide a structure of philosophical argument which is reflective of the key values and the vision of the scripture, but which relates those values in a more detailed and complex fashion to a range of secular, empirical issues. In this sense, the natural law use of reason and experience expands and specifies the moral vision of the scriptures; it acts as a bridge between the moral wisdom of revelation and a changing secular environment which puts new questions to the biblical vision in each age.

The second function of the natural law ethic is to provide a method of moral reasoning and a mode of discourse which can be shared with the civil community at large. Here the natural law provides a possibility of framing an area of moral consensus beyond the community of faith. The Consistent Ethic, like the two pastoral letters of the episcopal conference, explicitly addresses the ecclesial and civil communities together. The pastoral letters commit extensive sections to the biblical themes that establish the church's focus on both peace and the economy, but the policy sections of both pastorals are elaborated in a fashion which is open to examination, argument and agreement by those who are not committed by faith to the revealed word. The Consistent Ethic lectures are less explicit methodologically and are cast almost exclusively in the language of a natural law ethic. Like the pastorals the Consistent Ethic proposal has the objective of joining the ecclesial reflection on a range of issues with the civil debate about them.

The natural law lineage of the Consistent Ethic is also evident in the categories of analysis it invokes. Cardinal Bernardin has returned often to the point that the Consistent Ethic is not designed to reduce a series of issues to one general problem of "respecting life." Both the Fordham University and the St. Louis University addresses invite a two dimensional analysis. First, an examination of the distinct moral arguments made in the church on abortion, war, capital punishment, et al; then an assessment of where "linkage" does and does not exist, normatively and empirically. At both stages of analysis the moral argument is that of natural law: the specific positions—on abortion and war for example—use a philosophical rather than a theological rationale, and the appeal to relate the issues in terms of a consistent and comprehensive defense of human dignity and human life is similarly developed with a natural law framework.

The choice of the natural law model for the Consistent Ethic involves both assets and liabilities. The value of the model, as illustrated by the experience of the pastoral letters, is that it allows a religiously grounded but philosophically articulated social vision to be used by many institutions and individuals in a pluralistic society like the United States. Perhaps the most important role of the pastoral letters was their catalytic function—they became public property, extending beyond the ecclesial community to whom they were orginally addressed, and eliciting both agreement and criticism from a cross-section of the public policy and academic communities in the country. The style of the Consistent Ethic offers a similar opportunity, even though its multiple issues make it more difficult to focus the public debate in the fashion of the pastorals.

The limits of the natural law model are encountered in both the civil and ecclesial debates. While the just-war arguments of *The Challenge of Peace* and the social policy analysis of *Economic Justice for All* provided a framework for the ecclesial-civil dialogue, it cannot be concluded that those in the civil dialogue find the natural law ethic itself a satisfying method of moral argument. One could more safely assume that aspects of the tradition were used by many respondents in a selective fashion as they engaged the views of the bishops. Even within the ecclesial community, it would be prudent to distinguish the support which the social aspect of natural law theory finds in the theological and academic communities, as distinct from the controversy which surrounds many of the natural law arguments in medical and sexual ethics. Since the Consistent Ethic precisely moves beyond the sphere of the two pastoral letters to the medical-moral questions, its objective of shaping a consensus on a spectrum of issues is more difficult to achieve than were the objectives of the two pastoral letters.

The State: The natural law character of the Consistent Ethic is evident in its extensive use of the language of rights, duties and social solidarity. Hence it is not surprising that a key idea which runs through the Consistent Ethic argument is its conception of the state—a basic category in the natural law moral theory. The Consistent Ethic is not "statist" but it does advocate an activist role for the state on particularly controversial issues. The position on abortion seeks to use the coercive power of civil law in defense of fetal life, thereby restricting substantially the legality of abortion in the United States. The controversy which this position evokes from the left of the political spectrum is matched by equal dissatisfaction on the political right with Cardinal Bernardin's assertion that:

> Consistency means we cannot have it both ways: we cannot urge a compassionate society and vigorous public policy to protect the rights of the unborn and then argue that compassion and significant public policy to protect the rights of the unborn and then argue that compassion and signficant public programs on behalf of the needy undermine the moral fibre of society or are beyond the proper scope of governmental responsibility.[7]

The point here is not to argue that the issues of abortion and social welfare are the same morally, but to focus attention on the moral conception of the role of the state in society. The inherent tension which Fr. Murray identified in *We Hold These Truths* between a Lockean social contract view of the state and the more organic conception of a natural law ethic is part of the argument which the Consistent Ethic has resurfaced in the church and civil society.[8] The range of positive moral responsibilities which the natural law argument attributes to the state (and civil law) encounters dissent—for different reasons—across the political spectrum in the United States today. This was particularly evident in the public debate surrounding *Economic Justice for All*. Perhaps the single most persistent criticism of the pastoral was that it placed excessive emphasis on the role of the government in the economy. To respond adequately to this critique one would have to distinguish two levels of its meaning. At a tactical level there is a broad spectrum of possibilities in deciding which functions the state performs effectively; at this level of prudential judgment a continuing debate will mark socio-economic policy. But the critique offered of the pastoral letter often went beyond the tactical question. The often unexpressed differences with the letter lay at the philosophical level of how the moral repsonsibility of the state is to be understood. The activist role for the state argued in the Consistent Ethic is a philosophical position which finds expression in both the abortion issues and the social welfare issues. In both instances the argument about the Consistent Ethic will go more deeply than tactics.

If the argument is joined, the Consistent Ethic should, in my view, be cast in terms of an activist role for the state in society, but an activism limited by two other concepts drawn from Catholic social teaching. First, regarding the role of civil law in a pluralistic society, the Consistent Ethic should be argued in terms of the concept of public order found in the *Declaration on Religious Liberty* of Vatican II. The public order criterion assumes that the state has positive moral responsibilities, but it sets limits to the use of the coercive power of the state through civil law.[9] The limit is set by the requirement that an issue must be shown to affect directly the core values of public order (i.e. public peace, defense of rights and public morality) before an appeal can be made to invoke the prohibitions or prescriptions of civil law. The use of the public order criterion is first found in Catholic teaching in Vatican II; the previous guide for civil law had been the more expansive concept that the state and the law should be invoked to protect the common good. The relevance of the public order concept for the Consistent Ethic argument on abortion is that it places the responsibility on the church to demonstrate why abortion is a public order issue. The case can, I believe, be made, but it requires a social argument about the meaning and consequences of abortion as well as a rationale for invoking the civil law in this case. Too often the Catholic argument has assumed that the public order implications of abortion are self-evident. In fact it is often not even considered in the public debate, yet the Consistent

Ethic's call for use of the civil law to restrict abortion requires—by the standards of Catholic teaching—that the case be explicitly made.

Second, the activist role prescribed for the state on social welfare questions in the Consistent Ethic is limited in Catholic teaching by the principle of subsidiarity. The saliency of joining the right-to-life argument about abortion with a strong social welfare position is that the link is too seldom affirmed in ecclesial and civil debates. But the scope of state activity and the tactics of designing effective social welfare policies should be tested by the subsidiarity principle inherent in the same natural law social ethic which affirms an activist role for the state.

The Taking of Life: A third theme of Catholic social ethics found throughout the Consistent Ethic is the position it proposes on the morality of taking human life. As Fr. John Connery stressed in his commentary on the Consistent Ethic, Catholic teaching has sustained Augustine's assertion that some taking of life is morally legitimate in a sinful, limited human environment.[10] The consequences of this assertion engage the Consistent Ethic's positions on war and capital punishment, but also on abortion and care of the terminally ill. At one level the Consistent Ethic can be seen as bringing together the classical conclusions of Catholic teaching on these diverse questions. On closer examination it is clear that there are three issues just below the surface of the Consistent Ethic which are changes from the classical arguments. First, following *The Challenge of Peace* Cardinal Bernardin stresses the increasingly stringent limits placed on modern warfare since Pius XII. While he does not play out the full meaning of these restraints in the style of the pastoral letter, it is clear that the respect for life which the Consistent Ethic advocates envisions these limits as minimal conditions.[11] Second, the opposition to capital punishment found in the Consistent Ethic follows the distinction the U.S. Bishops have employed for the last decade. In a departure from Aquinas and later papal teaching, the case is made on prudential grounds that other means than capital punishment should be used by the state to protect basic values in society. Third, the specific discussion of warfare and the general advocacy of respect for life in the Consistent Ethic inevitably surfaces the differences found in the church today between the natural law arguments allowing some taking of life and the more biblically articulated argument for a totally nonviolent moral posture for the church. While the Consistent Ethic argues in the classical mode, differentiating just and unjust taking of life, its call to the church and society to stand consistently for life underlines the fundamental difference between these two positions which the Christian church has struggled with for centuries and which has now developed again in Catholicism.[12]

III. The Consistent Ethic: Ecclesiology, Ethics and Politics

To analyze the public policy potential and implications of the Consistent Ethic requires a threefold assessment: ecclesiological, moral and political. The first level seeks to locate the church's position on the Consistent Ethic in the political process. The second level seeks to test the relationship among the issues in the Consistent Ethic. The third level addresses questions of strategy and tactics.

A. Ecclesiology: The ecclesiological questions touching the Consistent Ethic involve the church *ad extra* and *ad intra*. The external issue is where the Consistent Ethic places the church in the wider public policy spectrum of the United States. The proposal of the Consistent Ethic did not develop new policy positions for the U.S. Bishops; it simply brought existing positions into a new configuration. This new configuration of the issues, however, did seek to build upon a reality which developed progressively in the 1980s. The bishops had shaped a public policy posture which cut across the conventional divisions in the U.S. political system. By joining opposition to abortion with opposition to the arms race; by linking a right-to-life agenda with an expansive social welfare policy, the bishops projected a position distinct from any other major institution in the country. The result was that they had fervent allies on specific issues, but very few individuals or organizations who would follow them across the spectrum of their agenda. The position illustrates both the strength and the liability of the Consistent Ethic. As a broadly defined philosophical framework it serves to test other positions in the public debate; as a practical program its range of concerns makes creation of a stable constituency very difficult. Since the church clearly should not be trying to create a voting bloc or a political organization the liability is not a fatal flaw. But the question of how to move the Consistent Ethic beyond the testing of more narrowly defined positions toward realizing its objectives remains unanswered. It may be the case that the church fulfills its particular function in the political process precisely by making a case which is broader than any organized political force is pursuing, but the projection of the Consistent Ethic has created expectations which have not been realized in practice. *Ad extra* the Consistent Ethic places the bishops in the policy debate but at times isolated in the political process.

This description leads to the *ad intra* question—the role of the bishops in proposing a policy vision which includes quite specific recommendations on abortion (a constitutional amendment), on nuclear policy (no-first-use), on the economy (specifically targeted public employment programs) and on Central America (opposing aid to the Contras). The general reception given the pastoral letters welcomed religious leaders who were prepared to press beyond the statement of values and principles. But there were dissenting voices, some based on political or tactical grounds, others like Fr. Avery Dulles who dissented from episcopal specificity on theological grounds:

> Generally speaking, I believe the episcopal conference should devote itself primarily to teaching, leaving the concrete applications, when these are not obvious, to lay persons regularly engaged in secular affairs.[13]

I can only repeat here in the context of the consistent Ethic what I have previously argued in response to Fr. Dulles' position. While agreeing with him that episcopal conferences in making specific policy judgments "should clearly identify them as such," I cannot agree that the bishops are restricted by either theological reasons or political prudence to simply stating general moral or theological principles. My difference with Fr. Dulles rests on three different arguments.

The first is ecclesiological: the logic of *Octogesima Adveniens* calls the local church precisely to the task of specifying general principles which the magisterium sets forth. While the phrase "Christian communities" in Paul VI's text clearly goes beyond the local hierarchy, it does not seem to exclude them. If such bodies stay purely at the level of principle they seem to sacrifice their comparative advantage derived from pastoral experience and knowledge of the local situation.

The second is moral: Catholic moral theology is characterized by two assets, its structure of principles and its willingness to press a moral argument through to specific conclusions. The Catholic tradition has done this in social ethics as well. There is undoubtedly a risk of absolutizing in either area what is at best a prudential choice or a complex and contingent moral conclusion. But there is also a risk in stating principles so abstractly that all acknowledge them, then proceed to widely divergent conclusions while claiming support of the principle. The danger of this is particularly acute in the public policy arena where all parties seek moral protection for specific positions.

A third argument is either political or pastoral. It arises from Fr. Dulles' persuasive commentary on what gives an ecclesial statement moral authority which commands assent. He says:

> Assent is never a matter of sheer obedience, but one of responsible judgment.... In the final analysis authority is only a means to an end, namely, the production of documents that effectively address real and urgent questions. In actual practice the influence of conference documents, like that of encyclicals and even conciliar statements, depends less on the formal authority with which they are issued than on their intrinsic merits.... If discerning readers find it persuasive and enlightening, it can produce an impact in excess of its juridical or official weight.[14]

I would contend that on issues like nuclear policy or the economy, "the intrinsic merits and persuasive quality" of episcopal statements are enhanced if the bishops show—with appropriate modesty and limited claims of authority—a willingness to engage the specific dimensions of problems. Obviously the test of such an approach is the quality of reasoning which joins the ethical and empirical elements of a problem. The formal object quo of an episcopal statement should be its moral-religious perspective. But its material content can extend to specific policy conclusions—explicitly defined as such.

This debate on how specific bishops should be in advocating a morally grounded course of action arose particularly during the preparation of the pastoral letters, but it has application to the Consistent Ethic proposal. To follow the course I have advocated, shaping episcopal teaching to include both principles and specific conclusions, requires an understanding within the church of how specific episcopal judgments are to be received. Precisely because such judgments will be a mix of principles and contingent applications, there must be room for contrary applications within the church. Such an approach will require more attention than has been given thus far to the limits and dynamics of a legitimate pluralism within the Catholic community. The pluralism has been explicitly accepted on social teaching in magisterial documents, but the Consistent Ethic includes issues which have been much less open to pluralistic interpretations. An example would be the proposals for legislative redress of the abortion situation in the United States. Distinguishing between the moral position on abortion and its legislative remedy at least opens the question of why pluralism would not be acceptable on the legislative front.

232 A Consistent Ethic of Life

B. *Moral:* The moral question which directly influences the Consistent Ethic's public policy application is whether it is necessary or possible to elaborate a hierarchy of issues within the Consistent Ethic. In considering how to press the multiple concerns of the Consistent Ethic is it the case that some issues will always have greater public policy significance? Can or should candidates, parties and legislative priorities be measured against a defined scale of issues which is determined by the intrinsic significance of certain issues?

These questions arise because the scope of the Consistent Ethic embraces very different kinds of problems which in turn are related to different moral obligations. The linking of these diverse issues is viewed by the supporters of the Consistent Ethic as its comparative advantage. It is seen by the critics of the proposal as a threat to clear moral thinking, because it confuses different moral responsibilities.

It is clear that substantially different issues and obligations exist along the spectrum of the Consistent Ethic—abortion on the one hand and failing to protect the civil rights of a person are both moral faults but of a qualitatively different kind. Beneath the difference of issues lie distinct moral obligations: in traditional Catholic teaching the negative duty of not taking innocent human life binds always and under all conditions; the positive duty to aid the poor admits of diverse modes of fulfillment depending upon the capabilities of different individuals. In terms of the intrinsic nature of these duties and the issues to which they are related, it would be theoretically possible to rank the issues and obligations in the Consistent Ethic.

Does this mean that such a hierarchy can or should be transposed to the public policy arena? It does not seem that such a move is either obligatory or even advisable. The direct illation from a statement of moral theory to public policy would inevitably fail to address precisely those issues which are the central factors in the wise shaping of social policy. In another context John Courtney Murray pointed to these factors in a critique made of an exclusively personal conception of moral theory: "It did not understand the special moral problems raised by the institutionalization of human action. It did not grasp the nature of politics, the due autonomy of the political, the limiting factors of political action or the standing of success as a political value."[15]

Murray categories could be used as a grid to test whether ranking the Consistent Ethic's issues would take due consideration of "the institutionalization of action and the nature of politics." The intrinsic significance of limiting or preventing abortion through civil law must be tested in light of whether such a goal is possible at a given moment. If it is not, the importance of the issue remains the same, but the public policy agenda of the church might focus primary efforts at other points on the spectrum. In the American public debate of the 1980s, diverse groups identified the prevention of abortion or the prevention of nuclear war as "the" moral issue before the nation. The Consistent Ethic allows for a recognition of the comparative importance of either of these issues versus others on the moral spectrum, but would balk at translating these statements into a firm ranking of political priorities. That task—ranking issues, relating them coherently to a policy vision and pursuing its implementation in the political arena—is rooted in moral theory but belongs to strategy and tactics.

C. *Strategy and Tactics:* Even if the Consistent Ethic is understood as a framework and not a political program, the logic of the proposal requires that it be thought through in terms of the pragmatic dimensions of the political process. Hence the need to conclude this section with a series of specific questions and recommendations:

1. *Single Issue Advocacy:* In strictly political terms there are arguments to be made for a single issue approach to the public policy process. Such a well defined objective makes it possible to concentrate a committed constituency on a precise goal. There are several examples of how such an approach has been successful; they run from resisting efforts at gun control to the civil rights legislative victories of the 1960s. But on ecclesiological and moral grounds I would argue that the logic of the Consistent Ethic compels the church to resist a single issue strategy. Ecclesiologically, there is the responsibility of the church to set a tone and an atmosphere in the civil life of society which it cannot do by focusing exclusively on a single-issue. Such a posture risks depicting the church as simply an interest group in a political struggle. The effect of single-issue voting strategies is to reduce the chance that parties and candidates will be judged by standards which test their vision of society and their capacity to address the basic needs of the common good. Morally, a single-issue strategy forfeits many of the resources of the moral teaching of the church. To highlight one question as the primary and exclusive objective in the policy process is to leave too many issues unattended and risks distortion of the single-issue itself.

2. *The Church and Parties:* The Consistent Ethic finds its best testing ground in the assessment of party platforms. It is precisely in this context that the church can evaluate the consistency of a series of positions and the scope of the moral vision being proposed by a party. Although it is clearly

understood today that the church should not tie itself to a political party, the Consistent Ethic can be used to insure that no perception of this kind exists. Precisely because the Consistent Ethic cuts across conventional political alignments in the United States, it is the most effective instrument for the church to use in offering a framework of judgment during a campaign, while keeping its own positions distinct in the public mind.

3. *Candidates and/or Elected Officials:* To move from evaluating party platforms or pieces of legislation to assessing candidates or elected officials is to encounter new complexity. The platforms deal with issues in broad terms; legislation takes one topic at a time. But candidates are pressed, as they should be, on wider range of topics: personal character as well as public positions, the relationship of personal convictions on issues to specific votes or decisions; candidates are asked not only what positions they favor or oppose, but what strategy they will use in achieving their objectives.

How useful is the Consistent Ethic in this testing of candidates. At one level, candidates run on platforms, so the assessment of the platform and the candidates' general positions are a single piece. Here again the Consistent Ethic tests the scope of the candidate's vision; it sets an agenda the candidate must meet, usually pushing a candidate to address issues not of his/her choosing.

The neuralgic case is the instance where a candidate says he/she agrees with the moral basis of the Consistent Ethic's position on an issue, but sees no way to realize the objective in practice. The issue can be abortion, capital punishment or nuclear testing. In each instance the step from moral analysis to a practical remedy does allow for several views to be held about tactics and strategy. The experience of the 1984 campaign on the abortion question (candidates personally opposed but not legislatively active on the issue) leads me to two guidelines for dealing with candidates. On one hand the total split between personal conviction and public posture is unsatisfactory. Part of what attracts voters to candidates is their personal character and conviction—what they stand for in light of what I as a citizen and voter stand for. If the candidate severs the link between personal conviction and public choices, the voter and the general public lose a key test of who should govern in a society. Candidates should be pressed to make explicit how they relate conviction and choice. Such a dialogue should produce a complex model of decisionmaking since not all personal convictions can be translated into law, policy or programs. Here my second guideline comes into play; while resisting the personal/public split for a public official, it is necessary to leave a candidate a legitimate range of prudential choice about when and how he/she is willing to move an issue from moral conviction to a proposal for law on policy. Candidates should feel the pressure of both the principles and the particular conclusions of the Consistent Ethic, but the legitimate freedom of debate about concrete choices which is recognized as necessary within the church, should have a particular relevance for testing candidates. If a candidate failed to do anything to implement what he declared to be a morally necessary objective, it could, or course, be grounds for citizens not to support him/her. But it is a different judgment to say that such a candidate has gone beyond the bounds of what is morally acceptable. The fault would lie at a more pragmatic level and judgment would be something less than moral censure of the candidate.

The Consistent Ethic's contribution to public policy lies less in making final judgments about candidates than in sharpening the church's own moral vision, so she can be a source of wisdom to others seeking to protect life at every stage of its development.

Notes

1. J. L. Bernardin, "A Consistent Ethic of Life: An American Catholic Dialogue" and " A Consistent Ethic of Life: Continuing the Dialogue" in this volume, pp. 1-19. These addresses were published as *The Seamless Garment* (Kansas City: The National Catholic Reporter, 1984).

2. For a sampling of the literature cf: R. J. Neuhaus, *The Naked Square: Religion and Democracy in America* (Grand Rapids, MI: William B. Eerdmans Publishing Co., 1984); R. P. McBrien, *Caesar's Coin: Religion and Politics in America* (N. Y.: Macmillan Publishing Co., 1987); A.J. Reichley, *Religion in American Public Life* (Washington, D.C: The Brookings Institute, 1985); R. W. Lovin, ed., *Religion and American Public Life: Interpretations and Explorations* (N. Y.: Paulist Press, 1986).

3. Neuhaus, cited; M. Stackhouse, Understanding the Neo-Evangelicals: Religious Right: New? Right?, *Commonweal* 59 (1982) p. 52-56.

4. Neuhaus, p. 3-19.

5. E. Troeltsch, *The Social Teaching of the Christian Church* (N.Y: Harper and Row, 1960) vol. I.

6. For a commentary on the categories and history of this development cf: J. C. Murray, *We Hold These Truths* (N.Y: Sheed and Ward, 1960) p. 295-336; J. N. Moody, ed., *Church Society: Catholic Social and Political Thought and Movements* (N.Y: Arts Publishers, 1953); A. P. d'Entreves, The Case for Natural Law Reexamined, *Natural Law Forum* 1 (1956) p. 1-50.

7. Bernardin, cited, p. 9 in this volume.

8. Murray, p. 306 ff.

9. For commentary cf: J.C. Murray, The Problem of Religious Freedom, *Theological Studies* 25 (1964) p. 529-30; *Declaration on Religious Freedom*, #2, 7; with Commentary by J.C. Murray in W. Abbot, ed., *The Documents of Vatican II* (N.Y: Guild Press, 1966) p. 685 ff; fn. 20, p. 686.

10. J.R. Connery, A Seamless Garment in a Sinful World, *America* (July 14, 1984) p. 5.

11. The discussion of limits on nuclear weapons is found in *The Challenge of Peace*, #146-161; 178-185. The debate about limits has been a major subject in commentary on the letter; cf: J. Nye, *Nuclear Ethics* (N.Y.: Free Press, 1986); W. O'Brien, Just War Doctrine in a Nuclear Context, *Theological Studies* 44 (1983) p. 191-220; D. Hollenbach, Ethics in Distress: Can There Be Just Wars in the Nuclear Age?, in W.V. O'Brien and J. Langan, eds., *The Nuclear Dilemma and The Just War Tradition* (Lexington, MA: Lexington Books, 1986) p. 13-30.

12. Cf: T. Shannon, ed., *War or Peace? The Search for New Answers* (N.Y: Orbis Books, 1980) ch. 1, 6, 12; P. Murnion, ed., *Catholics and Nuclear War* (N.Y: Crossroads Books, 1983) p. 117-146.

13. A. Dulles, What Is The Doctrinal Authority of a Bishops Conference?, *Origins* 14 (1985) p. 533.

14. Same, p. 532, 533.

15. Murray, cited, p. 277.

Response to J. Bryan Hehir, "The Consistent Ethic: Public Policy Implications"

Sidney Callahan

My response to Bryan Hehir's fine paper will be more of an amplification than a critique. My basic agreement with Hehir, along with the limits of time and space, precludes a more extended discussion of the public polity implications of the consistent ethic of life. I will limit myself to a brief reflection stimulated by two questions posed by Bryan Hehir's paper. The first question is:

(1) Why now? Why are we here in this conference engaged in what Hehir calls "the increasingly visible and complicated intersection of religion and politics in the U.S.?" Why are we now witnessing "the new intensity of religion and politics?"

The second question is a pragmatic one:

(2) How can we "involve the wider society and influence the public agenda" toward the consistent ethic of life?

(1) Why Now?

The current intensification of moral ethical and religious concerns in U.S. politics arises partly because the Catholic Church is ready to speak to American society in a new way—and American society is ready to listen as it has not before. Yes, as Hehir notes, these new moral concerns are partly induced in response to technological developments in medicine and nuclear energy, but more also seems to be at stake. Other developments within the Church and within American culture are also intersecting in new ways.

The internal development of the modern Catholic Church has been launched on a new course since before Vatican II. Believers will see this as a sign of the work of the Holy Spirit who makes all things new and so creates ferment, change and growth. As the Church's understanding of the Gospel message is ever more thoroughly assimilated, new concerns for the dignity of each individual person emerge. Catholic social thought is constantly reformulated. Since the second world war many different movements within the Church have appeared, focusing upon the dignity, equality and sanctity of human life. Popes and bishops have taught, and from the members at large groundswells emerge as various new Christian movements devoted to work, family life, women, peacemaking, and justice for the poor. As these movements and currents appear it has become necessary for the Church as a community to try and integrate a response, theologically, reflectively and pragmatically. In America one fruitful response has been the articulation of the consistent ethic of life.

New psychological understandings of human nature can help us understand the internal developmental progress in which articulation follows activity. Piaget has pointed out that as children mature they can often do things before they can conceptually say what they are doing. The child's actual response to a problem confronted in reality remains for a time preconscious, and can only later be consciously conceptualized and accurately described. This human development process reflects an innate human drive for rational conceptualization and rational consistency. We human beings as the rational species, seem driven toward integrity and consistency. We can see the Church's recent developments and articulation of social thought, its movement toward a consistent ethic of life, as a human effort to articulate and put into practice what is implicitly given in the Gospel message.

More specifically we can see that American Catholics are now ready to engage in public policy efforts in a new way. The new movements within the Church have met special conditions in the U.S. Here after a hundred and fifty years the Catholic Church has moved beyond its earlier immigrant minority status as a foreign sect. Today Catholics are assimilated and confident enough to try and shape the mainstream of society. Sects are content with toleration and can only hope to shape the morality of their own members; they withdraw from the larger world and concentrate on private moral behavior. Only a mainstream majority Church, which is not an established Church, can dare to challenge Caesar and morally contend with the secular powers that be. The consistent ethic of life agenda is in one sense a mark of U.S. Catholic maturity and strength. Ironically, the conflicts and arguments now taking place within the American Church are also an indication of security and maturity. It is no longer necessary for American Catholics to suppress dissent in order to maintain a common front against hostile persecutions.

Indeed, American society in the last half of the twentieth century is no longer actively hostile to religion. Many have seen this new openness as "the Catholic moment" in U.S. history. This new moment and readiness to listen has arisen because of several converging cultural movements. After the convulsions of the sixties and the crises brought on by Vietnam, Watergate and the ongoing series of scandals, much of the older assurance and moral authority of the past Protestant and secular establishment has been dissipated. When the best and the brightest of the old elites have led us into disaster after disaster one can no longer believe in the triumph of traditional republican virtues. A mood of disillusionment and the perception of America's moral decadence has been growing.

Neoconservatives, conservatives and religious fundamentalists have grown in strength as liberals have admitted that secular humanism and due process may not be enough to maintain a morally effective society. What has been called the liberals' "thin theory of the good" emphasizing only liberty, individual autonomy and due process, has not been effective in socializing new generations of Americans. As the quip goes, one cannot raise children on the ideology of the ACLU. Earlier generations may have lived off "the value fat" of implicit moral understanding of the common good, a moral resource which has been depleted by lack of cultivation and continued ideological assaults.

There is a new realization that moral relativism has become widespread and with its cultural dominance there has been a corresponding disintegration of those socializing institutions needed for a culture to flourish. The family and educational institutions break down if there is no moral authority and no commitment to commonly held moral truths. Conservatives and religious fundamentalists rush into the moral vacuum with energetic efforts to return to past pieties and the unquestioning allegiance to older orthodoxies.

Yet strategies to return to the past are doomed to failure, because of other equally potent new currents in science and social science. Old certainties in science and psychology have also collapsed at this critical juncture in our society. We are now in the midst of the development of postmodern scientific paradigms which challenge older worldviews and assumptions. As we read of superstrings, and chaos, open systems and the onrush of galaxies to who knows where, it becomes clear that we don't understand what matter is or the nature of our universe. The most basic challenges come from the challenges to the objective analytic methods in which the secular dogmas of the enlightenment put so much faith.

Only in the social sciences and psychology has there been a paradoxical effect. The collapse of the old mechanistic deterministic models of nature increased the role of human reason and free choice as causes of events. In psychology's cognitive revolution there is more room for a nonreductionist view of the rationally functioning human person who interprets and shapes his own destiny. The new fascination with how people process information and solve problems has forced a new appreciation of human choice and freedom to affect the environment. Behavior reductionists have been more or less routed. Thus education, rational persuasion and the power of thought have been rehabilitated in new ways, even as old mechanistic models and certainties have disintegrated. The growth of the "new age movement" reflects many of the cultural contradictions now existing.

Such a moment in our society may indeed be the Catholic moment. Catholicism has always flourished when old secular ideologies break down and the barbarians are at the gates. In times of ferment, when the old center does not hold, the Catholic center has been able to muster new synthesis, new support, new energy, and provide creative leadership toward a new future. Catholic thought has been able to create new cultural wholes from the best of the old, reenergized with the moral and spiritual fire of the evernew Gospel message. The consistent ethic of life embodies many of the goods in the older individualistic liberal traditions, while incorporating these moral values into a more communitarian commitment to the common good. It is rational and spiritual. As an ethic it appeals to good reasons, and to the best of our human emotions and ideals. There is a chance that this creative new approach can decisively shape our collective future—which brings us to question number two.

(2) How Can We Involve and More the Larger Society Toward a Consistent Ethic of Life?

If our society is at a critical period and in a condition of social and intellectual ferment there is a chance that it can be moved toward a consistent ethic of life. The first requirement for those seeking change is to believe that social change is possible. Social scientists have studied how change is effected. One irony pointed out by the sociologist Albert O. Hirshman is that often those who study social systems are the least open to the possibility of rapid and deep social changes. His thesis is that focusing attention upon all the ways that an operating system functions and analyzing how a status quo is reinforced, produces a "gloomy vision" that blinds an observer to the potential for change.

But there are historical periods when "history suddenly accelerates" and social worlds are overturned or transformed. Those persons who with "passion for what is possible" do not "rely on what has been certified as probable by factor analysis," go out and effectively change the world. Only after the fact will other analysts see why such radical changes happened— why for instance the Russian revolution improbably took place and succeeded. A different and more instructive example for those seeking to move toward a consistent ethic of life is the historical change that took place toward the morality of slavery, which in England was effected very suddenly within twenty years or so. While generations of Quakers and other marginal groups had fought against slavery without success, the cause finally moved from the periphery to the center of the society's moral concern for reform. We in the twentieth century have also seen the world quickly change—in both moral and immoral directions.

Another acute analysis of social change has been given by the social psychologist and philosopher of science, Rom Harre. He uses two instructive analogies to describe social change. One is the mutation analogy in which a new social practice arises in a small group and spreads just as a new biological mutation can become a new species. If the new way of life is not summarily destroyed by the larger system which it threatens, the innovation may triumph. Christianity, itself, might be an apt example of the spread of an innovative way of life.

One source of the social change and mutation which then spreads is the increase and straining of an operating system to the breaking point, a strain arising from tensions and inner contradictions. Suddenly an old system shifts and radically readjusts in a new configuration. The gestalt figure or elements in the whole reorganizes. The dialectic tension has become too great to sustain. Many others who analyze social change also take a systems approach. Change occurs if one can simultaneously increase pressure on weak points and remove obstacles in the surrounding environment blocking change. All of the above analogies can be helpful in thinking about strategies to move our society toward a consistent ethic of life.

Moving our society toward a new agenda will take the shrewdness of the serpent and the innocence of the dove. Such a change will come about through the adoption of new and better rational analysis; through appeals to new feelings and emotions, and through new actions in the private and public sphere. Individuals influence institutions and groups and the other way round. Human beings are themselves microsystems operating in larger social systems—all of which interact in dynamic ways. Persuasion and movement can take place on many levels at once in many different places; Christians must be able to outthink, outlove and politically outmanuever their opponents.

And Catholics committed to a consistent ethic of life will make progress toward our goals by specific campaigns. I agree with Bryan Hehir that it would not be enough for the Bishops to ennunciate global principles and give their moral analysis without struggling for specific enactments of specific policies and legislations. Lay Catholics are not united in a political group and can be empowered by the corporate witness and supportive actions of their moral leaders to increased political effectiveness. In such efforts, specific policies and laws must be grappled with in a spirit of dialogue and prudential judgments.

What we do, individually and collectively, changes the way we think and feel, as well as vice versa. Love and commitment must be shown in deeds, not only through words and worship. God is in the details and by their fruits you shall know them. The belief in the Incarnation drives the Church to struggle in the world for love of the world. As Christians we are especially called to be advocates for those without worldly power, the poor the vulnerable, whose interests are so often sacrificed to expediency. We must do what no one else in the society will do. So of course as a Church we must be engaged on many fronts at once; prudence and different vocations will determine where we put our individual and group efforts. But we can not preach justice and charity if we are not ready to act consistently on our commitments.

A consistent effort to further a consistent ethic of life returns us to some of the concerns voiced by Richard McCormick in his paper in this symposium. We cannot be taken seriously in the larger world in our preaching of love and justice if we do not practice these virtues in our own Church among our own members. "Justice is love's absolute minimum," as Paul the Sixth said. If we love one another we must be a just community. The sin of sexism and the misuse of authority gives great scandal and weakens our effectiveness in the legislatures, media and marketplace. If we do not listen and respect one another in our own community, who will listen to us in the world? Our methods and means of living together in community must be reformed.

We as Catholics give many messages to many people on many levels at once. If we are inconsistent while preaching consistency we are as a sounding gong. Our commitment to the fetus will be measured by our commitment to women and children; our commitment to peace by the way we deal with internal dissent, our commitment to the poor by the way we deploy our resources in our own institutions. Love and justice begin at home.

We follow a Lord who persuaded others and changed the world. The method was an extremely consistent one: If one wants the world to change then one must *be* different. The Christian counsel to doubters was the essence of simplicity, "Come and see for yourself." We who are committed to the consistent ethic of life have the same challenge. As we work and struggle we have to be able to witness to the unity of love and truth in our lives. The historical moment is propitious, we should persevere in hope...

Notes

Rom Harre, *Social Being, A Theory for Social Psychology*. New Jersey, Littlefield, Adams & Co., 1980. Chapter 15 "Social Change: Theories and Assumptions," pp. 335-355.

Albert O. Hirschman "The Search for Paradigms as a Hindrance to Understanding," in *Interpretative Social Science A Reader*, Edited by Paul Rabinow and William M. Sullivan. Berkeley: University of California Press, 1979, pp. 177, pp. 163-179.

"The Consistent Ethic of Life: Stage Two"

Symposium on the Consistent Ethic of Life
Loyola University, Chicago
Joseph Cardinal Bernardin
November 7, 1987

On December 6, 1983, I gave an address at Fordham University entitled, "A Consistent Ethic of Life: An American-Catholic Dialogue." Although the specific occasion for this lecture was the U.S. Catholic Bishops' pastoral letter, "The Challenge of Peace: God's Promise and Our Response," I used the opportunity to discuss the broader relationship between the Catholic moral vision and American culture. That presentation in the Bronx four years ago marked the beginning of Stage One of the consistent ethic of life, although, in effect, I was simply articulating the moral vision underlying the U.S. Bishops' Respect Life program from its inception in 1972.

I cast the Fordham address as "an inquiry, an examination of the need for a consistent ethic of life and a probing of the problems and possibilities which exist within the Church and the wider society for developing such an ethic." I immediately added that I did not "underestimate the intrinsic intellectual difficulties of this exercise nor the delicacy of the question—

ecclesially, ecumenically, and politically." I asked for a discussion, and I got one!

Four years ago I had no idea of the extent to which the inquiry which I was proposing would become a significant part of my pastoral ministry. Frankly, I am very pleased that my basic message has been heard so widely and supported by so many. Four years ago I did not imagine that it would be the subject of a symposium such as this. I am very grateful to Loyola University, its President, Father Raymond Baumhart, and all of the participants for making this possible.

In the time allotted to me this afternoon, I will (1) briefly explain why I decided to develop the consistent ethic theme, (2) point out the need for collaboration between pastors and theologians in its further development, and (3) respond to some of the issues raised by the major speakers. As with some of the other addresses at this symposium, my published text will be somewhat longer and more detailed than this oral presentation.

1. Why Develop the Consistent Ethic Theme?

During the past four years, many people have asked why I introduced this concept, why I invested so much precious reflective time and exerted so much limited energy in its development. The answer is as simple, and as complex, as my ministry as a bishop.

As a pastor, I have the responsibility to proclaim Jesus Christ and his gospel "in season and out." This means that I must present an evangelical vision of self-sacrificing love and profound respect for the dignity of all human life. And I must do this in a way that is *faithful*—to the Word of God and to the Spirit-guided tradition of the Church as taught by the Pope and the bishops.

Moreover, this proclamation of the gospel does not take place in a vacuum. It is situated in a particular historical moment and a specific place. That is why my pastoral responsibility includes searching for an ever-increasing understanding and penetration of Christ's message in light of current realities and critiquing the quality of life in contemporary society in light of the gospel. I do this as a co-disciple with all other members of the community of faith as, together, we seek to be "like a leaven" in the world and to transform our culture so that God's Kingdom might truly come.

Our engagement with the world is not superfluous or marginal either to our lives as believers or to the world in which we live. Rather, it is something desperately needed. The vision and the values which we proclaim and seek to develop in the form of principles and strategic choices can enrich and transform both our own lives and our world.

Each of us experiences the weaknesses and the limits of our own personhood and the world. We encounter forces that oppose what we affirm and tempt us, as individuals and as a society, to be less than we would like to be and can be. We know that sin and evil are real—not merely in ourselves, but in others and in the world around us. Nonetheless, we also acknowledge that we dream of becoming the full persons and the perfect community that God intends for his creation. And we believe that the Spirit of our loving God is with us to assist us in bringing this dream to reality.

The pursuit of this dream motivated me to develop the consistent ethic of life. I am convinced that such an ethic gives us and other people of good will a unique perspective on such matters as international justice and peace, economic justice and business ethics, civil and human rights, family and interpersonal relationships, the protection and nurturing of human life and stewardship of the environment. Such an ethic provides both the vision and the norms needed to guide and direct individual and communal behavior in a great variety of contexts.

2. The Need for Collaboration in Developing the Concept

While I believe deeply in the concept of a consistent ethic of life, I also know that there are limits to what I, as a pastor, can and should do in regard to its development. If the consistent ethic is to be adequately developed and truly engage our contemporary society, then it requires the expertise of theologians and other scholars to refine and flesh it out. As I have intimated, from the very beginning I have not underestimated the difficulties of developing such an ethic. That is why many of my major presentations about it have been deliberately addressed to Catholic university audiences. Such institutions of higher learning should engage in the tasks of enriching U.S. culture through the study and sharing of Catholic wisdom and enhancing our understanding of the Catholic faith by drawing on both the riches and the poverty of this culture.

From what I have just said, it should be obvious how fitting it is that this symposium should take place, and that it should occur *here*. Fitting because it takes place at Loyola University, an institution of higher learning that is faithful to its Catholic, Jesuit, and American roots. Fitting also because the symposium brings together scholars of national and international stature to engage the concept, test it, critique it, and further develop it.

I would like to indicate briefly how I see the distinct but complementary roles of pastor and theologian in this dialogue.

As I have indicated, I come to this discussion as a pastor, not as a theologian. Nonetheless, part of my pastoral ministry is to teach—to conserve the faith handed on to us by the apostles, to explain the teachings of the Church developed over the centuries, and to provide guidance for proper living to individuals and society.

To fulfill this ministry, I must rely on the assistance of others, especially theologians. As I have said on several other occasions, theologians are explorers. Their work implies searching, casting about for deeper understandings of the mysteries of the faith in light of contemporary life. They look to the past, they look to present realities, and they look to future possibilities in order to provide a deeper understanding of what God is saying to us. They do not create revelation, but they help us assimilate, make our own, and apply the mystery of God's saving love to our particular situation.

Because theologians are explorers, they search for new areas of understanding, new approaches to old realities. Because they are explorers, they must have an appropriate amount of freedom. And because they are explorers, we must expect that their searches will not always be successful, that there will be mistakes.

We have gathered here today with mutual, complementary responsibility within the Church. The relationship between theologian and bishop should be characterized by complementarity, mutual respect, and dialogue, even though the bishop's overseeing ministry determines what results of theological exploration can or should be accepted by the community of faith.

3. Responses to the Four Major Papers

In this spirit of a pastoral teacher who needs the help of theologians and has invited the exploration of the strengths and limits of the consistent ethic of life theme, I will now respond to some of what has been said here today. I trust that the manner of my response will be in accord with the appropriate relationship between pastor and theologian that I have just described. Just as all the participants have spoken with great conviction and respect, so will I.

It is not possible for me to respond in a detailed way to everything that has been said here today. Nor should I even attempt to do so, because it is proper that much of what has been said today should be seen as a dialogue between fellow explorers over a particular concept. It is my hope that this discussion will continue and in this way refine and enrich the concept of a consistent ethic of life.

I will briefly examine each major presentation in light of the others and offer two observations on it. My response will not follow the order of presentation but will begin with the more abstract or ontological concerns and then move to the more concrete or specific.

a. Professor Gustafson

I will begin with Professor Gustafson's paper. I tend to agree with his hypothetical suggestion that a different theological point of departure might give different weights to matters under discussion, leading to some different ethical conclusions. I also share his concern about what he describes as an "anthropocentrism and ultimately the individualism" that he finds in my addresses. Fr. McCormick also raised the issue of individualism in another context.

Professor Gustafson suggests that theology must be more theocentric. With that in mind he proposes his central ethical statement: "We are to seek to discern what God is enabling and requiring us to do as participants in the patterns and processes of interdependence of life in the world."

At first reading I agree with the intent of such an ethical statement. We *are* called to discern the on-going movement and action of the divine Spirit in the events of everyday existence. And we are responsible to do this in a way that respects the fact that we have intrapersonal relationships and interpersonal relationships, as well as relationships with society and the world around us. And within those relationships there must be a sense of the awesomeness of God who is their origin and their ultimate end.

Nonetheless, where Professor Gustafson and I might differ is in the matter in which we discover this divine pre-eminence. Roman Catholic natural law tradition has insisted that when one turns to the natural world, one can find God's plan and purpose. Consequently, divine pre-eminence can be mediated to us in and through our experience of our humanity and of the world.

However, such an inductive experience of the divine carries with it the danger of reducing the divine to the experience through which it is mediated. And that is why this so-called "natural" experience of divinity must always be enriched by and accountable to the face of God revealed in Scripture and worship, and expressed in the Church's teaching. In them we encounter the "mysterium tremendum" that shatters our temptation to build our own golden calves. We must then maintain a proper balance between the "naturalness" of the Divine and Divine pre- eminence.

I would like to address another dimension of Professor Gustafson's central ethical statement: the relationship between the individual and the social. He is correct in his reading of the development of Catholic thinking when he suggests that a priority has been given to the *individual* "made in the image and likeness of God." It is no secret that the *social* dimensions of Catholic theology have been advanced, in large measure, only over the course of the last century, and primarily at the prompting of the great social encyclicals of recent popes. And the consequences of this expanded vision have been explored in recent discussions about the so-called European "Political Theology" and the "Liberation Theology" of developing countries in Latin America, Africa, and elsewhere.

I have sought to be attentive to the interrelationship of the personal and the social as I included in some of my addresses the distinction between private and public morality. Moreover, the U.S. Catholic bishops, in their pastoral letter on the economy, clearly acknowledged the ethical impera- tives of economic policy just as they did other social imperatives in their pastoral letter on war and peace.

Although we have recognized this social dimension of theology and ethics, we have not fully addressed the tension between the personal and the social. When we do so, we undoubtedly will find the ambiguity which Professor Gustafson intimated. I affirm the need for greater work in this area and respect the challenge which this offers. At this time, however, it still seems to me that, in moments of conflict between the individual and the social, the individual must predominate for it is here that the fullest presence of the Divine is to be encountered.

b. Father McCormick

This last point of Professor Gustafson serves as a bridge to my response to Father McCormick's presentation. He moves from the more theoretical question of the proper relationship between the individual and society to the specific methods used in social and personal ethics. Father McCormick is not the first to highlight what many perceive as an inconsistency between the two approaches as they are found in the documents of the ecclesiastical magisterium. And, as a pastor who searches for consistency in ethical discussions, I, too, at times experience some of the same difficulty.

In a sense, this brings us back to Professor Gustafson's point that, in fact, the Church's moral teaching has given a priority to individual or personal ethics and that its moral valence is stronger there than in the social realm. And consequently, apart from other concerns which I will mention later, the result is that there seems to be greater room for an inductive approach in regard to social ethics than in the area of personal ethics. This brings me to my next point.

Father McCormick also engages the consistent ethic in a critique that originates in his dedication to an ethical method known as proportionalism. As one of the most respected and eloquent proponents of that method, he correctly enters into a discussion of the maxim, "no direct killing of the innocent."

It would be inappropriate for me to engage in a point-by-point response to his cogent observations. However, I must point out, respectfully, that proportionalism has not been accepted by the ecclesiastical magisterium. While some aspects of this approach are commendable, it has led to some conclusions that have, in fact, not been approved by the magisterium. This is why the magisterium has not accepted this method as an equally valid alternative to the Church's traditional moral methodology.

I am not disclosing a secret when I say this. And Father McCormick is correct in saying that the current tension in the Church about this matter *does* soften the underbelly of the consistent ethic. But it also threatens to do much more than that. The debates over moral methodology and concrete moral imperatives is draining vital energy from the lives of individual believers and the Church as a whole. And, at times, I myself become frustrated because I do not see a way in which we can move beyond this debate.

This simply means that continuing dialogue is needed. It must take place among theologians and between theologians and bishops. It must be marked by a spirit of civility and mutual respect. There is no room for caricature that inhibits understanding and the search for truth. Similarly, there is nothing inherently wrong with theological debate about points which are in conflict. Historically, such debate has given life and purpose to the various theological schools which have enriched our understanding of the Christian faith.

At the same time, it is not proper to ignore the distinctive teaching charism of the ecclesiastical magisterium and its right to expect at least a religious assent of mind and heart to what it proposes, as described in *Lumen Gentium.* I hope that through such dialogue we can move beyond current divisions to agree upon an ethical methodology that will integrate the wisdom of both ethical perspectives.

c. Professor Finnis

Let me begin by expressing my appreciation for Professor Finnis's lengthy and detailed written paper which is much longer than his oral presentation today. His three propositions and his analysis of them provide a scholarly overview of many of the criticisms directed at the consistent ethic by some in the Catholic Church.

In particular response I would like to discuss the manner in which we elect public officials. Professor Finnis says initially that he agrees with the principle enunciated by the National Conference of Catholic Bishops that one should not vote in terms of a single issue. Rather one should be concerned about the *character* of the candidates. But, in analyzing that character, he says, a different weight should be given to their position on infanticide than on affirmative moral responsibilities. In fact, he suggests that one may properly use candidates' positions on infanticide as litmus tests of their good or bad character and give little or no weight to their preferences on other public policies.

I agree that the character of a candidate for public office is an important consideration for the electorate. I also affirm the priority which should be given to candidates' positions on matters pertaining to the life of the unborn. I am uncomfortable, however, with seeing that position as a singular litmus test. My reason for saying this is *not* a lack of commitment to elimination of the crime of abortion in our land. Throughout the 35 years of my priestly and episcopal ministry, and especially since the 1973

Supreme Court abortion decisions, I have vigorously worked to eradicate this grave evil. Rather it has to do with the complexity of the political process in a pluralistic society.

To insist that the only person a Catholic may vote for must pass a litmus test based on how a person has or presumably would vote on a particular issue apart from an evaluation of the overall political process and the position of the candidate on other pro-life issues could eliminate us as a political reality in our society. What we must find is a way, without compromising our fundamental convictions and, in particular, our commitment to the life of the unborn, that we can credibly remain as participants in the development and transformation of public policy.

The second issue I wish to discuss is his view about the role of bishops in the development of public policy. It has been my experience, and I believe that of other bishops in the United States, that the Church's social and moral teaching can be effectively introduced into public discussion on a wide range of political issues. It is necessary to be very clear about what is meant here: The bishops should not be political partisans, but they can specify, examine, and press in the public debate the *moral* dimensions of issues as diverse as medical technology, capital punishment, human rights, economic policy, and military strategy.

The experience of our U.S. episcopal conference in addressing the issues of nuclear and economic policies has shown us the need to give high priority to this teaching task. Our critics have said we have entered too deeply into the political order, that we are too specific in our teaching, and that we are usurping the proper role of the laity in the secular and, particularly, the political order. I addressed this issue in my intervention during the recently concluded Synod of Bishops.

It is my conviction that this is a mistaken criticism. While attributing a lesser degree of authority to our applications, we have nonetheless thought it necessary to show how principles are to be applied in our contemporary circumstances so that the principles and their implications will be correctly understood. In the final analysis, moral teaching involves concrete choices.

In truth, the distinct teaching role of bishops in addressing the political order complements the indispensable role of the laity as participants in the political process. And for that teaching role to be fulfilled, the character of the moral teaching must meet three requirements. (1) It must be morally credible; that is, it must have the theoretical capacity to illuminate the human values and dimensions of political questions. (2) It must be empirically competent in its assessment of problems. (3) And as noted above, it must lead toward specific recommendations and conclusions which are realizable. Teaching which combine these characteristics is a permanent mode of the Church's contribution to the political process.

At the same time, both the theology of the lay vocation and the political requirements of effectiveness demand that the Church's direct engagement in the political order be through lay people. Nonetheless, if this crucial role is to be filled well, those who undertake it need solid grounding in the faith and the Church's social teaching, as well as political skill and empirical competence.

Endowed with these capacities, Catholic lay men and women who enter the political process, whether by election or appointment, should have the encouragement of the bishops in undertaking this vocation. They must be addressed and treated as professionals in their sphere of competence. While commentary and critique of public debate, public policy, and specific political choices are necessary parts of the Church's social ministry, the freedom to exercise professional judgment and the virtue of prudence must be accorded those in public life. It is the task of Catholic politicians, in cooperation with others of good will and a wide range of political coalitions, to grapple with how the moral teaching should be joined with the concrete choices of the political order and the requirements of building public support for needed policies.

When we fulfill our role as moral teachers and help prepare lay people for the political vocation, we exercise a ministry of co-discipleship.

d. Father Hehir

Finally, I will address Father Hehir's paper, focusing on two concrete issues facing the implementation of the consistent ethic.

Father Hehir suggests that, in debating public policy, the Church should not try to create a voting bloc or political organization. Rather it helps test other positions in the light of a consistent philosophical vision. However, because this vision encompasses the full range of human life issues from conception to natural death, it is difficult to create a stable constituency for it. So, as Father Hehir rightly pointed out, the consistent ethic "has created expectations that have not been realized in practice."

I am acutely aware of this. While the phrase "the consistent ethic" has become a part of the U.S. Catholic vocabulary and seems to resonate with the ethical instincts of many Catholics, its systematic and analogical nature makes it difficult for individuals to apply it consciously or reflexively in their civic and political choices.

At times this difficulty leads me to believe that we need to find better ways to communicate the principle. In some way we must take what is an abstract principle and make it more understandable in the concrete. And for that to happen, we will need the expertise of pastoral ministers and religious educators.

While acknowledging this need, I also know that, in the Catholic tradition, other principles, also complex in their theological explanation, have become both familiar and helpful to individuals in their every-day ethical decision-making. Why? Because the moral intuition behind the ethical theory may be absorbed and used without the sophistication of its theological articulation. If the acceptance and integration of the fundamental insight or linkage of life issues found in the consistent ethic of life were to become "second nature" to people, then it will have served a great purpose.

The second issue I would like to address is Father Hehir's reflection on the evaluation of candidates for public office. I agree with his guidelines that reject the legitimacy of a split between the public and the personal positions of a candidate but allow a legitimate range of prudential choice about how to move from moral conviction to legislation or policy.

Some will disagree with the second of these guidelines. And this issue could become a source of division during next year's national elections.

What seems to be at stake is the acceptance or non-acceptance of the teaching of the Second Vatican Council about the nature of the state and the role of civil law. It is clear that the Council shifted the criteria by which we evaluate and understand civil law. No longer is the law responsible for the full and complete realization of the common good and, consequently, the expression of all moral teaching. The law's scope is limited, and its development must be evaluated by the criteria of the freedom of the individual, the public order, equitability, and enforceability.

This implies that candidates who unequivocally subscribe to the consistent ethic of life in its full scope, as well as in its moral analysis of distinct issues, could sincerely disagree with others about strategies for the implementation of that principle, could oppose legislation supported by some, could support legislation opposed by others, or could decide that it is not in the best interests of the state to seek particular legislation or to enact it at a given historical moment. Although we might disagree with such candidates and might not vote for them because we disagree with their prudential judgments, in this context it would be inappropriate to say that such candidates or public officials are either acting immorally or that they should be otherwise castigated or ostracized.

Even if one were to disagree with this teaching of the Second Vatican Council, the history of our ethical reasoning on the making and enforcing of public law is more complex than some would suggest. From the time of Augustine it has been recognized that law must be applied according to the human condition. In fact, it has even been possible to tolerate evil in certain situations. What has been required of the lawgiver was *prudence*. This remains an appropriate criterion to use in evaluating whether candidates or public officials are faithful to the consistent ethic: Are they acting prudently? Such a criterion is faithful to the nature of the consistent ethic as well as the legitimate role of pluralism in our society.

I am very pleased that the consistent ethic of life theme has been taken seriously by many people in the last four years—including our distinguished speakers and respondents at this symposium. This is not the end of a long process but simply the beginning of the *second stage* in the development of the theme. Thoughtful, complex questions have been raised, and I trust that I can count on all of you to continue this dialogue with me and my fellow bishops.

Symposium Resource Persons

Joseph Cardinal Bernardin is Archbishop of Chicago, and one of the sponsors of this symposium. He has been Archbishop of Cincinnati and president of the National Conference of Catholic Bishops. He has served as chair of the committee which drafted the bishop's pastoral on war and peace. Currently he serves as chair of the pro-life activities committee of the National Conference of Bishops. Over the last years, he has written and talked extensively on the theme "a consistent ethic of life."

John C. Finnis is Reader in Law, Oxford University, and Fellow of University College, Oxford. A native Australian, he has been advisor to the Australian and British governments. He is presently a Governor of the Linacre Center (for Medical Ethics), London, and Member of the International Theological Commission (Vatican). His published works in philosophy include *Natural Law and Natural Rights* (Clarendon, Oxford 1980) and *Fundamentals of Ethics* (Georgetown 1983).

James M. Gustafson was until 1988 University Professor of Theological Ethics at the Divinity School and on the Committee on Social Thought at the University of Chicago. Ordained in the United Church of Christ, he has been president of the American Society of Christian Ethics, is a Member of the Council of American Academy of Arts and Sciences, and a Fellow of the Institute for Society, Ethics and the Life Sciences. His recent books include: *Ethics from a Theocentric Perspective,* 2 volumes (University of Chicago 1981, 1984), and *Protestant and Roman Catholic Ethics: Prospects for Rapprochement.* (University of Chicago 1978).

J. Bryan Hehir is Senior Research Scholar in the Kennedy Institute of Ethics and Research Professor of Ethics in the School of Foreign Service,

Georgetown University. As Secretary, Department of Social Development and World Peace, U.S. Catholic Conference, he has been advisor to the American Bishops, particularly for the pastoral letters on the economy and on war and peace. Fr. Hehir has been Stillman Professor of Catholic Thought at Harvard, and has published in *Foreign Policy, Worldview, Social Thought*, and *Review of Politics*.

Richard A. McCormick, S.J., is currently John A. O'Brien Professor of Christian Ethics at the University of Notre Dame. In 1974-86, he was Rose F. Kennedy Professor of Christian Ethics at the Kennedy Institute of Ethics, Georgetown University. Fr. McCormick has published 5 volumes of *Readings in Moral Theology* (1979-84), has contributed many chapters to books such as *The Future of Ethics and Moral Theology*, (1979-84), has contributed to journals including *Christianity and Crisis, America, Commonweal*, and the *Journal of the American Medical Association*.

Respondents

Frans Jozef van Beeck, S.J., teaches systematic theology at Loyola University of Chicago, where he holds the John Cardinal Cody Chair. Fr. van Beeck is the author of six books, including *Christ Proclaimed* (Paulist 1979) and *Catholic Identity After Vatican II* (Loyola University Press 1985).

Lisa Sowle Cahill is Associate Professor of Theology at Boston College, where she teaches Christian ethics. She has published *Between the Sexes: Foundations for a Christian Ethics of Sexuality* (Fortress and Paulist 1985). Her articles have appeared in *Theological Studies, Journal of Religious Ethics*, and the *Journal of Medicine and Philosophy*.

Sidney Callahan has lectured at over 165 colleges in the U.S. Her books include *Abortion: Understanding Differences* (co- edited with Daniel Callahan, Plenum 1984) and *The Illusion of Eve: Modern Woman's Search for Identity* (Sheed & Ward 1968). She is Associate Professor of Psychology at Mercy College, Dobbs Ferry, New York.

James J. Walter is Professor of Theology at Loyola University of Chicago. He is co-author of the book *Conversion and Discipline: A Christian Foundation for Ethics and Doctrine* (Fortress 1986), and has published in Europe as well as the United States in *The Heythrop Journal* and *Louvain Studies*.